Governments and Tourism

Governments and Tourism

David Jeffries

BUTTERWORTH
HEINEMANN

OXFORD AUCKLAND BOSTON JOHANNESBURG MELBOURNE NEW DELHI

Butterworth-Heinemann
Linacre House, Jordan Hill, Oxford OX2 8DP
225 Wildwood Avenue, Woburn, MA 01801-2041
A division of Reed Educational and Professional Publishing Ltd

$\mathcal{R}$ A member of the Reed Elsevier plc group

First published 2001
Reprinted 2001

British Library Cataloguing in Publication Data
Jeffries, David
    Governments and tourism
    1. Tourism – Government policy
    I. Title
    338.4'791

ISBN 0 7506 4478 8

For information on all Butterworth-Heinemann publications
please visit our website at www.bh.com

Typeset by Avocet Typeset, Brill, Aylesbury, Bucks
Printed and bound in Great Britain by MPG Books Ltd., Bodmin, Cornwall

Contents

Preface

Throughout a career spanning 45 years, the author has had occasion regularly to brief policymakers on tourism. Very often they were public figures and business leaders who had little or no previous knowledge of governments and tourism. Dr Patrick Roper, who has contributed a key chapter on host community responses to tourism, has more than 30 years experience in the field, both within the public and private sector. This book is first and foremost for the policymaker, recently appointed to a responsible position – perhaps as a member of a local tourism committee – who is willing to invest time and effort in gaining a good general grasp of the subject and, as it were, a competitive edge. The book is for readers worldwide. The author offers insights and works towards conclusions that he hopes many will find relevant within the particular countries and communities they serve in public office.

However, in introducing the subject to non-specialists, the author also frequently takes a line which he hopes may give pause for thought to the managements of official tourism organizations and other professionals, provoking debate within specialist circles.

The book serves too the needs of lobbyists, researchers, consultants, travel writers with an interest in tourism policy, teachers and the policymakers of the future, students. The author has had special regard for the interests of student readers on postgraduate courses and degree courses in tourism.

There is to the best of his knowledge no general introduction to the subject of governments and tourism in one book. At the risk of oversimplification, it may be stated that much of the existing academic literature – chapters in books, articles in journals – is focused either on the legislation under which official tourism organizations have been established or on policy directives governing their operations or on technical aspects of their work. These have had a rather narrow perspective. Official tourism organizations represent only a very small part of total government involvement in and impact on tourism. The potential field of study is vast. That is why the author claims for the book no more than the status of an introduction.

Finally some remarks seem necessary on the connection between government and host communities. It is taken as axiomatic that in a truly democratic system there is a close cooperative relationship between government and community. The issues discussed are those encountered by governments in deciding how best to formulate and execute tourism policies for the well-being of the community. A number of questions immediately spring to mind. Why should governments be involved anyway? What government structures are required? How realistic is it to expect governments to participate in the management of tourism or is this really 'mainly a matter for the private sector'? Such controversial questions are or should be of considerable interest both to governments and the communities they serve. They are relevant in an increasing number of countries and places worldwide which are at the receiving end of the continuing rapid growth in world tourism.

D.J. Jeffries

Abbreviations

ACP	Africa Caribbean Pacific
AFCI	Assembly of Chambers of Commerce (France)
AIEST	International Association of Scientific Experts in Tourism
APEC	Asia Pacific Economic Cooperation Secrétariat
BTA	British Tourist Authority
CEU	Commission for Europe (World Tourism Organization)
CVB	Convention and Visitor Bureau
DCMS	Department of Culture, Media and Sport
DETR	Department of the Environment, Transport and the Regions
DG XXIII	Directorate General XXIII (European Commission)
EC	European Commission (Commission of the European Communities)
EDF	European Development Fund
EIU	Economist Intelligence Unit
ERDF	European Regional Development Fund
ETB	English Tourist Board
ETC	European Travel Commission and English Tourism Council
EU	European Union
GATS	General Agreement on Trade in Services
GDP	Gross Domestic Product
HDI	Hotel Development Incentives
HMSO	Her Majesty's Stationery Office
IACVB	International Association of Convention and Visitor Bureaus

IPA	Institute of Practitioners in Advertising
IUOTO	International Union of Official Travel Organizations
KEF	Kent Economic Fund
KTSG	Kent Tourism Sector Group
LBL	Learning and Business Link
MTRI	Montana Tourism and Recreation Initiative
NTA	National Tourism Administration
NTO	National Tourism Organization
OECD	Organization for Economic Co-operation and Development
OEEC	Organization for European Economic Co-operation
OTA	Official Tourism Administration
OTO	Official Tourism Organization
RTB	Regional Tourist Board
R and D	Research and Development
SEEDA	South East England Development Agency
SEETB	South East England Tourist Board
SET	Selective Employment Tax
SICTA	Standard International Classification of Tourism Activities
SMEs	Small and medium sized enterprises
STB	Southern Tourist Board
STCG	Scottish Tourism Consulting Group
TCSP	Tourism Council of the South Pacific
TDAP	Tourism Development Area Action Programme
TIA	Travel Industry Association of America
TIC	Tourist Information Centre
TPC	Tourism Policy Council
TSA	Tourism Satellite Account
UK	United Kingdom of Great Britain and Northern Ireland
UN	United Nations
US	United States
USA	United States of America
USNTO	United States National Tourism Organization
USTTSA	United States Travel and Tourism Administration
WEFA	Wharton Econometric Forecasting Associates
WTO	World Tourism Organization
WTTC	World Travel and Tourism Council

Acknowledgements

It was Professor S. Medlik who encouraged me to undertake this book and whose guidance was invaluable as it took shape. Rik, as he has been known to his many friends and to me since the beginning of my career, receives my heartfelt thanks. Of those who have given many hours to researching material for this work and to its production, I must thank first my wife, Joëlle, for handling all the related correspondence and Margaret Abel for typing the whole text. Thanks go to Patrick Roper for contributing a vital chapter and for much digging and delving, with the help of his son, Charles, on the Internet.

There are many others without whose encouragement and help the book would not have been possible. John Fosbrooke of the English Tourist Board was dedicated and tireless in researching the historical background to tourism in the UK. His colleague, Michael Dewing, also gave valuable assistance. Other members of Britain's National Tourism Organization were most helpful: Sue Garland, Deputy Chief Executive of the British Tourist Authority and her colleagues, Gareth James in London and Nicholas Markson in Brussels.

The British Tourist Authority/English Tourist Board Library and Archives in Hammersmith, London, retrieved a mass of material which has informed the book. My local Public Library at Sanderstead, Surrey, gave help throughout by locating scores of published sources which have enriched the bibliography. I am grateful to the staff of both libraries for their courtesy and patience.

Numerous are those who have given time to briefing me on specific topics and I extend my thanks in particular to:

- Patrice Tedjini and Peter Shackleford, respectively Head of the Documentation Centre and Regional Representative for Europe, at the World Tourism Organization in Madrid.
- Richard Webster, Director, Legislative Affairs, Travel Industry Association of America, Washington, DC. Helen Marano, Director of Tourism Development, US Department of Commerce, Washington, DC. Dr Douglas Frechtling, Chair, Department of Tourism and Hospitality Management, George Washington University, Washington, DC.
- Matthew Cohn and Pam Gosink, respectively Director and Group/Overseas Marketing Manager at Travel Montana, Helena, Montana. Kate Russell-Cobb, London representative of Rocky Mountain International. Norma Nickerson, Institute for Tourism and Recreation Research, Missoula, Montana.
- René Baretje, one of the best known tourism experts in France, and Jean-Jacques Pringué, International Relations, Regional Tourism Committee, Nord–Pas de Calais.
- Richard Bifield, Past President, Tourism Management Institute, Telford, England and Andrew Grieve, Managing Director, Discover Britain, Worcester, England.
- Robert Chenery, Director of Development, London Tourist Board.
- Rajeshwar Singh, Director of Tourism, Ministry of Tourism, Fiji and Stanley Wilson, advisor to the Tourism Council of the South Pacific, both based in Suva, Fiji.

Throughout the book I have quoted from a range of previously published material. Every effort has been made to acknowledge the full source and copyright holders, but if any has been inadvertently overlooked the publishers and I will be pleased to make the necessary arrangements at the first opportunity. Material on Languedoc Rousillon by A. Clarke in Chapter 11 is reproduced from the *Annals of Tourism Research* (copyright 1981) by permission of Elsevier Science; OECD copyright material is reproduced from *Tourism Policy and International Tourism in OECD Member Countries*, 1989 and 1993, with permission from OECD; Parliamentary copyright material from Hansard and Commons Select Committee Reports is reproduced with the permission of the Controller of Her Majesty's Stationery Office on behalf of Parliament. Acknowledgement of permission to reproduce published material is also due to the British Tourist Authority, the British Council, the World Tourism Organization, *Caterer &*

Hotelkeeper, *Journal of Travel and Tourism*, *Tourism Management*, *Travel and Tourism Intelligence* and Prentice Hall International (Englewood Cliffs, NJ). Quotations from P. Yale are reprinted by permission of Pearson Education Ltd © Longman Group Ltd (Harlow, Essex).

I am particularly grateful to those who read and commented on selected draft chapters: Professor David Airey of the University of Surrey; Colin Clark, Director of Horwath Consulting and formerly Secretary to the Board of BTA and ETB; Ian Rickson, Head of the Evaluation Unit, BTA; Fred Cubbage, Managing Director, South East England Tourist Board; Simon Curtis, Tourism Development Coordinator, Kent County Council; and our daughter, Elisabeth Jeffries, MSc (Tourism).

I thank our daughters Claire and Beatrice for seeking out published sources in France. Finally, I am grateful to our son, Richard, and youngest daughter, Cécile, who egged me on with the regular question 'When are you going to finish that book?'.

D. J. Jeffries

Part One

General Scenario

Introduction

Tourists and tourism

It is necessary only to scan the mass media in the English speaking world to conclude that a widespread, popular conception of a tourist is of a person travelling away from home for a sightseeing tour or a beach holiday. The term means much more than this to managers and administrators. Tourists are persons travelling not only on holiday but on business, on courses of study, on pilgrimage and on many other grounds. To be comprehensive a tourism statistical system must cover all of the activities of persons travelling to and staying in places outside their usual environment for not more than one consecutive year for leisure, business and other purposes. (Source: United Nations, New York (1994, p. 5), Recommendations on Tourism Statistics)

The existing, official, internationally favoured definitions of tourism are the product of debate extending over 60 years. Gee, Choy and Makens (1984, p. 5), in *The*

Travel Industry, record the League of Nations definition which was drawn up as early as 1937. Intergovernmental organizations sought to refine definitions after the Second World War. Campaigns sponsored by the United Nations, the IUOTO and OEEC sought to reduce frontier formalities and barriers to travel. They called for agreement on what constituted a tourist so that, in turn, governments could agree on how tourists should be treated at international frontiers. Governments were also increasingly interested in gathering comparable data to guide policymaking in what was recognized as a field of growing economic and social importance.

By the 1940s, the notion already existed that tourism excluded permanent residence and any earning activity within the place visited, according to a definition developed by Hunziker and Krapf and quoted by Burkart and Medlik (1982, p. 41) in *Tourism Past, Present and Future*. Later, official definitions treated an international tourist as a person staying temporarily in a country other than his own for purposes *other than remuneration from within the country visited*. This strongly suggests the following. In seeking to distinguish between these international travellers and permanent migrants or visiting workers, governments sought a definition that would help identify 'outsiders' who were evidently economically attractive in that they would bring extra spending into their national economies. This was at a time when many governments gave high priority to the earning of foreign exchange. Earning revenue from tourists was the equivalent of an export. Most states were disposed in principle to a 'free trade' in tourism. Over many years, frontier formalities for tourists, as defined, were reduced.

The Australian Bureau of Statistics (no date) in its *Framework for the Collection and Publication of Tourism Statistics* (pp. 4 and 5) has summarized neatly the WTO distinction between travellers, visitors, tourists and same day visitors. A traveller is:

Any person on a trip between two or more countries or two or more localities within his/her country of usual residence.

Travellers are broken down into 'visitors' and 'other travellers'. The category 'visitors' provides the means for identifying those persons whose activities constitute 'tourism'. A 'visitor' is defined as:

Any person travelling to a place other than that of his/her usual environment for less than twelve months and whose main purpose of the trip is other than the exercise of an activity remunerated from within the place visited. 'Visitors' are further divided into 'tourists' staying a night or more and 'same-day visitors'.

In the shorthand of policymakers, the activities of both tourists, as formally defined, and same-day visitors and the business of providing for them are often referred to as simply 'tourism'. For example, this is the sense in which the British Government uses the word in its latest strategy. (See Department for Culture, Media and Sport, *Tomorrow's Tourism – A Growth Industry for the New Millennium*, 1999a). There is no such word as 'visitorism'. It would be too cumbersome to repeat 'tourism and same-day visiting' at every turn.

So far discussion has centred on international tourism and the crossing of international frontiers by persons who are generally attractive, as 'outsiders', to receiving countries. There are some differences in the way in which domestic tourism is handled statistically depending on the purpose of the statistics. The Australian report quoted above explains these (p. 6). However, domestic tourism has been, and still is, widely understood to refer to the activities of persons travelling within their own country but away from 'their usual environment' for the broad range of purposes which have already been indicated (i.e. not just for holidays but for business, study, pilgrimage and so forth). Again they are divided into tourists and same-day visitors. Once more they are implicitly economically attractive 'outsiders' from the point of view of the places visited within their own country *for they do not include travellers remunerated from within these places*.

In effect, there are administrations at every level, from sovereign states downwards, which are keenly interested, for broadly the same reasons, in identifying tourists as well as in measuring their movements and expenditures. They include regions, counties or unitary authorities, districts and parishes within England which may be interested in movements of persons travelling into their respective territories for defined purposes, whether from within their country or from abroad. Administrations take a similar view elsewhere, for example, US regions (groups of states), states, counties and cities within states. In France, the equivalent local levels are *regions*, *départements*, and *communes*.

Regular measurement of movements inwards to these levels is difficult and expensive. International border controls, even where much reduced as in Europe, facilitate the identification of international tourists. Tracking movements within a country presents obvious challenges. Statistical information is consequently partial and fragmented. It is often based on national sample surveys of households and on the recent history of journeys taken by their members. This method gives far from complete information on destinations or places, at the different levels visited.

Sample survey results cannot be broken down reliably into small units (areas or localities). Also, for practical reasons, an arbitrary cut-off point is adopted. Only trips over a specified distance or incurring an absence away from home for more than a specified minimum time may be included in the survey. For example, the *American Travel Survey*, 1995 collected information on trips of the US population of 75 miles or more away from home (WTO, 1996b, p. 84). In the UK the Countryside Commission's *UK Day Visits Survey* (1996) counted as 'tourism' only those trips lasting 3+ hours and not made on a regular basis. In recent years advances have been made in methods based not on surveys of people at home but on data collected on the spot. At a seminar in 1998 on Measuring the Local Impact of Tourism, the UK's Department of Culture, Media and Sport (DCMS) issued a guidance pack with three items: *Measuring the Local Impact of Tourism; Practical Guide to Local Area Tourism Models* and the *EU Tourism Statistics Directive*. The number of UK local authorities carrying out their own studies is on the increase. The growth of potential interest in the UK reflects increasing development of incoming tourism. From 1982 to 1995 the number of local authorities in England and Wales employing Tourism Officers (or Tourism Units) grew from 172 to 232, according to the Municipal Yearbook. The DCMS documents were a response to local area administrations' preoccupation with the spending of tourists as an injection of new money into their communities.

How do local communities distinguish tourism from other activities with which it clearly has close affinities? How does it coincide or overlap with recreation and leisure? These latter terms may be used to describe the purposes of some important groups of tourism and same-day visiting. They are also often used loosely to designate activities similar to those of tourists but in which people engage *within* their own neighbourhoods or 'usual environment'. In the British context this usage is implicit in practice rather than explicit. *Leisure and Recreation*

Statistics is an annual report on expenditure by local authorities in England and Wales. It is produced by the Chartered Institute of Public Finance and Accountancy, London. The types of facility covered – swimming pools, sports halls, leisure centres, golf facilities, art galleries and country parks – are typically subsidized for the benefit of local communities. All spending on the provision of facilities is grouped under the heading 'Recreation and Leisure' while the only reference to tourism is an item for 'tourist promotion' which includes tourist information centres and expenditure aimed at attracting tourists to the area (1998 edition). The tourist is quite clearly an outsider. Tourism units tend to be located within overall leisure departments (though this practice is changing). They specialize in publicity and information, that is, in marketing in its narrowest sense.

Implicitly, in this context, out-of-home or neighbourhood recreation and leisure seekers, for whom provision is made often under public control and with public subsidy, are different from tourists in that they move about within their usual environment. Local government can be expected to have a special care for them. They are local electors and taxpayers and their families. These users and tourists may make use of the same theatres, museums and parks, fish on the same river banks and swim in the same pools. In making provision, local authorities and others involved have to take account of the requirements of all users and potential users. These must be aggregated into one mix. A policy covering supply is likely to be an overall leisure and recreation policy with tourism subsumed as one element. In many countries there is mixed use of services on the ground. Tourists and locals will be present together on, say, beaches or on the occasion of local cultural events and festivals. Tourism is normally clearly isolatable as a function of government only in the context of external marketing. In some exceptional situations, notably in developing countries where there is little or no local demand, tourism does concentrate in enclaves where production and marketing focus exclusively on the needs of 'outsiders'. But in highly developed countries local recreation and leisure are often the bedrock upon which tourism is built.

Drawing on US and Canadian experience, Mill and Morrison (1992, p. 313) state:

Goals for tourism have to be set before policy statements can be developed. In so doing, it is crucial that these tourism goals be not set in isolation. For example, there is a very close link between tourism and recreation. It can be argued that tourism is a form of recreation involving overnight travel or a certain distance away from home. In addition, both tourists and residents often share the same recreational facilities ... tourism policy cannot be separated from recreation and leisure policy. The use of attractions and facilities by the local population has to be considered as a possible constraint to tourist policy.

Elsewhere, the close inter-connection of different elements has long been recognized. French legal texts and policy statements frequently link *tourisme* and *loisirs*. This is manifest in new laws of 1987 and 1992 on the organization of tourism quoted by Pecqueux (1998, pp. 251–7).

There are sound operational as well as political and administrative reasons for treating out-of-home leisure activities, recreation and tourism as an entity. They depend on a wide range of common management and personnel skills and use the same technologies, for example, reservation technologies. They all entail hosting, taking care of and entertaining people away from their homes.

The tourism industry

Some industries are relatively easy to visualize and to isolate statistically: vehicle manufacturing, construction, textiles etc. Until the 1990s the tourism industry was identified by reference to tourists. Conceptually the industry was the amalgam of enterprises that interfaced with tourists together with ancillary back-up enterprises. Two difficulties were inherent in such an approach. First, such enterprises might already be classified as part of other industries in their own right. Second, their customer base extended well beyond international and domestic tourists and even beyond local recreationists. Much depended on location. A restaurant might derive only part of its business from these groups. New methods, TSAs (Tourist Satellite Accounts), bring suppliers more effectively within the framework of official statistical systems and take account of the extent to which they derive their receipts from tourism. TSAs are discussed in Chapter 2.

Even accepting that new methods will succeed in clarifying the identity of the tourism industry, there will probably still remain a body of sceptics. The DCMS document on *Measuring the Local Impact of Tourism* already referred to, remarks on the familiar view that 'there is no such thing as the tourism industry'. Mill and Morrison claim (in their Preface) that 'tourism is not an industry. Tourism is an activity.' Jefferson and Lickorish (1991) describe it as a 'trade' throughout. The issue has been discussed at greater length by Thomas Lea Davidson: 'What are travel and tourism: are they really an industry?' (1998, p. 22). The author indicates the conditions that must normally be met by an industry to qualify as such. One of these is that it should group firms producing and selling a common product, i.e. the product of one firm is a substitute for the product of another. Tourism is thought to fail this test. It is pointed out that tourism depends on parts of different industries and on a range of activities which complement one another. But this argument does not allow for the fact that groups of interests performing complementary functions for tourists in particular locations do compete with groups elsewhere with substitute offerings.

Could any reasonable observer, walking through Blackpool in England, Benidorm in Spain or Disneyworld in Florida, deny the industry's existence? In such heavy concentrations of tourism an ensemble of different enterprises cooperates to bring together the elements of one or more destination products. (Consider also the discussion of products in Chapter 4.)

Tourism is easiest to identify in common sense where it is the prime economic activity of a locality. Where it is dispersed, it is more difficult to seize and shape or influence, even though its overall effects may be important in national terms. Concentrated or dispersed, the existence of the tourism industry is very widely recognized in the whole body of literature presented in the references. It is not infrequently described as 'the world's biggest industry'.

Leiper (1990) has a definition which is now widely quoted. The industry:

> consists of all those firms, organizations and facilities which are intended to service the specific needs and wants of tourists.

The definition does not embrace all those ancillary activities which provide back-up goods and services for the industry and which have to be taken into account in assessments of the overall impact of tourism.

Official Tourism Administrations

National Tourism Administrations (NTAs) exist in well over 100 countries. WTO (1996a) reviewed the budgets of 109 NTAs but the coverage was not comprehensive. The WTO offers the following definitions of NTAs and their subsidiaries, NTOs:

1 The National Tourism Administration (NTA) is defined as the:
    (a) Central government body with administrative responsibility for tourism at the highest level, or
        Central government body with powers of direct intervention in the tourism sector.
    (b) All administrative bodies within national government with powers to intervene in the tourism sector.
2 Other governmental or official bodies of lower rank – either incorporated within a higher body or autonomous – may be regarded as NTA executive bodies. These may also include central organizations legally or financially linked to the NTA. One prime example is the National Tourism Organization (NTO) – also known as the National Tourist Office – defined as follows:
        An autonomous body of public, semi-public or private status, established or recognized by the state as the body with competence at national level for the promotion – and in some cases, marketing – of inbound international tourism.

Below the national level there exist in most countries official organizations with roles similar to those of NTAs and concerned with particular regions, sub-regions and localities. Like NTAs their principal functions are to encourage provision for and to attract tourists from outside their boundaries. At these levels there are dual structures too, regional or local government departments constituting the senior, policymaking element, with subsidiary bodies to take charge of operations, in particular, external marketing. At these levels a very wide range of different names are given both to the policymaking and operational arms across many countries. For convenience, they will be referred to in this book as Official Tourism Administrations (OTAs), preceded by the qualification regional or local. Occasionally the term OTA on its own will be used to embrace all types of official tourism administration from the national level downwards. The term OTO will refer to the subsidiary or operational arm.

The structure of the book

Part One, including the present introduction, gives an overview of tourism and of a number of terms commonly used in the formulation of tourism development and marketing policies. Tourism is itself controversial. How communities should organize themselves to cope with tourism also gives rise to controversy. The language used by policymakers and their advisers to discuss the sector and what to do about it is sometimes imprecise and can give rise to misunderstandings. Tourism has existed for a long time but policymaking is still prone to amateurism. Therefore the reader is invited to consider the author's reflections on some of the most commonly used terms before proceeding to the core of the book.

Major issues were exposed in early debates on tourism in the UK. These are discussed in some detail at the beginning of Part Two. It will be implicit in the rest of Part Two and indeed in the rest of the book that such issues have not been peculiar to the UK or to one particular phase in the development of tourism. They are virtually universal and recurring. They are a permanent feature of the landscape of tourism and have to be kept continually under review.

Parts Two and Three take discussion beyond initial identification of issues to the way in which they have been addressed over several decades since the advent of mass tourism and more recently in a selection of leading countries.

Finally, Part Four attempts to draw the threads together. Highlighting the main lessons to be drawn from past experience and taking into account the likely long-term context, this concluding section will offer guidelines to the tourism policymakers of the twenty-first century.

Choice of countries for illustrative purposes

The book as a whole draws on experience in a very wide range of countries but it will be clear that certain issues are pursued in greater depth by reference to a limited number. Those selected are the USA, France and the UK, especially the UK. The tourism industries in the three countries are among the most advanced and sophisticated in the world, drawing on vast international markets and on their own domestic markets. Together they offer every known category of tourist product. There are some significant differences in their approaches to tourism development and marketing which are instructive.

The commentary on the USA, France and the UK is extended by means of a limited number of regional and local examples. Successful tourism policy depends ultimately on the organization of space. The author has chosen two contrasting parts of the world – first, one of the least visited and most thinly populated areas of the USA, and second, one of the most densely populated and heavily visited corners of Europe and of the globe.

Points of detail

References to the UK and its constituent parts may be confusing to some readers unfamiliar with this 'compound unitary state'. Government policy is sometimes applicable to the country as a whole, that is, to Great Britain and Northern Ireland, but the main body of tourism legislation and policy relates to Great Britain (or simply Britain), which is comprised of England, Scotland and Wales. Tourism is handled somewhat differently in each of the constituent parts. Comment on the UK in the book majors on England, which accounts for 85% of the UK's tourism.

Finally, British spelling is generally used but US practice is followed in a limited number of cases where this differs from the British and where the US source is quoted verbatim. The translations of quotes from French text are the author's.

2

The case for the encouragement of tourism: pro-tourism lobbies

If one is to look for a single, authoritative, collective statement which best supports the view of tourism as the supreme good of modern civilization, then a prime candidate must be the resolution passed unanimously by the United Nations XXI General Assembly designating 1967 as International Tourism Year. This, quoted by Burkart and Medlik (1982, p. 59), stated that:

> tourism is a basic and most desirable human activity deserving the praise and encouragement of all peoples and all Governments.

The clearest indication that the principle has been widely recognized by States is the growing body of legislation that has given employees the right to paid annual leave. Within the European Union, for example, every employee is entitled by law to a minimum of four weeks' paid leave per year and in some European countries the figure is much higher. In the UK the minimum was four weeks from the end of 1999 (Department of Trade, 1998). This does not mean that all entitled workers use their paid leave for a holiday away from home, although in developed countries a high proportion do.

The thinking behind the UN Declaration has been developed over the years. The 1980 Manila Declaration adopted by the WTO's World Tourism Conference stated that the right to use of leisure and, in particular, the right to access to holidays and to freedom of travel and tourism were recognized as an aspect of the fulfilment of the human being by the Universal Declaration of Human Rights. WTO's Bali Declaration 1996 proclaimed that tourism, which was now enjoyed by all social strata, had become an important human need and 'not just a leisure activity'.

Individual commentators have written of the phenomenon in glowing terms. For example, the American authors McIntosh, Goeldner and Ritchie (1995, p. 191) present Chapter 10 of their wide ranging study with the following heading and introduction:

Cultural and International Tourism for Life's Enrichment: … The highest purpose of tourism is to become better acquainted with people in other places and countries, as this furthers the understanding and appreciation that builds a better world for all. International travel also involves the exchange of knowledge and ideas – another worthy objective. Travel raises levels of human experience, recognition and achievements in many areas of learning, research and artistic activity. In this chapter, we discuss travel as it enriches our lives.

There exists a wide if rather uncritical convention that tourism is *a good thing*, especially for tourists. But what about the receiving or host countries and communities? The rest of this chapter focuses on the claims made for tourism as a positive contributor to economic, social and cultural development *in the places visited* and as potentially a force for conservation and environmental protection.

The enthusiasm typical of those who built the modern tourism industry in the UK may be gauged from these words by a businessman to a gathering of political and industrial leaders in 1979. At a lecture to mark the 50th anniversary of the start of official promotions of Britain as a tourist destination, Sir Peter Parker (a Board member of the British

Tourist Authority from 1970 to 1976 and Chairman of British Rail at the time of the address) said:

> This is a great occasion, charged with the energy of a half century, and the daring. What we are celebrating is, above all, the will of people who dared against the odds of their time 50 years ago, to accentuate the positive in the teeth of a prevailing negative wind …
>
> And, of course, it has been more than a campaign, it has been a movement of people, of minds and of hearts, it has grown and formed with all the passion of a crusade if without the piety. So we speak about a great industry, about a success story, about a theme that rings out with challenges. That is how I see the theme of the last 50 years. I see it as the story, the saga rather, of the emerging industry of tourism; an industry still not fully understood, still not even clearly defined because it is a complex part of so many industries, and an industry of risk-taking and risk-making.
>
> An authoritative definition comes formally from the Tourism Society:
>
> *Tourism is concerned with the temporary short term movement of people to destinations outside the places where they normally live and work, and their activities during their stay at those destinations.*
>
> But for this occasion, for such an assembly, we can describe the theme more sweepingly. I am talking of a vast set of activities crucial to the country's prosperity; it is perhaps one of the single largest economic activities in the country. Good for trade. Good for business. Good for people. And it is a growth trade, and it has been so for 100 years with a few warlike interruptions.

With the passing of time, governments worldwide and the business community have adopted a more cautious style as tourism has grown apace throughout the world. The enthusiasm of the 1970s has gradually given way to a more critical climate in which even the most expansionist promoters of the industry, whose favourite word is 'growth', will feel duty-bound to recognize the need for 'sustainability'.

In the immediate years after the Second World War, official pronouncements laid great stress, almost exclusively, on the economic benefits of tourism – above all on its potential contribution to international balances of payments. This may be illustrated again with a UK example. Following a review by Government and a decision in 1950 to establish one organization as the agency for the promotion and development of tourism, Harold Wilson, then President of the Board of Trade, wrote to the Chairman of the new British Travel and Holidays Association in the following terms:

> Our present economic circumstances render it imperative that in all aspects of its work the primary, and indeed paramount, aim should be to increase to the maximum the number of tourists from the dollar area who come to this country. … the primary objective must be to create conditions which will be as attractive as possible to visitors from the dollar area, and will enable the country to maximize its earnings of dollars.

The full text of the letter is on pp. 22–5 of the British Tourist Authority Report (1975), *The British Travel Association 1929–1969*.

> But the UK's situation was not unique. The OECD Tourism Committee (1989, p. 15), in a succinct review of government policy and action over 25 years to 1988, commented:

> In the immediate post-war years the leaders of the European countries that were to become Members of the OEEC and then the OECD were rapidly confronted with a shortage of hard currency. Promotional activities under official auspices were thus seen as a means of bringing in hard currency.

The same report referred briefly to the emergence during the 1980s of new concerns in OECD countries: regional development, rural development and job creation and, by implication, acknowledgement at policymaking level of the potential benefits of tourism as well as problems in these areas.

In the 1990s advocates of tourism worldwide added to their portfolio a new sheaf of benefits, both economic and non-economic. The former (economic) are discussed first.

Fresh impetus was given to the economic debate by two events in the 1990s:

- the UN's publication of Standard International Classification of Tourism Activities (SICTA); and
- the invention of Tourism Satellite Accounts (TSAs).

For many years before this decade, assessment of economic impacts on destinations had been derived to some extent from bank reports but largely from estimates of tourists' expenditures on accommodation, food and drink, transport, shopping and other items. The sources were in many cases official surveys which collected the information direct from representative samples of tourists. *Ad hoc* multiplier studies here and there attempted to assess the full impacts of this injection of new money, or first round of spending, as it flowed in successive rounds of spending through the economy. Such methods were unsatisfactory. They were expensive and random. Good data were difficult to obtain. These techniques did not give a full picture regularly enabling proper comparisons to be made between countries and between the tourism industry and other industries.

Under the leadership of WTO, WTTC and the OECD, considerable advances have been made in the development of TSAs. These are derived not from demand and from estimates of first rounds of spending but from the producers of goods and services for tourists and their suppliers. They are more comparable with standard government accounts for other industries. Several governments have developed and made use of TSAs. There is an excellent introduction to the subject and review of progress by Sonpal in the *Journal of the Tourism Society* (2000, p. 23). The WTO is promoting the wide application of TSAs in more countries. Work in this field has already given visibility to a new generation of data. A WTO publication entitled *The Economic Impact of Tourism – Using Tourism Satellite Accounts to Reach the Bottom Line* (1999a) carries the sub-title '*Proving the Economic Importance of Tourism*'. The introduction to the report notes that it will take some years for the new standards to be implemented globally but that 'quite a bit is already known about tourism around the world'. Impacts on GDP, export earnings and employment are discussed. The contribution to the GDP of several types of countries is indicated. It is extremely important in tropical islands such as the Maldives and Jamaica and substantial in a range of countries such as Canada, Italy, Spain and Switzerland.

The WTO estimates that there are 115 million direct tourism jobs

17

worldwide or approximately 4% of the world total. Creation of new jobs has been 1.5 times faster than the world average in the past 15 years. Millions more indirect jobs can be attributed to the tourism sector.

The document lists the main headings under which TSAs can produce persuasive results:
1 Tourism GDP
2 Ranking of tourism
3 Tourism employment
4 Investment
5 Tax revenues
6 Tourism consumption
7 Tourism balance of payments.

Finally, the publication details the experiences of six very different countries in the use of TSAs. The quote from the Canadian Tourism Commission, which has led the field in the development of this method, is illuminating:

> In 1995, the government was looking for industries that could help Canada climb out of a recession. As a result of our Tourism Satellite Account, we had solid figures to put on the table and tourism was identified as a strategic sector for economic development. A new public–private entity was formed to develop the tourism industry and over the past four years we have seen Canada's tourism promotion budget grow tenfold from C$13 million to C$130 million through a combination of public and private financing.

It will probably be many years before a significant number of countries follow Canada's example in the publishing of regular TSAs. The WTTC, a private enterprise organization, no doubt impatient for a global system to come on-line, has commissioned *simulated* satellite accounting research to produce estimates of tourism impacts on the global economy in 1999. These appear in the WTO publication already quoted and are summarized as follows:

Travel and Tourism Industry GDP	US$1328 billion
% of total GDP	4.4%
Travel and Tourism Economy GDP	US$ 3,549.9 billion
% of total GDP	11.7%

Jo Coleman

Information Update Service

Butterworth-Heinemann

FREEPOST SCE 5435

Oxford

Oxon

OX2 8BR

UK

Keep up-to-date with the latest books in your field.

Visit our website and register now for our FREE e-mail update service, or join our mailing list and enter our monthly prize draw to win £100 worth of books. Just complete the form below and return it to us now! (FREEPOST if you are based in the UK)

www.bh.com

Please Complete In Block Capitals

Title of book you have purchased:...

....

Subject area of interest:...

Name:...

Job title:..

Business sector (if relevant):...

Street:..

Town:.. County:..

Country:.. Postcode:.....................................

Email:...

Telephone:...

How would you prefer to be contacted: Post ☐   e-mail ☐   Both ☐

Signature:.. Date:...

☐ Please arrange for me to be kept informed of other books and information services on this and related subjects (✔ box if not required). This information is being collected on behalf of Reed Elsevier plc group and may be used to supply information about products by companies within the group.

FOR OFFICE USE ONLY

Butterworth-Heinemann,
a division of Reed Educational
& Professional Publishing Limited.
Registered office: 25 Victoria Street,
London SW1H 0EX.
Registered in England 3099304.
VAT number GB: 663 3472 30.

BUTTERWORTH
HEINEMANN

A member of the Reed Elsevier plc group

Travel and Tourism Industry Employment	67.8 million
% of total	3.1%
Travel and Tourism Economy Employment	192.3 million
% of total	8.2%

Source: WTTC/WEFA

Note: Travel and Tourism Industry identifies the impact of goods and services directly produced for visitors, while Travel and Tourism Economy identifies the broader impact of travel demand as it flows across and through the economy).

A selection of comments, made at the highest levels in different world regions, illustrates how widely the economic case has been promoted and the extent to which it has been developed in detail.

Asia

At the WTO seminar on Asian Tourism Experiences in Kyoto, Japan, 1998, Shogi Ishizuki, Chairman of the Japan Tourist Association, stated:

WTO reported that the international tourist arrivals in the world in 1996 reached 596 million people. In the year 2000, it will increase to 660 million and it will further increase to 940 million in 2010. As for the international tourism income, in 1996 it was US$436 billion. Tourism accounts for 10 per cent of world GDP and employment and tourism is the largest generator of both GDP and employment. In ten years, the tourism share in GDP is expected to increase to 11 per cent. These forecasts of further growth of tourism makes us feel really encouraged about the bright future of tourism. (WTO, 1998a, p. 11)

Europe

In a background paper for the WTO/CEU Joint Seminar on the Responsibilities of European Governments in April 1997, Keller and Smeral wrote:

Tourism demand is an important income and employment generator which, directly and indirectly, affects many different branches and services. The most important are hotels, restaurants, the retail trade, transport, sports, entertainment, culture, travel agents, tour operators, guides and several personal services. These branches need inputs from other branches such as the construction industry, agriculture, food and beverage industry, clothing industry, machinery, consultants, lawyers, tax accountants, etc. so that the value added directly created in the first round increases additionally with the degree of specialization and decreases with the sizes of the different import quotas.

According to EUROSTAT estimates, the value added share created directly and indirectly from tourism in the European Union (EU) – international and domestic tourism – amounts to approximately 5% of the aggregated GDP of the EU. Countries such as Italy, Austria, Portugal, Spain or Switzerland have a significantly higher value added share than the European average.

Tourism is also a powerhouse in terms of generating employment – especially for young people. It ranks as one of the major sources of jobs in most OECD and non-OECD member countries. In the EU, the average share of employment is 6% (3% to 4% of the average share is related to the work force of the hotel and restaurant industry). …

Tourism in Europe is dominated by SMEs (small and medium sized enterprises). SMEs boost regional and local economies as well as labour markets. Tourism discourages migration from rural and mountain areas, therefore reducing regional disequilibria. According to EUROSTAT, 96% of the 1.3 million hotels and restaurants in the EU are small firms with less than nine employees. Most of the firms are family owned. (WTO, 1997, pp. 3–4)

North America
In the preamble to the United States National Tourism Act 1996, the Congress finds that:

1 The travel and tourism industry is the second largest service and retail … industry in the United States and travel and tourism services ranked as the largest United States export in 1995, generating an $18.6 billion surplus for the United States.
2 Domestic and international travel and tourism expenditures totaled $433 billion in 1995. $415 billion spent directly within the United States and an additional $18 billion spent by international travelers on United States carriers traveling to the United States.
3 Direct travel and tourism receipts make up 6 per cent of the United States gross domestic product.

4 In 1994, the travel and tourism industry was the nation's second largest employer, directly responsible for 6.3 million jobs and indirectly responsible for another 8 million jobs.

5 Employment in major sectors of the travel and tourism industry is expected to increase 35 per cent by the year 2005.

6 99.7 per cent of travel businesses are defined by the Federal government as ... small businesses. (*Source:* Library of Congress, Washington, DC)

Developing countries

In a communication from the Commission of the European Communities to the Council and the European Parliament, it was declared that:

> Tourism can have a marked impact on the economy, especially in developing countries, and can account for a substantial portion of GDP: in the past, growth in international tourism has ushered in structural changes in certain developing countries, sometimes ousting traditional productive sectors. Tourism has a major effect on job creation, being labour-intensive, whatever the level of skills required. It also stimulates activity in many other sectors of the economy such as transport, construction and food industries. Its growth prospects hold out real opportunities, not just for those international concerns already very active in the sector but also for the many small and medium-sized firms, including those active in rural areas and among social groups experiencing difficulties in the job market, such as young people, women and less skilled workers. (Commission of the European Communities, 1998.)

In summary, advocacy of tourism has broadened to take account of its role not only as an earner of foreign exchange for participating countries but as a source of new income, a promoter of a wide range of businesses and professions, a very significant base for the development of small and medium enterprises, a stimulus to job creation, a support for poor regions and locations within countries and a replacement for declining or lost industries.

It was observed in a WTO report (1996b, p. 59) that:

> If this nation [the USA] is serious about its commitment to economic growth, to economic opportunity for all Americans, to the expansion

of world trade, and to a continually improving quality of life, it must be concluded that tourism activity and the industry that facilitates it has a major role to play.

But in the late 1980s and throughout the 1990s increased attention has been given to analysing and promoting tourism's *non-economic* benefits. Official statements have tended to add these in to an overview of all benefits. This suggests that a bolstering of the economic case has often been sought by the industry and its allies. Extracts from a number of WTO declarations illustrate the breadth of this overview:

Osaka 1994

... tourism is the greatest producer of world gross domestic product and employment, plays a significant role in promotion of mutual understanding between the peoples of the world and in maintenance of peace through people-to-people exchanges, and thus contributes to the prosperity of many countries and regions.

Bali 1996

... tourism can really enhance the quality of human relationships, regardless of the ethnic, racial, religious or socio-cultural differences and has a great role to play not only in promoting mutual understanding and relations among nations but also in helping to bring about world peace.

Malé 1997

... there is a recognition and appreciation for the uniqueness and diversity of natural environments, peoples, cultures, and heritages of the Asia-Pacific countries and their importance for tourism's potential for cross-cultural learning, international understanding, and world peace ...

Manila 1997

Improved living conditions for local populations, increased employment and income, upliftment of women and disadvantaged social groups, and, overall, poverty alleviation, are some of the areas which fall within the purview of social impacts of tourism ...

The WTO's *Guide for Local Authorities on Developing Sustainable Tourism* (1998b) held that carefully planned, developed and managed tourism could bring sustainable benefits to local communities. Besides listing a wide range of direct economic benefits such as job creation, the report (p. 29) observed:

Tourism requires that adequate infrastructure, such as roads, water supply, electric power, waste management and telecommunications be developed. This infrastructure can also be designed to serve local communities so that they receive the benefits of infrastructure improvements. Tourism development can help pay for the cost of improved infrastructure.

Tourism can provide new markets for local products such as agricultural and fisheries items, arts and handicrafts and manufactured goods and thereby stimulate other local economic sectors. Developing tourist facilities can help support the local construction industry.

Tourism stimulates development of new and improved retail, recreation and cultural facilities, such as speciality shops and improved shopping districts, parks and recreation, cultural centres and theatres, which local residents as well as tourists can use. Tourism often helps pay for cultural facilities and activities such as theatre performances which local communities could not afford without tourism.

The overall environmental quality of an area may be improved as a result of tourism because tourists prefer to visit attractive, clean and non-polluted places. Land use and transportation patterns may also be improved because tourism serves as a catalyst for redevelopment of some places.

Tourism can provide the justification and help pay for conservation of local nature areas, archaeological and historic sites, arts, crafts and certain cultural traditions because these features are the attractions for tourists. Therefore they must be maintained and often enhanced if tourism is to be successful and sustainable.

Tourism encourages a greater environmental awareness and sense of cultural identity by residents when they see tourists enjoying the local environmental, historical and cultural heritage. Often residents develop a renewed sense of pride in their heritage when they realise that tourists appreciate it. In this respect tourism may stimulate revitalisation of certain aspects of the cultural heritage that otherwise are being lost through the forces of modern development.

23

These views were drawn from experiences in different countries during the 1980s and 1990s in which the non-economic elements were being, as it were, added to the mix. The British Tourist Authority was among the first to promote them with vigour. The Authority's Chairman remarked in the 1983/84 Annual Report (1984, p. 9):

It is difficult to believe that even today, there are those who fail to appreciate the manifold benefits of tourism, both economically and socially. They complain about the number of tourists who come to this country and, generally question the importance of the industry. It is argued that the presence of large numbers of overseas visitors imposes an undue strain upon services and the environment.

But the truth is that tourism can and does enhance the quality of life in Britain by the provision of amenities and attractions which would not exist if it were not for overseas visitors. Tourism, in fact, conserves and does not destroy those very features of British life and the British scene which draw visitors to this country from all parts of the world.

How many theatres in Britain, particularly in London, would have rung down their curtains permanently had it not been for overseas visitors and their spending? How many restaurants and stores would have put up their shutters for good? And how many historic houses and gardens would have vanished, bulldozed into the ground, to make room for a new supermarket or car park? And how many jobs would not have been created and how many jobs would have been lost?

Tourism today is contributing much to the regeneration of inner-city areas and to the economic and social wellbeing of rural communities. Most important of all, it is creating jobs, especially jobs for young people.

So far, this chapter has covered the case for the encouragement of tourism which has been put repeatedly to a wide audience of potential supporters. In *Sustainable Tourism* (1998, p. 6) Middleton and Hawkins summarized the attractions of tourism to governments specifically. Their view is that:

It is especially attractive to governments in the economically developing world because of the opportunities inherent in the industry; specifically its:

- Massive size, recent growth and widely forecasted potential for future development.
- Ubiquity – there are few areas in the world in which travel and tourism is irrelevant either as a region of origin or destination for visitors – or both.
- Significance for the economic, foreign currency and employment needs of most, if not all countries of the world – especially for many smaller developing countries with otherwise limited resources to sustain the economic demands of their growing populations.
- Conferment of potential economic values in natural, cultural and other heritage resources such as scenery, wilderness, historic structures, biodiversity in flora and fauna and environmental quality, all of which have intrinsic values measured in world environment terms, but typically have no obvious trading value to most resident populations. Environmental values, with important exceptions in certain cultures, are largely irrelevant to subsistence level or starving populations.
- Contribution to the quality of the lives of virtually all residents, especially in economically developed countries.
- Relatively low pollution output of servicing organizations, compared with other major global sectors of the economy, such as intensive agriculture, fisheries, chemical industries, much of manufacturing, and extractive industries.

Many of the studies, papers and seminar reports which have furnished this chapter balance or attempt to balance, advocacy of tourism with a recognition of its potential problems and negative impacts. The overwhelming message, however, is that these can be overcome by means of intelligent policy frameworks, sound public and private sector forward planning and management to achieve sustainability. Indeed the 1990s have been characterized by intense debate on theory and practice of management. There has been not only an unprecedented explosion of official, industrial and academic comment, but this has focused on issues of management and control, as distinct from 'boosterism', promotion and publicity.

The need to achieve economic growth while minimizing negative environmental effects was recognized at least in principle by a new international force which emerged from the early 1990s. The World

Travel and Tourism Council is a global coalition of 70 Chief Executives from all sectors of the travel and tourism industry, including accommodation, catering, cruises, entertainment, recreation, transportation and travel related services. Its goals are:

to convince governments of the strategic and economic importance of Travel and Tourism, to promote environmentally compatible development and to eliminate barriers to growth of the industry.

Its membership includes the leaders of many of the best known international and multinational corporations in the sector. The WTTC has been active in promoting globalization, economic liberalization and open markets, particularly in air transportation. It has vigorously promoted its 'Principles of Intelligent Taxation', which WTTC claims 'will result in both increased resources for governments and strong competitive economies', in the clear conviction that taxation policy is a crucial determinant of the industry's development. (See *Issues in Tax Policy*, WTTC, 1994a, which carries the slogan 'The World's largest industry and generator of quality jobs'). While militant in the promotion of growth and in lobbying for the elimination of 'unfair' tax burdens to that end, the WTTC joined forces with others to promote sound management. Together with the WTO and Earth Summit, the WTTC moved to apply the principles of the 1992 Rio Earth Summit to its own sector. *Agenda 21 for the Travel and Tourism Industry – Towards Environmentally Sustainable Development* (no date) was the combined statement, widely distributed throughout the 1990s, which 'took a strategic look' at the implications of 'Agenda 21 Travel and Tourism' and announced a number of WTTC initiatives such as its Green Globe environmental management and awareness programmes for companies in the sector.

3

The case against tourism: doubters and sceptics

Patrick Roper

The concept of tourism as something that needed a new word to describe it emerged at the end of the eighteenth century and, in Britain at any rate, had a pejorative cast from the outset – as the Oxford English Dictionary puts it, 'originally usually deprecatory'. There was a patronizing, sneering feel about the terms 'tourism' and 'tourist'. When William Thackeray wrote in 1830, 'No doubt ere long the rush of London tourism will come this way' he was not suggesting that this was a good thing.

Much anti-tourism commentary has been triggered by this negativity embodied in the words 'tourism' and 'tourist'. Interestingly, the pejorative connotation does not seem to apply in French, where virtually the same words are used, ostensibly with the same meanings. In 1930 *Time & Tide* magazine commented that 'the office of the commissioner of tourisme [*sic*] in France ... was organised to clip as many petty annoyances as possible from the routine activities of visitors'. This is a telling contrast to the stated aims of many tourist boards today, which set out to help the industry and the balance of payments rather than the consumers.

The term 'tourism' was, of course, coined essentially to describe the phenomenon of the much larger number of visitors that improved methods of transportation, increasing wealth, literacy and the availability of travel information were generating. Inevitably this set in train the overcrowding, environmental damage, vulgarity and other downside phenomena associated with tourism and which I discuss later in this chapter. Prior to this though, there had been commentators who were doubtful about the virtue of travel, both from the point of view of the traveller and of the destination.

Plutarch (75 AD) in his life of Lycurgus, who lived in the ninth century BC, observed that he tried to fill Lacedaemon (modern Messini in south west Greece) with proofs and examples of good conduct so that the citizens would follow them unquestioningly. In order to protect this situation he forbade his people to travel abroad and:

> banished from Lacedaemon all strangers who would not give a very good reason for their coming thither; not because he was afraid lest they should inform themselves of and imitate his manner of government, or learn anything to their good; but rather lest they should introduce something contrary to good manners. With strange people, strange words must be admitted; these novelties produce novelties in thought; and on these follow views and feelings whose discordant character destroys the harmony of the state. He was as careful to save his city from the infection of foreign bad habits, as men usually are to prevent the introduction of a pestilence. (trans. Dryden, n.d.)

Today Messini is a popular tourist destination, but some of what Lycurgus feared is borne out by the disorderly activities now prevalent, and popular, in certain Mediterranean resorts.

Plato in his *Laws*, written about 360 BC, pointed out that the legislator has to consider what to do about his own people travelling abroad and the reception of strangers from elsewhere. He added:

> the intercourse of cities with one another is apt to create a confusion of manners, strangers are always suggesting novelties to strangers.

When states are well-governed by good laws the mixture causes the greatest possible injury, but seeing that most cities are the reverse of well-ordered, the confusion which arises in them from the reception of strangers, and from the citizens themselves rushing off into other cities, when anyone either young or old desires to travel at whatever time, is of no consequence. (trans. Jowett, n.d.)

As Europe emerged from the Dark Ages the Benedictines, who did so much to bring civilization to wild and lawless places, were not expected to enjoy travel. The Rule of St Benedict ordained that any brother sent out on business for the day should:

not presume to eat while he is out, even if he is urgently requested to do so by any person whomsoever.

The Benedictines were, of course, wonderfully hospitable, but the monks or nuns were not expected to enjoy the company of their visitors:

on no account shall anyone who is not so ordered associate or converse with guests.

St Benedict might have had a good point when one contrasts this with the situation described by Bender (1996) – himself a tourist – in the Daitokuji Zen Temple in Kyoto following the advent of modern tourism in the 1990s:

Walls which gave shelter to the gardens had been ripped out to give the tourists faster access. Loudspeakers under the veranda gave an intrusive speech to each tour group. Visitors were being strongly pressured to buy a tea ceremony. Monks were selling autographs and joking boisterously with visitors.

Better educated people in Europe would, until relatively recently, have had a Classical and Christian education and may have been aware of these earlier reservations about travel. Thomas More, in *Utopia*, for example, said that people wanting to travel needed to get permission and have a limit on the time they could spend away. He adds that they were always treated hospitably by other Utopians but would be expected to do some work if they stayed for more than one night. For shorter journeys out of his own city the traveller needed only 'his father's permission and his wife's consent'.

Today many of these ideas seem strange but there are still countries who are reluctant to see their citizens travel abroad, and not solely for the adverse effect it has on the balance of payments.

Arguments against tourism today fall into several different types based on the disbenefits that people believe the industry may bring. I have divided these as follows, though in many cases they overlap, or occur in combination.

1 Dislike of strangers and xenophobia. A simple dislike, fear or mistrust of strangers, or simply a reluctance to associate with them, perhaps because they have caused difficulties in the past, but usually because they have a strongly contrasting lifestyle that is thought to damage the lifestyle of the host destination.
2 Change of a destination's character. This is one of the commonest causes of argument against tourism and is often promulgated by tourists themselves, the 'discoverers' proclaiming that a place they liked has been spoiled by 'the hordes'.
3 Social and cultural damage. Tourism can undoubtedly create problems among communities that have had little exposure to people from the richer places of origin from which tourists are usually drawn. This is a complex situation and one that can give rise to the accusation that tourism eventually destroys the things the tourists go to see. Events, for example, that have arisen spontaneously within a culture to serve its own social and spiritual needs may become no more than tourist spectacles.
4 Economic damage. The purpose of tourism is usually said to be to create wealth and employment, but it is often claimed that most of the money returns to the original, non-indigenous investors, that jobs are low-paid, menial and seasonal and that other groups not involved in tourism may be marginalized or dispossessed by development.
5 Environmental damage. This covers a very wide range of issues, many of which are found equally in the case of non-tourist developments. Areas of high biodiversity are often destroyed by development and wildlife can be interfered with by trampling and disturbance. An increased number of people, especially wealthy people, can cause pollution, reduction in water tables, an increase

in local high chemical input, cash cropping to provide the range of foods demanded by the industry and so on. There is also the general global damage caused by increased consumption of fossil fuels through air and other travel and similar phenomena. These often affect places other than those the tourists visit in any quantity, though everywhere may suffer. An example of the former is the high ultra-violet levels in Tierra del Fuego caused by damage to the ozone layer from the action of chlorine and bromine released from chemical compounds used largely in the developed world.

6 External control or colonialism. Tourism from developed areas to Third World destinations is sometimes described as a new form of colonialism, a concept notoriously difficult to define and one that has to be carefully distinguished from imperialism. One definition of colonialism that most closely equates with that of some manifestations of tourism is that of T.R. Adam (1955):

the political control of an underdeveloped people whose social and economic life is directed by the dominant power.

I shall cover these six categories in turn.

Dislike of strangers and xenophobia

Xenophobia, deriving from Greek and meaning 'fear of foreigners', is perhaps too strong a term for the now rather few groups who would prefer it if outsiders stayed away altogether. Certain remote tribal peoples, often with good reason, fear outsiders because they are aware of a very wide range of undesirable consequences that may flow from an association with them. With these groups 'tourists' are probably not normally distinguished from other outsiders: all are bad.

There are other communities with highly distinctive lifestyles that are objects of great curiosity to people from elsewhere, but who simply do not enjoy being a kind of peep show or human zoo. According to Gork (1998), the Orthodox Jewish community of Mea Sharim in Jerusalem, for example, want to protect their beliefs from outside influence and their spokespeople have declared tourists officially unwelcome, though other members of the community may not agree with this, a situation which in itself shows how tourism can create internal tensions.

Mea Sharim illustrates another aspect of tourism. Traditional customs and habits are seen as a kind of living history, 'unchanged for generations' to use guidebook language. Their attraction to outsiders is that they stand in strong contrast to the increasingly homogenized appearance of the developed world in the twenty-first century. Often they are thought to represent a better way of life which was more certain and secure, with strong community and inter-generational bonds. The Jews of Mea Sharim are as they are because they live according to strict rules. Originally from Poland, they founded the neighbourhood in what is now Israel in the late nineteenth century and were, at that time, regarded as progressive. Today with the men in black coats and fur hats and women in long dresses and head shawls they are inevitably in danger of becoming just another 'sight' on the tourist itinerary and this is not a condition they relish.

According to an anonymous report on the Internet, the Amish community in North America have similar problems with tourism. Many are now moving from Holmes County, Ohio, with which they are closely associated, to the less well known Knox County because, in the words of one of them:

> Holmes was full of tourists and we wanted to find a farm we could afford … I guess we were looking for a place where it could be suitable for a group to move in.

One of the very few places in the world almost completely off limits to tourists is the island of Ni'ihau in Hawaii (Global Town's Ni'ihau, Internet Report, 1999). This has been privately owned since 1864 and the population of around 250 is largely Hawaiian Polynesian and Hawaiian is the main language. As an island in the group that is one of the world's major tourist destinations, Ni'ihau is a conundrum to the outside world. Over the years the impact on the Hawaiian culture and environment by non-Hawaiians has changed most of the islands beyond recognition. Puhipau, a Hawaiian who argues passionately against what he believes to be further damage to his home country, has said:

> I beg you please don't come to Hawaii. Tourism is killing us, it is literally sucking the life out of us.

The Ni'ihauns, as American citizens, are free to come and go as they please, though if they choose to live somewhere else, they are not permitted to return to their island permanently. The fact that they continue to stay on Ni'ihau indicates that life there is not unsatisfactory for them and they are undoubtedly aware of what other parts of Hawaii are like and that the wider world is a very different place.

The policy of almost absolute exclusion of tourism from Ni'ihau is in contrast to the situation of St Kilda, the small archipelago in the wild north Atlantic 115 miles (185 km) west of mainland Scotland. I was once told by a former chair of the Highlands & Islands Development Board that tourism had been a key factor in causing the 2000-year-old island community to lose its cohesion and contentment to the point where, in 1930, they were, at their own request, moved to mainland Scotland, leaving their ancient traditions behind and the islands uninhabited. Ironically, the islands are now a World Heritage Site for their 'magnificent sea cliffs, teeming sea bird colonies, and remains of past human settlement'. While, no doubt, there were many incentives for the St Kildans to move to places with a wider range of facilities and services, their problems began when early visitors started buying the tweed they made. Previously this activity had been controlled by the McLeod clan, but the new 'free' market enabled some rather more entrepreneurial families to make more money than others. In a community where co-operation was essential, this created a discord which, with other factors, eventually made an abandonment of the islands seem the only course of action.

It is easy to see how tourism, in a case like this, has had a damaging effect on a remarkable culture. One wonders, however, if tourism had not taken place at all, whether the St Kildans would have been happy to continue living as they did indefinitely, knowing they were increasingly out of step with the modern world and not able to enjoy most of its material benefits.

Today Ni'ihau is under pressure. Tour operators circle round it like wolves on the basis that forbidden pleasures are especially desirable. There is a dispute between the island's owners and the federal authorities about access rights. The owners claim their property rights extend offshore, but the Hawaiian police are only prepared to charge individuals who venture beyond high water mark. Thus some landings are made by boat for people wanting to beach comb, or fish from the beach (but, in reality, to say they have been to the 'forbidden island'. The island administration also runs a helicopter for emergencies and organizes over-flight tours, though these keep well away from the main settlement of Pu'uwai. The income from this makes an important contribution to the island's economy so, while tourists may not be welcome on Ni'ihau, the money from tourism is.

Change of a destination's or its people's character

Clearly much of this overlaps with section 1 above. Contact of one human group with another, from whatever cause, changes both. Particularly in the underdeveloped (in Western terms) world, observation of the morals and manners of new visitors sets off irreversible trains of thought in those being visited. How do they come to be like this? How do they get rich enough to visit us? Do they behave like this all the time?

The cycle of tourism resembles that of exploration, discovery and development. The first travellers set out and survive all sorts of dangers and privations to bring news of a distant country. They are followed by pioneers who develop matters further, then by increasingly conservative groups until the possibilities of the place originally discovered may be said to be fully developed.

In tourism the trailblazers are not the explorers or genuine travel writers, but backpackers and similar usually young adventurers, or sometimes the very wealthy who will pay substantial sums to get to destinations rarely visited by people from their particular culture, or by people at all.

Nowadays a salutary, but sobering, exercise is to scour a world atlas for very remote places then use the World Wide Web to see if one could arrange a trip there. By this method I discovered within minutes that I could book a holiday to the heart of the Tibesti Mountains in the central Sahara or cruise to the remotest Arctic Islands off the north coast of Siberia, both in relative comfort.

This urge for the remote, the almost unattainable, has turned places (with a twist of copywriting spin) that were once considered to be not worth a candle into sought-after destinations. Consider Macquarie Island roughly halfway between New Zealand and the Antarctic. According to Saffigna (1999), an Australian travel company that includes the island on some of their Antarctic cruises says:

In 1822 Captain Douglass gave his opinion on Macquarie Island – he thought it 'The most wretched place on earth of involuntary and slavish exilium that can possibly be conceived, nothing could warrant any civilised creature living on such a spot.' It's funny how times change! Today Macquarie Island is a highly sought-after adventure destination, valued worldwide for its unique geology, flora, fauna and history.

A defining characteristic of tourism, but one that is rarely considered, is that it is second-hand travel. Tourists, on the whole, are not explorers, they do not set forth like Captain Douglass into uncharted territory. As G.K. Chesterton (1936) once wrote, 'the traveller sees what he sees, the tourist sees what he has come to see'. The guidebook came into being at about the time that the term 'tourism' arose and started to make the recommendations with which we are all familiar today. As Roland Barthes (1972, pp. 81–4) pointed out in *Le Guide Bleu*, one of his essays in *Mythologies*, printed guides started to categorize phenomena in what we might now call a touristic way. Hilly and mountainous country was deemed better, more picturesque, than flat land; wilderness more worthy of visiting than cultivated areas. Churches, cathedrals, monuments and anywhere that monumental architecture was found were recommended with little concern as to whether the intending visitor had any interest in the purposes for which the buildings were created.

One of the common misunderstandings about tourism is that sightseers travel because there are particular things they want to see and that these things will then deliver insights and experiences that will be satisfying and revealing. In fact, as Dean MacCannell (1999, p. 14) points out, the majority of sightseers go to places they have previously heard of, read about or seen depicted to confirm they are there:

> In the establishment of modern society, the individual act of sightseeing is probably less important than the ceremonial ratification of authentic attractions as objects of ultimate value, a ratification at once caused by and resulting in a gathering of tourists around an attraction and measurable to a certain degree by the time and distance the tourists travel to reach it.

Sometimes, in fact, the reality is less impressive than the sales image. The 'oh yes, there it is' act of recognition is one of the factors that contributes to the image of tourists being dull and passive. The idea that tourists travel for the sake of new experiences overlooks the fact that tourism is also, as the advertisements so often say, about getting away from it all, of escaping, not of going somewhere but of leaving somewhere. If the destination is warm, welcoming, pleasant and affordable it may matter little where it is, so long as it is not home. Home, in contrast to away, has many constraints. At home or work the individual is well known to family, friends and acquaintances and is not in a position radically to change his or her behaviour. On holiday, however, a somewhat different persona can be presented. The taboos present in normal daily life can be more easily broken. Women from the Arab world often abandon the *hijab*, the veil, when visiting non-Muslim countries; shops in seaside resorts sell kiss-me-quick hats and rock false teeth that have no market in non-holiday areas. Nearly naked strangers mingle happily on resort beaches.

Such freedoms, attractive as they may be, tend to give tourism a bad reputation as being decadent. A report by Chachage (1998) records that a resident of a recently developed resort in Muslim Zanzibar anxiously remarked on a radio programme:

You can see the foreign women. They cross the way in our villages without any over-clothes. We see some of them walk in our areas half naked.

The Zanzibar Government has introduced dress guidelines for visitors, but having a dress code is one thing and implementing it another.

It is also interesting that people, on the whole, can only put up with the holiday level of freedom in short bursts; holiday satisfaction on longer visits usually peaks after a few days at a destination then declines over the remaining period until the individual wants to go home to renew their relationship with the cat and water the geraniums. As Paul Theroux once remarked, 'the grand tour is just an inspired man's way of heading home'. This fading syndrome was originally implied in the word 'honeymoon', a wonderful period that rose to fullness like the moon, then waned.

The morality, or lack of it, involved in some tourism is manifest in the remarkable quantities of alcohol that individuals often consume (again perhaps more a function of being away from home than from its low price) and the general relaxation of sexual mores. In many holiday destinations an abandonment of convention not only prevails, but is sought, and this again is because the individual is away from his or her normal environment with its many constraints. Tourists are then seen, often with justification, as rowdy, drunken and immoral, lacking in reasonable standards of decent behaviour and so on.

The pioneering tourist, whether backpacker or wealthy adventurer, usually has a 'get there first' (or 'almost first') mentality and it is often they who are the most vehement opponents of mass tourism. The Lonely Planet series of guides are particularly disparaging about these 'following packs'. Talking, for example, about Liguria, the Italy guide (2000) says:

> If you blink you'll miss the five magnificent villages of Cinque Terre, but you'll never forgive yourself if you do. The villages are wedged into impossibly mountainous countryside which borders coastal Liguria in the north-west of the country, and as yet the ravages of uncontrolled tourism have been kept in check.

Conflict also occurs when relatively sophisticated residents of places that have become popular tourist destinations decry the effects their visitors are supposedly generating. Journalists are often very adept at writing copy that knocks tourism, sensing that this will be popular with their readers (who are not normally tourists). The irony is that both journalists and readers almost certainly travel widely themselves and inflict the phenomena they profess to abhor on others (though, of course, they, like most individuals, do not categorize themselves as part of mass tourism, but as something on an altogether higher plane). Evelyn Waugh observed this with his acerbic wit when he said that the tourist:

> debauches the great monuments of antiquity, a comic figure, always inapt in his comments, incongruous in his appearance ... Avarice and deceit attack him at every step; the shops that he patronizes are full of forgeries ... But we need feel no scruple or twinge of uncertainty, 'we' are the travellers and cosmopolitans, the tourist is the other fellow.

An example of this contempt of tourism appeared in *The Times* (11 September 1999), when feature writer Jonathan Meades proclaimed that:

> Our cities are being killed by pedestrian zones which benefit only tourists and criminals.

(Note the juxtaposition.) Further on in the feature he adds:

> Leicester Square [London] is a pit lined by reeking fast food outlets and inhabited almost exclusively by gormless tourists and loitering representatives of the various trades that exploit gormless tourists.

He then asks if architect Norman Foster, then working on a scheme in the area, really intends that:

> a further swathe of epicentral London should be put off-limits and freed up to create a sort of trash sump for grockles[1].

As well as these various social and cultural shifts engendered by tourism, it undoubtedly changes the appearance of places and, to some, this is a matter of regret, whereas others welcome it. However, we live in a world that constantly changes and the art is to encourage the good and discourage the bad (however those two opposites are defined) in as sensitive and as sensible a way as possible. On England's south coast the land now occupied by two towns, Brighton and Peacehaven, would perhaps both be National Nature Reserves or similar heritage areas if earlier developers had not felt they had potential as both holiday and residential towns. Featured by Thompson (2000, p. 8) in the *Daily Telegraph*, Brighton now boasts some of the finest seaside architecture in the world, including the famous Royal Pavilion and the West Pier, which is currently being restored at an estimated cost of £40 million, of which over £14 million will come from the UK Government's Heritage Lottery Fund.

But poor Peacehaven, only a few miles east, has to put up with the 'amorphous rash of bungalows' kind of comment. To the untutored eye, both Brighton and Peacehaven are fascinating, but the received wisdom is that, qualitatively speaking, Brighton is light years ahead and the reason is that high quality architecture was opted for from the outset. Today these differences in character bring both advantages and disadvantages to those living in either place.

Neil (1990) notes that some of the undesirable consequences of tourism development in the European Alps have been highlighted by philanthropist Prince Sadruddin Aga Khan, president of the Bellrive Foundation and a former United Nations Commissioner for Refugees:

Slowly but surely the mountains are being eroded and in some places reduced to deserts. I blame tourism for this explosion of chaotic development of the mountains. There are too many ski lifts, too many hotels, too many chalets, and too many cars.

The Bellrive Foundation calculates that there are 40,000 ski runs throughout the seven Alpine countries, carrying 1.2 million passengers to summits each hour during peak season. Sadruddin added that:

Countless roads and highways carry more traffic than any other mountain system in the world. Exhaust fumes are killing natural wildlife and vegetation.

The Swiss Forest Institute estimates that at least 50 per cent of the trees in the Alps are dying, resulting in serious soil erosion.

Sadruddin said he was not against tourism but would like to see a moratorium on further development and that protective legislation was too often 'inappropriate, ineffective and ignored'. When he spoke in 1990, chain saws, bulldozers and cranes were clearing more natural habitat and farmland at Albertville in France for the 1992 Winter Olympic Games.

Social and cultural damage

One of the greatest problems in respect of the advent of tourism in places that have had little or none is that, as has been remarked above, it creates divisions and tensions within the community. The new visitors may not only bring in work and wealth, as Plato remarked. They bring in novel ideas that can create disharmony and they can easily generate envy, a desire to emulate the habits of people who clearly seem so rich and stylish, or cynical contempt. As travel writer Robert Byron said when writing of the view from Syria in the earlier part of the twentieth century:

If you can come from London to Syria on business, you must be rich. If you can come so far without business you must be very rich. No one cares if you like the place, or hate it, or why. You are simply a tourist, as a skunk is a skunk, a parasitic variation of the human species which exists to be tapped like a milch cow or a gum tree.

At the advent of the year 2000, a television programme in Britain ran a feature on the Greenwich Meridian, 0° longitude. One of the places visited was Yendi, a largely Muslim town in northern Ghana which, since it has no hotel although it is a substantial and fascinating place, was evidently not on any tourist itinerary. The presenter, Jon Snow, an experienced and widely travelled news broadcaster, was clearly surprised and pleased by the infectious welcome he was accorded. He was a traveller and an equal, someone from a distant land with whom information could be usefully exchanged and enjoyed. It made Yendi appear a wonderful place to visit but, if it were to be 'developed', how long would this unaffected pleasure in the arrival of strangers be maintained? To many, the garlanding with flowers on arrival at a South Pacific island airport is fun, part of what has been paid for. To others it is an embarrassing pastiche of a custom that once had some genuine feeling and significance, but which now demeans both host and visitor.

Ultimately this kind of tourism can generate two cultures: the 'replicated' South Seas with an eclectic mix of stereotypical elements the visitor might already be more or less familiar with and the real South Sea island out of sight of the tourists and where they may be unwelcome. This is the South Pacific of modern housing where people eat fast food and go to work in offices very much like those throughout the world. Presenting ersatz customs and culture of the past to tourists is like breaking wonderful and complex stained glass windows and putting them back together again higgledy-piggledy for the benefit of outsiders who just want to see a bit of colour.

Set against these examples of tension, a great deal of tourism has little or no discernible effect on those living in the places visited or the local environment, though this is usually only true when there is a small cultural difference between visitors and visited. In my home village in Sussex, for example, we have a hotel, several bed and breakfast establishments, a couple of restaurants and a picturesque goose-grazed green surrounded by ancient cottages. Throughout the year tourists must be present here, yet this is scarcely noticeable. They do not jam the road, take all the parking spaces, strip the shops of commodities, offer an incentive for the locals to go into prostitution, or create drunken disturbances. In fact they are surprisingly unobtrusive. A public footpath passes our house, a path that is signposted and marked clearly on all local maps. Tourists are said to enjoy walking but, in over 25 years' residency, I cannot say I have ever seen a single individual that I considered was most probably a visitor making use of this very attractive walk. But they do all the things that tourists are supposed to do, like create employment: often some of the younger people's first jobs enabling them to earn a small measure of financial independence, plus the experience of working and the social interactions.

Economic damage

The economics of tourism are often spoken of as deceitful. It is argued that a new development will create jobs and put cash into the local economy. Many believe the jobs available at the destination end will be low paid and that very little of the money spent by tourists will remain in the local economy.

Many words have been written about all this, but it is important to note that the strategic policy of both the destination and of the outside organizations responsible for the developments can be adjusted to correct some of the imbalances, provided the will to do so exists. If, however, the decision- and policymakers at the destination do not care a great deal about the fate of their less empowered citizens (which, sadly, is often the case) and developers are not especially interested in the welfare of those who will work for them and those who have, effectively, created the destination, then tourism will be seen as destructive. Many other industries can and do behave in exactly the same way: it is not tourism as such that is causing the problems, but the character and motives of those responsible for it, as well as the pressures they experience.

Sadly the growing stridency of criticism against this 'unacceptable face of tourism' has resulted in vested interests concocting a wide range of cosmetic schemes that give an appearance of virtue. Much so-called green and ecotourism comes into this category and has been dubbed 'greenwash'. It is of increasing importance, and widely acknowledged importance, to conserve energy, to reduce pollution and to encourage biodiversity and tourism can sometimes help to achieve these aims, but to create a set of problems, then pat yourself on the back for reducing them a few percentage points is clearly insincere and simply a device for alleviating any guilty feelings your customers might have and for making backers and stakeholders feel better by winning a few plaudits for responsible housekeeping.

Chachage (1998) has written about some of the more damaging effects of tourism in Zanzibar. The first tourist hotel was built by the Zanzibar Government in 1974. By 1983 there were ten tourist hotels and guest houses and by 1985, Zanzibar was producing policy and legislation concerning tourism, and the Zanzibar Tourist Corporation (ZTC) was formed. It was with the introduction of the Trade Liberalization Policy of 1985 and the Private Investments Act of 1986 that tourism became an important aspect of Zanzibar policies and plans. Chachage says:

> There were 95 hotel projects approved between 1988 and 1995. The total number of hotels and guest houses stood at 150 by 1995, and these, according to the ZTC were not enough to accommodate tourists. The Aga Khan Fund for Economic Development opened the Zanzibar Serena Inn in 1996 ... the investments were based on attractions such as kilometres of white sandy beaches, historical sites and monuments, the old stone town, etc.

When the tourism policy was introduced in 1986, Zanzibar received 22 846 tourists in that year. By 1996, with a few fluctuations, it was nearly 70 000 and:

> the contribution of tourism to the GDP was almost 19 per cent by 1995 and it was alleged that it was employing (directly and indirectly) about 10 000 people.

The author continues:

> Despite the fact that Zanzibar has always aspired to establish an 'organised sustainable high class tourism', a tourism which is culturally and environmentally friendly, the reality has been far from this. Tourism in Zanzibar has basically been the mass type of the sun, sex, sand, and added to this, drugs. *Africa Events* quoted one resident of Zanzibar town as having said the following on the character of the tourists in Zanzibar:
>> they are up to no good these tourists. All over the Island whorehouses are popping up to cater for them. The so-called hotels coming up by dozens on beach fronts are no more than dens of iniquities. Tourists lure our girls there with wild promises of foreign travel. They then get them into the cocaine habit. The next thing you know they are hooked. We do want foreign investment,

but not the sort that turns our sisters and daughters into whores and junkies.

It is with tourism development that drug abuse and drug-trafficking have become rampant. Some Zanzibari youths went to the streets to protest against tourism in the name of defence of Islamic faith. There were also condemnations of the industry from religious leaders in many parts of the country in that year. Sheikh Kurwa Shauri was imprisoned and finally deported to Tabora (mainland Tanzania) after demanding the government to abolish tourism.

Chachage cites much evidence to show that tourism, mainly from Europe, has been highly instrumental in developing the Zanzibar drugs trade:

Some of the tourism enterprises are widely believed to be involved in drug-trafficking and money laundering, and to use the tourist investments simply as a pretext. ... There were more than 150 Zanzibari youths serving long term jail sentences in India, Pakistan, Bangladesh, Turkey, Egypt and some European countries for drug-trafficking by 1995. Twelve of them had been sentenced to death.

Overall their studies have led to a very damning conclusion for the kind of tourism development that has taken place in Zanzibar. They point out that the tourist industry has the potential of creating new jobs, but mainly service jobs that are low skilled, low paying and often seasonal:

They are mainly menial and demeaning and the profits are repatriated to the West. Many companies and hotels tend to import most so-called skilled and specialized labour even if that labour is available in the country. Part of the reason for this is the fear that employment of locals, especially in clerical or office jobs, would lead to the exposure of some of the corrupt practices of these companies (e.g. tax evasion, under-declaration of incomes, capital flight, etc.). Another reason is the deeply embedded racism and class discriminatory nature of the structures of the industry, especially among the foreign-owned companies. The beneficiaries in this regard are the international tour and travel companies who arrange the packages and are paid most of the money: there is virtually no local control over tourism and the companies which exist in the Isles are mere agents. Such lucrative forms of accumulation have inevitably led to speculation in land earmarked for tourism development and conflicts with local communities in matters of land use. Conflicts over natural resources use as far as these investments are concerned have been on the increase because these investments have been hitting at the traditional land and resources rights. Many of these beach hotels and resorts have taken over areas which were being previously used by fishermen as fishing camps or landing sites. ... Most often, locals have had to sell their land, or face removal when the government has decided that the area is a tourist zone.

In *Rethinking Tourism and Ecotravel*, Deborah McLaren (1998) points out how:

Many governments are becoming international players as they claim to be developing ecotourism projects, yet these programs are coming at great expense to the environment. One of the worst acts of 'ecotourism' yet, according to a watch group in Thailand, is 'unbelievable'! In the name of ecotourism the Lao government has given the green light to the Malay Syuen Corporation to develop a mammoth resort [in a] national park ... to pave the way for the US$21 million 'Phou Khao Khonay-Nam Ngum Ecotourism Resort', including a mini-city of hotels, golf courses, casinos ... local residents have to move out of the area.

Unbelievable, maybe, because it does not seem to be true. The only ecotourism manifestation in the area appears to be the Lao Pako Resort on the Nam Ngum river in Lao. This, however, is a modest forest lodge and not the major development described to McLaren. Its ecological credentials seem sound enough, but its publicity material contains the following:

On the huge verandah which overlooks the river, there is ample space for just relaxing and taking in the view, reading the variety of books and magazines or playing chess, backgammon or cards.

It is an interesting reflection on modern tourism that people would travel thousands of miles to a remote tropical forest using high-energy consumption, polluting aircraft to stay in an ecologically sound lodge to read and play board games and cards.

Environmental damage

This has already been covered to some extent in the previous sections but, as well as massive changes to the character and culture of particular areas, tourism is often accused of destroying or damaging wildlife habitats and their flora and fauna, in other words the very things that help to make them attractive in the first place.

Part of the problem is that different societies, groups and people have different perceptions of nature. Henry Thoreau, the nineteenth-century American writer, once observed, on watching men clear-felling an area of North American virgin forest, that they stood back and regarded their work with the greatest satisfaction, while he was saddened by the destruction of another piece of wilderness. Many cultures simply do not understand the recent concern in the developed world for wildlife conservation. Others are horrified by the apparent lack of feeling we have for the land, and everything in it, as it is given.

It has been said that the anti-tourism commentary in the wildlife area usually comes from naturalists, amateur and professional, who are, in the main, tourists themselves. The study of wildlife requires peace and quiet and the presence of large numbers of other tourists who want to play ball games or hide and seek with half a dozen children does much to destroy the atmosphere and the satisfactions that naturalists seek.

However, some very busy areas are surprisingly rich in wildlife. Creatures like foxes, for example, find it more congenial in urban London than in the countryside where they may be hunted or shot and where food is often scarcer. I once lived for three years in a house in the centre of Alton Towers theme park in Staffordshire. There could be up to 30 000 people a day visiting the attraction and over 2 million visits annually between mid-March and early November, but the wildlife was remarkably varied and seemingly content. More so, apparently, than was the case on many of the neighbouring farms where modern methods of husbandry did much to reduce or eliminate anything that did not produce a cash return.

In some areas local naturalists will argue that one or another species is suffering as a result of disturbance by tourists, an assertion that may not always stand up to close scrutiny. In the Falkland Islands and the Antarctic, for example, an ever-popular draw are the colonies of nesting penguins. Some ornithologists have suggested that the approach of visitors to these very tame birds is causing disturbance and reducing their breeding success. On Anvers Island in the Antarctic this theory was tested by dividing a penguin colony in half with a fence, according to Smith (1997). One half was left in peace, as before, while the other half was visited by tourists on a regular basis. Upon the conclusion of the experiment it was found that the 'disturbed' penguins were not only less timid than their fellow penguins on the other side of the fence, but had no behavioural disorders. This does not mean that the colonies can be visited by any number of people without deleterious effects. If the birds are too distracted the ever-present skuas have more opportunities to steal their eggs. However, the proximity of human beings does not seem, *per se*, to have a negative effect.

Despite this there are undoubtedly many horror stories. A friend recently had a holiday in the Maldive Islands spoiled by other tourists who persistently broke off large lumps of the protected coral reefs as souvenirs. Similar problems occurred in East Africa near Mombasa, and the World Resources Institute (1998) published the following:

> The Mombasa Marine National Park is adjacent to the most heavily populated tourist beach along the Kenyan coast. The reefs are threatened by over-fishing, destructive fishing from beat-seining and spear fishing, organic pollution and sedimentation, and tourist damage from trampling. The reduction of predatory fish led to increases in burrowing sea urchins whose excavations began to reduce the reef framework to rubble.

The good news is that the creation of a marine national park here has reversed the damage. This is particularly encouraging as national park status often acts to increase tourism, rather than conserve wildlife, by generating publicity that appeals strongly, particularly to potential urban visitors, on the basis that a national park will have an infrastructure that enables them to enjoy it more easily.

A similar instance to the coral destruction is the case of 'Old Methuselah', a bristle-cone pine from the White Mountains of California that was long thought to be the oldest living thing on earth. It had to be protected against souvenir hunters who were pulling bits off and the nearby location of an even older recently found tree of the same kind has had to be kept secret in order to prevent this.

One sobering tale of how development and tourism can damage very things it sets out to give people the opportunity to enjoy is fc in the story of the Cornish chough. This attractive and engaging bl bird with bright red legs and beak is Cornwall's avian emblem and features on coats of arms, flags and in similar contexts. According to tradition, King Arthur is currently incarnated as a chough prior to his return to the world of humankind and thus the bird has a very special place in Cornish history and folklore. The chough is a bird of the sea-cliffs and coastal pastures and it is now extinct in Cornwall, though still resident elsewhere in remote parts of the British Isles. According to a report by Bellamy and de Savary (1990, pp. 31–8), the decline of the chough in the Duchy started with the arrival of the railway in 1860. This gave farmers access to distant markets and they began to cultivate many of the rough, cliff-top pastures where the choughs fed. Tourists also started to arrive by train in Cornwall in increasing numbers and are said to have disturbed the birds at their breeding sites by visiting the cliffs.

The latter may be another 'disturbed penguin' story, for many seabirds nest happily on the cliffs at Land's End and elsewhere despite the presence of large numbers of tourists. Nevertheless, it is another illustration of the kinds of conflict that can occur where development and the attraction of visitors can terminally damage many of the things that caused the area to be attractive in the first place. In summer 2000 zoo-bred choughs were released into the wild in Cornwall in the hope that the bird would once more become a feature of the Cornish cliffs.

External control or colonialism

Nicholson-Lord (1997) suggests that one of the ways in which tourism changes culture is by turning authentic traditions into profit-making performances:

> What's undeniable is that tourism, in one way or another, changes tradition and for many people, particularly in the Third World, that change looks and feels like degradation. Part of the problem is that tourism is colonialism in another guise – economic rather than political. Hence it rubs hard against the growing worldwide movement for local or national self-determination.

One of the most strident proponents of tourism as colonialism is McLaren (1998). She points to the setting aside of large areas of land for tourism development, or as national parks, as a manifestation of colonialism in the sense that they are available only to wealthy foreigners and out of bounds, or of restricted access, for indigenous people. Later in the same book she says:

> Tourism promotes the same colonial tendencies that agricultural export companies, missionaries, and others perpetrated in earlier centuries. Colonizing is not new, but tourism development as a form of colonizing is new and growing at tremendous rates.

She then cites the enormous growth of tourism in the last half of the twentieth century and adds:

> the numbers are remarkable and the effects catastrophic.

To help support her case, McLaren quotes Molner (1989), who said of the 1980s:

> The past decade has seen the colonization of the developing world by the tourism industry. Considering that international travel accounts for the exchange of more than $3 trillion a year, it may be safely said that tourism exerts a greater, more persuasive influence on the countries and cultures of the world than any imperial power ever has.

Interesting though these views are, they do seem to be forcing tourism into a mould it does not readily fit. Colonization, by most definitions, involves an attempt to settle permanently in another area regardless of whether anyone already lives there or not. The intention is not to return home again after a week or two. From the destination's point of view one can see that the year round replacement of one set of wealthy foreign visitors by another, and the establishment of facilities from their culture, may look like colonization (especially to those who have been colonized in the more recent past), but to draw the analogy too closely runs the risk of ascribing the consequences of tourism, and the intentions of tourists, to the wrong causes.

Trying to compare and evaluate the benefits and disbenefits of tourism can be a bewildering process. Many of the things alluded to in this chapter are summed up in an article by Kristin Huckshorn (1997) on a visit to Sapa in the mountains of Vietnam where the Hmong people live. On arrival, a group of local children welcomed the party with 'Hello! Goodbye! Money!' Huckshorn says:

> Visitors complained that booming tourism, poorly managed by local officials, had commercialised this once remote town, destroyed tribal customs and instilled bad habits in local children. The people the foreigners wanted to protect held a contrary view. Tourism put money in their pockets and improved living standards, minority villagers said. Where I saw exploitation, they smelled opportunity.

In 1993 Sapa had no electricity, one hotel and 3500 residents. About 20 backpackers would visit each month during the season. By 1997 electricity had arrived and there were 60 hotels and 10 000 residents. Up to 600 tourists can be in town over one weekend. The situation sounds chaotic and change is undoubtedly rapid. Many of the traditional attractions of a relatively undisturbed local people will, no doubt, disappear but, as Huckshorn remarks, and perhaps not dissimilar to the situation in St Kilda, 'the views are intoxicating'.

Talking about tourism development in Burma, broadcaster John Pilger said in February 2000 (BBC2, *Itchy Feet*):

> I don't think you can expect big business operations suddenly to turn into the tooth fairy and say 'well, that's all very nice, we won't do that any more, we'll withdraw our investment'. They are just like any other big businesses; they only respond to something that threatens their investment, that threatens their resources, their profits above all.

Hopefully more developments, whether for tourism or other purposes, will be controlled from the outset so that a reasonable compromise can be reached between the interests of all parties. If not it is very likely that much new tourism development will be destructive in some or all of the ways described above. Many believe that tourists themselves will boycott places where, for whatever reason, tourism seems to have an unethical dimension. Aung San Sun Kyi, the at one time imprisoned though elected leader of Burma (Myanmar), has asked people not to visit the country while under its present regime (who are courting tourists) but to come 'when the Burmese people are getting some benefit … and are not being exploited'. John Pilger says of such exploitation:

I think it's up to individual people to find out about that before they go, and if they feel strongly enough about it to boycott it, to go somewhere else. There's always an alternative. Always.

Fine words, but, in my view, unrealistic. The majority will simply read the brochures and listen to the travel companies: the policies and politics of particular destinations will only be of concern if they are seen as a threat to their personal interests.

One of the little-regarded elements in the various debates about the pros and cons of tourism is that concerning the motives of authors and commentators. Many books and papers that take a virtuous stance, or recommend virtuous future actions, are written by people who work in tourism and want to go on doing so. Not only does it provide them with a living, it enables them to get to many exotic destinations they would otherwise be unlikely to visit. Tourism is a seductive, and sometimes maybe even a Faustian, discipline.

There will be an increasing number of difficult questions asked about tourism in the twenty-first century. In order to secure its benefits and minimize the damage it can cause, ways should be sought of studying its effects and consequences by more people who do not have a strong vested interest so that travellers and hosts alike can be more confident, as is the case in so many other areas of human activity, that objective and responsible long-term policies are being evolved.

Note

1 'Grockles' is one of several mildly disparaging terms applied to tourists in Britain. It originated in Torbay, Devon and is reputed to mean that tourists look like little Grocks. Grock was an internationally famous circus clown whose characteristic prop was a suitcase and there may thus have been some resemblance between him and visitors who carried their suitcases from the railway station.

4

Language and concepts

Introduction

This book uses throughout a number of familiar sounding terms: development, marketing, tourist product, distribution, competition, segmentation, image and general brochure. These terms are reviewed in this and the following chapter as background to discussion and as a guide to further reading. The words 'tourist product' and 'image' are noteworthy victims of vagueness in many texts. An additional useful source is Medlik's *Dictionary of Travel, Tourism and Hospitality* (1996).

Development

This word has a specialized connotation in the domain of Official Tourism Administrations and their executive arms concerned with action to encourage the industry to develop and improve supply. The whole range of activities encompassed by the development function in its fullest sense has to be undertaken in totally new greenfield sites opening up to tourism for the first time.

Past examples have been the great Languedoc Roussillon regional project in France, the Cancún resort in the Mexican Caribbean and the Petite Côte resort strip in Senegal, West Africa. Current illustrations are the development of tourism in new, hitherto virtually unvisited National Parks in Africa, for example, in Tanzania and Zambia. An illustration of what is involved is in D.J. Jeffries 'Terms of Reference for a Project in Tanzania' (1993), prepared for the European Commission. These provided for development to begin with massive investment in infrastructure to underpin transport, utilities and telecommunications and on site preparation. This phase was to be followed by investment in superstructure, especially hotels and other forms of tourist accommodation and in other fixed installations requiring substantial capital. These would be supplemented by investment in equipment such as vehicles and sports equipment. Finally a workforce to manage and operate hotels and other installations and equipment would have to be put in place before a full product, or series of products, could be made available to tourists. In well-established destinations, the range and extent of actions required under the development heading can of course be much reduced when, for example, the infrastructure and superstructure are already in place.

NTAs worldwide have rarely had direct and exclusive responsibility for the very heavy, capital intensive initial phases of resort development which were handled higher up in government hierarchies. In the 1970s and 1980s, particularly in command-and-control economies, some NTAs had powers to invest in, build and run hotels and to operate tourism services such as bus fleets. From the mid-1980s onwards, liberal economic theory, deregulation and privatization have generally prevailed and the NTA development function has diminished. In some Western economies it was always relatively modest.

In the UK, while the public sector funded some major elements of infrastructure (such as roads, railways, ports and airports), superstructure, equipment and services were largely provided by the private sector. State support for the development of hotels for a short period in the early 1970s was markedly exceptional. That was the high noon of interventionism. Up to the late 1980s the NTOs for England, Scotland and Wales still had significant development functions and finance for capital investment. The latter has been reduced and, in England, terminated, while in Scotland the modest funds available have not been channelled through the Scottish Tourist Board. Paradoxically, some other national and local institutions have taken on this function. The European Union and British National Lottery have been the new sources of massive injections of capital into infrastructure and attractions with major potential impacts on tourism, leisure and recreation.

While development is clearly of great significance, it is a function which now largely bypasses the NTOs and even NTAs as a whole. Summing up the WTO/CEU–ETC Joint Seminar in 1997, the Secretary General of WTO said (p. 47):

> The oldest of our NTAs were created immediately after the First World War. In Italy, France and in other countries, the first offices abroad were opened between 1919 and 1921. And the very first international body, the predecessor of IUOTO, which itself preceded WTO, was the International Union of Official Tourist Propaganda Organizations. It is interesting to note that promotion, which was where things began, is perhaps, in certain cases, all that remains today.

Marketing

This is a term which stands for a philosophy of management but is also used to describe the function of a division, department or unit within an organization or enterprise. It is to be deplored that the founders of modern marketing did not stress this distinction. Marketing in the first sense might more properly have been substituted by 'market-driven management'. In a true, modern, market oriented environment, marketing personnel can logically be expected to have considerable power and influence since they are the main communication link between the marketplace and the production side under the aegis of the organization as a whole. Where the marketing function is at its most developed, it has major inputs into all decision making. Its precious and unique knowledge of the consumer is fed into decisions on what to produce for which target markets of consumers. It influences product packaging and presentation and handles all communications with the consumer, relations with and delivery to distributors, short-term pricing strategies such as discounting and after-sales service. In practice (see below) not all marketers have such a wide remit.

The number of definitions of marketing as an *overall management approach* is legion. Baker (1983, p. 5) quotes T. Levitt in 'Marketing Myopia' (1960) as follows:

> Selling is preoccupied with the seller's need to convert his product into cash; marketing with the idea of satisfying the needs of the customer by means of the product and the whole cluster of things associated with creating, delivering and finally consuming it.

Middleton (1996, p. 17) quotes Kotler (1991) as follows:

> The marketing concept holds that the key to achieving organizational goals consists in determining the needs and wants of markets and delivering the desired satisfaction more effectively and efficiently than competitors.

Middleton points out that the definition holds good for any form of consumer or industrial product marketing. He also writes that the Kotler definition is equally relevant to the marketing of people, ideas and places, and to any exchange process 'where target markets and organizational goals exist'.

Kotler and Armstrong (1999, Preface) have honed their definition into the following:

> Marketing is the business function that identifies customer needs and wants, determines which target markets the organization can serve best, and designs appropriate products, services, and programs to serve these markets. However, marketing is much more than just an isolated business function – it is a philosophy that guides the entire organization. The goal of marketing is to create customer satisfaction profitably by building value-laden relationships with important customers. The marketing department cannot accomplish this goal by itself. It must team up closely with other departments in the company and partner with other organizations throughout its entire value-delivery system to provide superior value to customers. Thus, marketing calls upon everyone in the organization to 'think customer' and to do all they can to help create and deliver superior customer value and satisfaction.

Kotler, in another text (1997, p. 784), has remarked:

The modern marketing department evolves through six stages, and today companies can be found in each stage. In the first stage, companies simply start out with a sales department. In the second stage, they add ancillary marketing functions, such as advertising and marketing research. In the third stage, a separate marketing department is created to handle the increased number of ancillary marketing functions. In the fourth stage, both sales and marketing report to a marketing and sales vice-president. In the fifth stage all of the company's employees are market and customer centered. In the sixth stage, marketing personnel work mainly in cross-disciplinary teams.

What of the marketing divisions and departments of NTOs? Marketing is the main task of NTOs. They are moreover concerned with assisting and supporting the industry's marketing rather than carrying out this task directly. In the UK context there have been phases in which marketing functions were relatively broad. In the 1970s to mid-1980s the English Tourist Board marketing division worked in partnership with the development division to assess market demand for the products of categories of enterprises and individual firms applying for finance for capital projects. The development of domestic, short-break tourism was initiated following identification on the marketing side of potential demand. The division persuaded hotel groups to provide a single weekend tariff, with dinner bed and breakfast, for a couple sharing a room. The tariff was marginally costed. The division briefed the group telephone reservation systems before the advertising launches. The division set up a system for measuring sales. Its function included the development of a product for a specific target market, the strengthening of distribution channels, all sales generating activity and monitoring of results. The division acted as overall coordinator. The test marketing for this operation with 200 hotels, was reported in the English Tourist Board's Annual Report 1972/73 (1973, p. 11). Its long-term development with over 1000 hotels under the brand name 'Let's Go' was documented in Jeffries (1985, pp. 15–17).

The long-term reduction in NTA/NTO activity in many countries has meant that the marketing function has narrowed. Budgets of National Tourism Administrations (WTO, 1996a) indicate that marketing for the most part is synonymous with promotion, that is, advertising, media relations and information. At annual travel trade fairs and exhibitions, such as the World Travel Market, London and ITB, Berlin, NTOs assist, to some extent, in the creation and improvement of distribution channels by bringing together commercial suppliers and buyers of tourist products. But, while there may be exceptions, their present role in development is slight.

Tourist product

Successful market analysis, according to thinking already explained, is the first step to successful product formulation. How does a tourist destination set about the development of a better tourist product than its competitors? It behoves all who are involved to have a common understanding of the term. Otherwise they stand little chance of working together to produce and market effectively one or more tourist products. The issue was central to one of the earliest applications of new techniques to destination marketing in proposals put forward by Jeffries (1968) which were implemented by the BTA. The proposals defined main British product lines to be marketed in France together with their target market segments. The approach was further developed in Jeffries (1971) and taken up by Medlik and Middleton (1973, pp. 28–35), who noted that 'As far as the tourist is concerned, the product covers the complete experience from the time he [*sic*] leaves home to the time he returns to it.' Thus, 'the tourist product is to be considered as an amalgam of three main components of attractions … and facilities at the destination and accessibility of the destination.'

General marketing texts focus on the distinction to be made between the product as acquired by the customer and the satisfaction which he or she enjoys as a result. Kotler (1997, p. 431) writes:

> In planning its [the firm's] market offering, the marketer needs to think through five levels of the product. Each level adds more customer value, and the five constitute a *customer value hierarchy*. The most fundamental level is the *core benefit*: the fundamental service or benefit that the customer is really buying. A hotel guest is buying 'rest and sleep'. The purchaser of a drill is buying holes. Marketers must see themselves as benefit providers.

There is not scope here to discuss the five levels in the tourist product. Our purposes are served by focusing on the two that are essential, namely, the 'basic product' and the 'core benefit'.

A typical basic tourist product might be a scenic tour to be developed and promoted by a UK coach operator. (In the UK a coach is a road passenger vehicle operating long distance services or tours.) It will be possible to specify what the production and operating staff are to provide and how the basic product is to be summarized and presented in the firm's brochure. The summary will outline what is to be offered to each customer: a seat on the coach, a room at a named or specified category of hotel at each stop, provision for meals and pre-booked seating at the restaurant, the services of a driver-guide and pre-paid entrances to historic places to be visited en route. Certain services will normally be taken for granted, for example, help with luggage. These are the tangibles and quasi-tangibles of this basic product. They can be offered to the prospective customer for one overall price. The presentation can be enhanced by branding, with a well-known brand name such as Wallace Arnold Tours. What is eventually delivered is objectively observable by a third party and can be made the subject of a contract (or, if not delivered after contract, a legal suit). The most tangible element is a series of linked spaces – a seat on a coach, a bedroom, access to space at a historic site – at specified times.

The space can be strictly defined in physical terms and with precise time limits – the coach seat – or more generally assumed – the floor space within a museum, the signposted viewing point by a waterfall. Space made available to the tourist will often be complemented by a service: a path for mountain trekking and a guide; use of fishing equipment at a lakeside angling hotel. Spaces and associated services add up to basic products which give access to environments, activities and experiences. It is from these which, it is reasonable to suppose, the 'core benefit' is derived – usually.

The core benefit is different from the basic product. The core benefit for one person taking a sightseeing tour might be improvement in education or status. This could be, for example, a teacher interested in history. Another might be a person in need of company, say, a recently widowed woman moved to take the tour to meet like-minded people and to make new friends. If the purpose is achieved, the core benefit has been enjoyed. Through observation and research, many marketers are aware of the ultimate motives of their customers (see Swarbrooke and Horner, 1999) but they are not necessarily in a position to guarantee satisfaction contractually.

The basic product is most readily observable in the offerings of the international package tour operator (or travel wholesaler in North America). It is a total trip product which it is convenient to visualize as consisting of *two* main components, rather than three *pace* Medlik and Middleton. These are the return trip to the destination and the destination component. The latter consists of sub-components provided by a number of enterprises that, in the simplest examples, provide local transport, accommodation, food and drink.

Yale (1985, p. 2), writing on the 'tour operator's product', remarks that most tour operators (in the UK) sell package holidays. She observes that the typical package holiday consists of three principal elements: transport, accommodation and transfers between the airport and the accommodation. (In Jeffries' preferred approach, the last two are sub-components making up the destination component.) Yale writes:

the transport part of the package may involve:
- A seat on a charter or scheduled aeroplane.
- A place on a ferry, hovercraft, hydrofoil or catamaran.
- A berth or a cabin in a cruise ship.
- A seat on a train.
- A seat on a coach.
- A hired car.

Usually the transport part of the package is there to enable the client to get from his/her home to his/her holiday destination. However, in the following types of holiday, the transport itself is a crucial part of the experience:
- Cruises.
- Coach tours.
- Luxury train trips, e.g. the Venice–Simplon Orient Express.

Yale continues:

The accommodation part of the package may involve:
- A room in a hotel, guest house, bed and breakfast establishment or pension.
- A self-catering apartment or villa.
- A cabin in a holiday camp.
- Space for a tent or in a pre-erected tent.
- A berth in a caravan.
- A room in a chalet or hotel.

The quotations serve to emphasize that the basic total trip product is structured on a promise of space or spaces. These are commonly expected to be enhanced by attractive décor and to be made available along with certain linked services, e.g. cabin service in a plane, or efficient and friendly reception at the hotel.

An illustration of a rather more complex product than the typical simple package noted by Yale may be derived from the programmes of Discover Britain. This British Incoming Tour Operator packages destination components for inclusion in the programmes of overseas tour operators and travel wholesalers who add the international transport elements for the purpose of marketing total trip products.

Ahead of the 1999 season, Discover Britain offered to Republic Tours, France, a destination component to be marketed as a seven-day scenic/historic sightseeing tour of Scotland. The tour appeared in the French operator's brochure as an eight-day *Grand Tour d'Ecosse et l'Ile de Skye* including travel by air from Paris to Glasgow or Edinburgh return, for an overall price of 7895 francs (£800 or $US1300). One of the departures in the summer of 1999 brought a group of 22 to Scotland. At the destination, Discover Britain, having made bookings beforehand, provided the following:

Transport within Scotland, driver and guide-interpreter, overnight accommodation in five Scottish cities, entrance tickets to Edinburgh Castle, Glamis Castle, Eilean Donan, Moray Firth Cruise, Scone Palace, Blair Castle, Cairnton Farm and Canal Cruise together with miscellaneous items such as porterage and Skye Bridge Tolls.

Discover Britain's charge to Republic Tours was £485 per person. The difference between this and the £800 charged to clients covered international transport and the French operator's mark-up.

This real example substantiates the claim that the basic total trip product has *time and price dimensions* and that the destination component is made up of sub-components which are linked by tourists or their representatives. The sub-component providers at the destination have potentially a common interest in coordinating their actions. Finally, the example brings home the reality that the basic total trip product has a *geographical dimension*.

Many destination components transcend political and administrative boundaries, a fact which has important implications for OTAs. The coordination of tourism across boundaries calls for intelligent appreciation. The geographical dimension of a product may be Europe, presented by the European Travel Commission in the North American market. Or it may be Great Britain, a typical sightseeing tour covering all three constituent countries. At another level the product's geography may be co-terminous with a particular area regarded by tourists as culturally or topographically homogeneous, such as 'Shakespeare Country' or the Cotswolds in England. The destination component may also be presented in the form of a route or 'trail': the Chateaux of the Loire in France, the 'Romantic Rhine' in Germany, the Pilgrim Route to Santiago de Compostela in Spain and the Lewis and Clark trail traversing many states of the USA.

Stating clearly the geographical dimensions of products to be developed and marketed helps to identify the public and private sector partners whose support should be enlisted. Their cooperation will often have to cut across cherished administrative boundaries.

The notion of a basic product is easy to follow and has practical applicability. But the problem of full product definition is extremely challenging. A number of very different approaches have been adopted in recent years. Some focus in reality on categorizing types of facility that provide specific sub-components, for example attractions and hotels (The Australian Bureau of Statistics and Bramwell, 1998, pp. 35–47). Other writers have acknowledged considerable difficulties in attempting broader definitions of what is termed the 'place product' (Ashworth and Voogd, 1990, pp. 65–7; Gold and Ward, 1994, p. 9). Middleton (1994, p. 337) has indicated that:

> the overall tourism product can be defined as 'a bundle or package of tangible and intangible components, based on activity at a destination. The package is perceived by the tourist as an experience available at a price.' It is central to the definition that the components within the 'bundle' can be, and should be, designed and fitted together in a variety of ways calculated to match consumer needs and the capacity of resources.

Middleton (1994, p. 337) includes in his definition destination attractions that are:

the elements within a destination's environment which, individually and combined, serve as the primary motivation for tourist visits. They comprise natural attractions, such as landscape, seascape, beaches, and climate; built attractions, such as historic townscape (e.g. London and Rome) ...

The broader approaches to definition attempt to embrace on the supply side absolutely everything that the tourist uses, consumes and experiences. This includes the host community's built, natural and human environments. Clearly these may often have wide cultural, social and economic significance. While their protection, conservation and development may have to take tourism into account, there are bound to be broader considerations. A mindset which regards the Taj Mahal, a rain forest or Ayers Rock as merely 'part of the tourist product' may tend to forget their broader meaning. That is why there is merit in making a deliberate and clear distinction between the basic product and the environment to which it gives access. This distinction should be reflected in policymaking and planning.

In practice the matter receives very little attention in policy documents and official strategies. While, for example, improvements in the product and its quality are commonly demanded, the terms themselves are seldom fully defined. Such policies are not meaningful and are open to widely varying interpretations.

Distribution

It has sometimes been argued that, while goods are normally distributed from the place of production to the consumer, the reverse happens in tourism. If this view is taken logically, it follows that the customer is distributed to the product. But this is to assume that transport to and from the destination is not part of the product. There can be unfortunate consequences for making this assumption. The first is that the significance of the cost of such transport can often be overlooked in assessing the competitiveness of alternative destinations. The second is that the availability, convenience and quality of transport access can also be ignored. Thus the significance of transport – as a service with features comparable with those on ground – can be left out of the equation. These include comfort, catering and décor. Vertically integrated tour organizations often put together transport and destination components as one brand (e.g. Club Med). It is absurd to imply that customers are distributed like parcels in a hold.

Total trip products may be purchased by tourists through a complex network of retailers (travel agents) and wholesalers or direct. When the product is purchased direct, it is the tourists themselves who assemble the sub-components by, for example, booking the travel ticket from the carrier or taking their own car, by booking accommodation or simply by turning up at the hotel and by booking their own site visits or theatre seats. Tourists may also make part of their reservations through intermediaries and part direct. Figure 4.1 presents three different models of distribution.

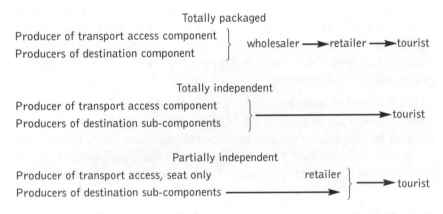

Figure 4.1 Models of distribution

Variations on these models are possible. Some customers purchase direct from wholesalers. Some make their own way to the destination but purchase a destination package. But all models embrace a total round trip or 'basic total trip product'. They are each in principle capable of delivering: to a German tourist, a ranch holiday in the American West; to a British tourist, a golfing tour of South Africa; to an Irish pilgrim, a visit to Lourdes; to a Japanese businessman, a convention in London.

The Scottish scenic/historic tour cited earlier could have been organized and booked entirely independently by a tourist from Paris following an identical route. Independent travellers might have wished to vary patterns from the standard package tour routes and there therefore existed variations in this scenic/ historic tour product. The1999 BTA *Digest of Tourist Statistics* (No. 22, p. 35) confirms that large numbers of package tour and even more independent holidaymakers tour Britain beyond London.

Mill and Morrison (1992, p. 471) in the North American context quote McIntosh's definition of a distribution channel as 'an operating structure, system or linkage of various combinations of travel organizations through which a producer of travel products describes and confirms travel arrangements to the buyer'. This description, say the authors, indicates that a tourism distribution channel has a twofold purpose:

> ensuring that the potential travelers obtain the information they need to make their trip arrangements and, having made their choice, to make the necessary reservations. Distribution may be direct or indirect. *Direct distribution* occurs when a carrier, supplier or destination marketing organization sells directly to the traveler; *indirect distribution* is when the sale is made through one or more travel trade intermediaries.

There are two processes that take place in tourism which are normally paralleled by one in physical goods distribution. In the tourism context, it is first, *title* to the product or product components which is transmitted direct or via intermediaries. Second, consumption begins when the entitlement is taken up, for example, when the customer boards the plane, train or ship, on the outward journey. The Scottish producers in the example distributed title to their space and services via Discover Britain and Republic Tours to the Parisian customers. Consumption began when they boarded the plane at Charles de Gaulle Airport.

In the classic physical goods distribution model, the factory delivers the products to the wholesaler which owns them till sold to the retailer which owns them till sold to the customer. The transfer of ownership and the physical movement of goods are concurrent.

5

Language and concepts (continued)

This chapter continues the discussion of familiar terms begun in Chapter 4. Here, competition, segmentation, image and general brochure are considered.

Competition

The example of the Scottish historic/scenic tour component, cited in Chapter 4, prompts the questions: Who was the competitor? How did Scotland compare? The first area of search was the brochure of the tour operator and the first candidate competitor was an eight-day tour of Ireland, a very similar basic product at a somewhat lower price (7195 francs compared with 7815 francs). Only further market research would have revealed how far these products were substitutable for one another. By placing them close together in the same catalogue of tour offerings, the tour operator recognized that they offered similar satisfactions for a similar investment in time and money.

Tour operators, like department stores, place similar, competing products and brands together. In department stores are to be found types of merchandise grouped in areas: luggage in one; photographic equipment in another. Different categories of groceries and pharmaceuticals are to be found in separate areas of supermarkets. Tour operators often group similar offerings within a single brochure, as do specialist tour operators (winter sports, ecotourism). This may be verified by an examination of such brochures in the travel agent shops in most Western countries. The brochure of a US travel wholesaler, Maupintour, picked at random, helps to illustrate the point. Its Europe 1999 programme offers a 15 day Alps rail tour from Vienna to Zurich and a 14 day rail tour from Berlin to Budapest at similar round trip prices from a number of US cities.

Tour operators, like other distributors, present products in *categories* from within which they offer a choice. Where customers are able to choose, there is competition.

Categorization of products as a preliminary to obtaining meaningful data on share-of-market, competitive position, differences between competing products, is poorly developed in tourism. Published information on independently arranged tourism is especially weak.

A.C. Nielsen in the UK produces a Holiday Booking Survey which regularly analyses business handled by the UK tour operating industry. A summary produced for the author, courtesy of this organization, tracks the volume of forward bookings in March 1999 of foreign package holidays in Summer 1999. The report shows separately the bookings of 15 leading tour operators and their expected carryings to all major overseas holiday destinations. Further analysis shows the volume of travel for different purposes, that is, it shows the bookings for different product categories, as follows:

Short Haul: beach holidays in hotels; beach holidays in self-catering; flight only/fly drive; city breaks; cruises; inland tours
Long Haul
Long Haul general
Long Haul: ski/lakes and mountains

The data could be re-worked to enable a destination to quantify its business derived from British tour operators and its share-of-market. A Mediterranean country could, for example, assess its own position in the short haul beach holiday market and changes over time. In other words, it could assess the performance of its beach destination components compared with other Mediterranean destinations.

A.C. Nielsen's work is outstanding, but its survey only covers package tours to overseas destinations favoured by British tourists. Similar data organized by product category are produced in some other countries but they are not widely published or available. They do have very considerable commercial value.

A unique contribution to thinking in this area was made by Edwards (1993) in his work for the Economist Intelligence Unit: *Price Competitiveness of Holiday Destinations*. In this he presented an analysis of the price competitiveness of tourism destinations from the perspective of four origin countries: France; Germany; Italy; and the UK. The analysis was carried out separately for three main holiday types: beach resort holidays; city break holidays (in short haul destinations only); and multi-centre touring holidays. This clearly was highly relevant to the interests of destinations providing these types of destination component.

With rare exceptions, destinations themselves have not organized their tourism statistics in terms of the types of holidays or tourism they provide. As a consequence they are missing opportunities to evaluate more effectively their own positioning, performance and prospects. Official data, when available, show volume of arrivals, purpose of visit (business, holiday etc.), length of stay, accommodation used and expenditure, presented in time series. From these it may be possible to derive very generalized market share figures capable of masking major shifts in the performance of particular product categories. Market-driven policymaking and management and marketing operations require more sophisticated information than is generally available at present.

An important source, available to subscribers only, is the *Euro Travel Monitor Survey* produced by IPK International, Munich, and based on interviews of very large samples of the population of 34 West and East European countries. This indicates the volume of holiday travel and the types of trip taken ('product categories purchased') divided into:

- sun and beach/waterside
- sightseeing/touring
- city break/holiday

- countryside recreation
- mountain recreation
- snow holiday
- health oriented
- sporting holiday (no snow)
- cruise
- yachting, boating
- visiting an event/show
- visiting a theme park

The data cover packaged and independent holiday-taking. They include the usual demographic material as well as destination and information on holiday satisfaction.

Each category title gives, albeit in highly abbreviated form, an indication of the basic product type 'purchased' plus the type of environment or activity to which it gives access.

The output of the *Euro Travel Monitor Survey* is relevant to both marketing and development. It is understood that the Spanish Government is one of the major clients for the unpublished results. It is not just in Europe that the need for this kind of information is recognized. The Australian researcher Roger March (1994, p. 413) has observed that:

> tourism products and services need to be classified in a more meaningful way ... The conventional means of classifying tourism products and services has been to equate 'tourism sectors' with 'tourism products': the accommodation sector comprises, therefore, accommodation products and the attractions sector involves attraction products ... Operational definitions of tourism product types need to be developed that provide more useful insights for tourism operators and promoters ...

The application of marketing theory and practice, gained in other sectors, to this complex service sector presents serious conceptual difficulties. Newcomers to the field need to be aware of the problem and of the present relatively primitive 'state of the art'.

Segmentation

According to Middleton (1996, p. 71):

Market segmentation is the *process* whereby producers organize their knowledge of current and potential customer groups and select for particular attention those whose needs and wants they are best able to supply with their products. In other words, since it is usually impossible to deal with all customers in the same way, market segmentation is the practical expression in business of the theory of consumer orientation. It is arguably the most important of all the practical marketing techniques available to marketing managers in travel and tourism. It is normally the logical first step in the marketing process involved in developing products to meet customers' needs ...

The techniques available to marketers to identify actual or potential segments of customers and their requirements in terms of products or categories of product are discussed by Middleton and others, notably Swarbrooke and Horner (1999, pp. 96–100). These are, however, generally difficult to use in overall destination development and marketing in the absence of well-developed systems for categorizing products. Unless data are available on each main product category, there will be a tendency to produce products for and address promotions to an amalgam of markets simultaneously, a practice incompatible with segmentation.

Image

The term is very widely used. Academic and other literature suggests that the task of projecting a tourist image of a country internationally falls to the NTO and the positive interest generated is followed up by commercial operators who convert this into bookings. There are several factors that invite considerable scepticism about this theory.

First, it is instructive to look at a given destination paired with one of its markets. The image or brand image of a destination may be heavily influenced by history, tradition and contemporary events. The French have a perception of England that has evolved over a thousand years. The French brand image of England is profoundly based and complex. The best the tourism marketer can do is to take the more positive elements in that image and build on them. There is, for instance, a strong following in France for Conan Doyle's stories about Sherlock Holmes.

French visitors are to be found almost daily, year round, gazing at Baker Street in London. Just off this thoroughfare there is the Sherlock Holmes Hotel, with its Moriarty's Restaurant and Watson's Bar. A tour guide may sometimes be seen dressed in Victorian apparel. (This is that part of tourism which is really popular theatre.) Throughout the world the half a million Burns suppers which are held annually to celebrate Scotland's national poet and to honour the culture of Scotland (letter to *The Times*, 30 January 2000) arguably sustain an image which greatly benefits that country's tourism industry. Films or television series powerfully spotlight particular places. The tourism industry and tourism organizations use them as springboards. The accumulations of history, real or imagined, and the outpourings of the media overwhelm the small voices of the tourism organizations.

At the other end of the spectrum from England and other destinations with well-established images, there is the completely unknown destination (increasingly rare). Here attempts may be made to create a positive image from scratch and, in theory, this may be done successfully provided there is an adequate budget and the image corresponds to the reality as perceived by the eventual tourist. The resources required are difficult to assess and these are likely to vary widely between different pairs of markets and destinations. However, there is little evidence that destination brand image advertising is routinely subject to formal testing, much less that it is successful.

Tests of such advertising are rarely published. The English Tourist Board archives contain a report (1983) on a pilot television advertising campaign designed to modify Londoners' perceptions of England's North Country during a three-year period in the 1980s. This was based on before and after tests of the ABC 1 socio-economic groups in the London population and on studies of control groups elsewhere not exposed to the advertising. Awareness of the English Tourist Board increased massively but there were only minor changes in the destination's image, with no traceable effects on the public's disposition to travel. Traditional perceptions of the region as highly industrialized did not change.

Highly sophisticated testing techniques are available at the start of the twenty-first century but apparently not much used by destination advertisers. The London based IPA Advertising Effectiveness Data Bank is claimed to represent 'the most rigorous and comprehensive examination of advertising working in the marketplace, in the world', according to *Advertising Works 10* (1999, p. 518). The IPA has made biennial awards for outstanding advertising since 1980 to agents and clients who submit papers on their campaigns, including brand image campaigns. These are required to give evidence of the results achieved and of the scientific rigour of measurement. The Data Bank contains reports of the campaigns of 650 winners since 1980. These are claimed to be examples of best practice across a wide spectrum of UK marketing sectors and expenditures. They feature organizations and enterprises as wide ranging as banks, insurance companies, automobile manufacturers, telephone companies, supermarkets, food and drink producers, institutions, charities and service organizations. Of the 650 documented cases only three in 18 years have been tourist destination bodies: the Torbay Tourist Board (1984), the Wales Tourist Board (1992) and the Israel Tourist Board (1994).

A clear distinction has to be made between pure destination image promotion and the broader range of marketing activities undertaken by destination promoters. The former must be represented, for example, by high exposure television and colour supplement advertising unaccompanied by specific product offer or price. But much destination advertising is about making specific products visible and available by naming both the destination and the product and the booking channel. In this the industry and NTOs engage separately and jointly, as may be verified by glancing through the travel sections of the press at the peak holiday booking times in main tourism generating countries. Visibility for specific, priced destination products is sought not only by NTOs but by tour operators, wholesalers, carriers, hotel interests and others. Tour operators – notably those at the 'quality' end of the spectrum and special interest operators – are selective in terms of destinations, not all-embracing or neutral. Their decision to include a destination in their brochures, or to exclude it, can have a significant effect on the destination and on its competitive position. The destination's struggle for visibility may perhaps be more clearly understood by means of an analogy with the presentation of consumer goods on the shelves of the supermarket. Grocery producers and marketers deploy large budgets to build brand images (note the IPA case studies of this sector). Customers are made aware of brands by advertising and other forms of communication *before* stepping into the supermarket – for example, by means of television at home and street poster advertising. Against this background the customer explores the shelf space in the supermarket. A very important part of marketing of most brands is the securing of such space and getting a more visible and more accessible space than the competitor.

It is proposed as a reasonable working hypothesis that the equivalent of the consumer goods producers' brand image promotion is, in the field of destination marketing, largely generated by history, tradition, culture and contemporary events which achieve high media exposure. Most tourism marketing activity performs the function in reality of 'claiming shelf space', that is, making tourist product visible and easily available both at the right time and the right place. Whether NTOs' 'pure' destination advertising effects fundamental changes in image remains unproven, at least as far as published records allow. Whether national, regional and local tourism organizations achieve measurable business as a result of their marketing is another matter. There is much evidence that joint efforts made with private sector partners featuring specific products do frequently secure sufficient visibility to produce bookings cost-effectively. (Note the analysis of BTA joint marketing schemes in Jeffries, 1989, p. 77.)

The contribution of NTOs to overall destination marketing is actually generally quite modest, though allowance must be made for the possibility of exceptions. Two sets of data are instructive, as follows.

An unpublished study for ETB in 1997 gave the total advertising spend on outbound travel from England by carriers, tour operators, NTOs and others as £247 million (around US$ 400 million), of which £35 million (around US$ 56 million) were spent by NTOs – that is, about 14%.

Beaver (1993, p. 675) noted that the UK travel industry was estimated to have spent some £150 million annually on brochures alone (around US$ 240 million at that time). This equalled the entire *worldwide overall marketing* budgets of the NTOs of the top six destinations for British holidaymakers: Spain, France, Italy, Greece, the USA and the Irish Republic (WTO, *Budgets of National Tourism Administration*, 1996a; BTA, *Digest of Tourist Statistics,* No. 22, 1999).

General brochure

The general brochure is the stock-in-trade of the Official Tourism Organization. This may be verified by making a written or telephone enquiry, visiting an OTO's information office or visiting its stand at any of scores of travel exhibitions which take place annually in most source countries. Individual OTOs produce a variety of brochures – some on specialized topics such as golfing or historic sites open to the public – but most will have a glossy *general* brochure which presents the whole area: its culture and history, its landscapes and buildings, major events, other attractions, gastronomy, accommodation and so forth.

The more sophisticated and professional OTOs produce 'segmented' literature to fit in with segmented marketing, that is, material that is clearly written for and distributed exclusively to particular segments in order to maximize 'conversion rates' or the proportion of recipients who actually become buyers or travellers to the destination, thus reducing wastage. A good example of such a practice is Travel Montana's annual mailings of special literature to registered snowmobile owners in the USA.

Many forms of communication are available to marketers which, depending on circumstances, can be more efficient than producing and distributing one's own printed matter, for example, paid advertising space in manuals distributed to travel agents, or taking commercial radio programme time. OTOs are quickly adapting to new opportunities presented by the Internet. Nevertheless, the general brochure remains almost obligatory. Why is this? One explanation is that the brochure is not only for the consumer but is also a document which offers within the destination tangible evidence that the industry as a whole is receiving 'fair' exposure. It may be the projection of a political and administrative entity and only coincidentally meaningful from the consumer's point of view, offering too much information in some respects and not enough in others. A patchwork of neighbouring communities, each of which now has its own general brochure, might do better in future to merge their identities. They might then undertake marketing activities that would be both sectoral and segmented. They would thus concentrate on a specific product category, say, golfing holidays, and achieve economies of scale by promoting them jointly as a clearly identified brand to specific external markets. Indeed, recognition of the need for efficient sectoral marketing is evident in some well-known national schemes that benefit a large number of host communities. Perhaps one of the best examples developed since the 1950s is the promotion of country cottages and other rural properties across the whole of France which may be booked through reservation centres in some major world capitals and within the country itself under the auspices of the *Féderation Nationale des Gîtes de France*. Sectoral marketing is also practised by other countries, including Britain. For instance, the BTA promotes English Walking Holidays as a brand.

Part Two

Policy Issues

6

History introduces the policy issues: the 1960s and the Development of Tourism Act 1969

The OECD review of 1989 briefly quoted in Chapter 2 describes the evolution of government policy and action in member states. These accounted for 70% or more of international tourism movements worldwide in the period covered. The review addressed mainly the development of policy in the 1960s and 1970s, a period of unprecedented expansion and change, to the early 1980s, when the broad lines of OECD member countries' tourism policies were in place. The state's role was seen as having developed through four phases concerned, in order, with promotion, stimulation, intervention and coordination. Initially, the main concern of states was to boost international tourism which was 'gradually becoming a mass phenomenon'. In some countries promotion and advertising expenditure virtually took up all the funds allocated to the statutory tourism bodies. But state involvement in this sector became increasingly complex and frequently controversial. According to the report, 'few major sectors had seen their resources and institutional framework challenged as often as tourism'. This, the authors indicated, was in part due to the weaknesses of the national tourist authorities and an almost excessive emphasis on promotional activities which helped to explain why social and economic policymakers in some countries did not regard tourism as being really important. In many cases, they observed, statutory bodies were ill-equipped to deal with new problems posed by the boom in tourism. As a result, 'the very bodies which should have been directing tourism policies had to contend with a growing compartmentalisation of policy'.

To meet the growing demand for private travel, governments had to provide appropriate infrastructure. Up to the mid-1960s this was mainly a question of building enough of it. Travel by car and by air expanded rapidly. The report continued:

After having concentrated on expanding tourism, national tourism policymakers now had to contend with congested urban centres and major roads, particularly during peak periods. The fact that travel was becoming within the reach of more and more people pushed up demand for medium-grade hotels and for supplementary forms of accommodation. Governments had to inject a massive amount of public funds to compensate for the private sector's initial lack of interest in this type of accommodation. As for higher-grade hotels, the shortage of trained hotel staff obliged governments to set up schemes to train them.

In the 1960s a new dimension was therefore added to the national tourism policies of many Member countries. Policies focused increasingly on channelling as well as increasing tourism. This concern went hand in hand with land use planning. New developments in the regions drew tourists to them. In Europe, coast lines were developed and new tourist routes built to ease the congestion on major roads. New airports were built in the regions, which also helped to start a shift in tourism to them. ...

The initial general enthusiasm soon ran into the problems inherent in any rapid growth in demand. In the early 1960s a surge in the prices of tourism services prompted governments to implement price controls to protect both the consumer and the international competitive position of their respective countries. Governments were henceforth responsible not only for attracting tourists but also for protecting them as consumers during their stay. The prices of tourist menus and tariffs were controlled, more stringent grading systems for hotels were adopted, and during the period some countries introduced optional insurance for tourists.

... National tourism policies were gradually adapted to meet the needs of tourists who had become more demanding. The emphasis started to shift from quantity to quality.

... The disillusion that marked the end of the 1960s in several areas also affected tourism. In some cases, the hopes that had been placed in tourism as a means of solving the developing countries' problems were cruelly dashed. In Europe, some countries discovered how vulnerable their tourism industry was to factors completely outside their control. In all the OECD Member countries, local communities demanded the right to benefit from tourism as much as foreign visitors. Governments increasingly had to translate their regional planning objectives into structural measures and to make government bodies more effective. These developments had a major impact on government tourism policy. In 1970, national tourism bodies were restructured in the United Kingdom, the United States, Italy, the Netherlands, Norway and Canada. All Member countries introduced stricter eligibility criteria for official financial assistance.

... During the 1970s, national tourism bodies thus had to take account of new factors; among other things they had to reconcile the need to devote an increasing amount of resources to co-ordination with the need for more effective monitoring of market changes. The constraints on their resources made necessary a new division of responsibilities between public sectors, and encouraged them to implement promotional programmes in co-operation with the private sector. In a similar vein, national tourism bodies began to decentralise tourist development by providing local and regional bodies with both financial assistance and technical assistance with drawing up development plans.

The uncertain economic climate prompted a more cautious approach on the part of tourism authorities. In particular, at the start of the 1970s they sought to identify those areas that would enable tourism to develop on a more stable basis. The unpredictable nature of international tourism, and its vulnerability to events over which governments had no control, encouraged several countries to pay more attention to domestic tourism. A programme to encourage Canadians to visit their own country was launched in 1971, while France, Germany, Italy, the Netherlands, Sweden, the United Kingdom and the United States conducted in-depth surveys of the travel habits of their inhabitants. Many Member countries also began to place increased emphasis on promoting tourism in the lower price bracket. The oil shock of 1973 and its aftermath showed that domestic tourism had a marked stabilizing effect on total tourist demand; the role of national bodies in promoting domestic tourism was confirmed.

The OECD commentary is an excellent general background. It is possible to complement this by reference to trends in tourism policymaking in particular countries. The UK exemplified these trends in many ways but presented some interesting variations, as was evident in the events leading up to the 1969 Development of Tourism Act, the Act itself and the early years of its implementation. Study of these confirms all the important issues of the time, common to many countries though not necessarily addressed in the same way. The Act affected Great Britain, that is England, Scotland and Wales, but did not affect directly Northern Ireland, which was already covered by the Development of Tourist Traffic Act 1948.

The Bill that was to become the 1969 Act, after much debate and modification, was pushed through by a Labour (Socialist) Government. In the decade of the 1960s the country had experienced strong growth in tourism. Several distinct events had intensified pressure for change and reorganization. In 1966 the Government had introduced the Selective Employment Tax (SET), the purpose of which was to force investment and labour out of service industries into the manufacturing industry, whose contribution to exports and hence to earning foreign exchange was to be stimulated thereby. But this discouraged one of the most important new 'export' industries, namely tourism, when its prospects were improving dramatically, due to several factors. These were growing world demand, the devaluation of the pound sterling and an expected massive increase in airlift to be brought about by the introduction of regular jumbo jet services to London in 1970.

The Government introduced a temporary scheme to promote urgently the rapid expansion of hotel capacity. The Government also foresaw a need to regulate the hotel industry and to introduce consumer protection measures. Finally, pressures from Scotland and Wales for greater autonomy in developing their own tourism industries prepared the ground for new arrangements for these very distinctive parts of Great Britain.

The Government therefore put forward a Bill designed to strengthen institutions and to give them the force of law as well as to make provision for a massive injection of funds into the Hotel Development Incentives (HDI) Scheme and for some financial aid to tourist amenities and facilities. The legislation provided a framework for compulsory registration and classification of accommodation (lodging) for tourists, details of which would have to be worked out and put forward for government approval after the Act was passed.

The Bill did indeed become the Act after much debate and modification. Its provisions hinged on the creation of a new national (British) tourism organization. A national tourism organization already existed. This was the British Travel Association and the implication was that this would be reduced in status, fade away or be wound up. The Association had been established in 1950 with government support and encouragement and had evolved from a succession of private sector organizations established as early as 1929 (British Tourist Authority, 1975). However, from the 1950s onwards it was very far from being a purely private sector organization. Although a company limited by guarantee, its Chairman and eight of its Board members were appointed by the government. Seven were elected by an electoral college of subscribing members and four represented the Scottish, Welsh and Northern Ireland Tourist Boards. By 1968 a government grant-in-aid covered 80% of its expenditure and it was mainly concerned with promotion and publicity, particularly overseas (Minister's statement in the House of Common, 13 November 1968). The Association operated through a well-developed network of 24 overseas offices. The Board of the Association was served by a number of committees, which drew on the expertise and influence of a wide range of leaders in the public and private sectors. The organization was indeed a hybrid – on one hand the government-chosen instrument for the promotion of tourism and, on the other, a forum for trade associations, lobbies and pressure groups which helped to inform a steady flow of representations to the central authorities on fiscal, regulatory and other matters affecting the industry.

Except where otherwise stated, the following summary account of debates on the Bill is based on a reading of House of Commons Parliamentary Debates (Hansard) from 23 February and 23/24 June 1969.

When the intention to introduce a Bill was first announced in Parliament on 13 November 1968, the Cabinet Minister concerned (President of the Board of Trade), said that an existing voluntary body such as the British Travel Association would not be suitable for the administration of new policies covering, for example, the HDI Scheme and the compulsory registration and classification of hotels. He said that the proposed new Boards for the British Tourist Authority, Scotland and Wales would be 'compact and functional' and that members would 'not be representatives or delegates for particular sectional or geographical interests'. (Eventually, similar principles were to be applied to the English Tourist Board, the need for which was recognized later during the passage of the Bill.) On the First Reading, the Minister reinforced this point of view by stating that it did not seem appropriate that a purely voluntary body should be the body to distribute 'substantial Government and taxpayers' money'. On the Second Reading he added, 'We will draw their [the Boards'] membership from people of experience and ability in tourism, industry, commerce, economics and administration' but ' … not advocates of any particular interests'.

The Bill in its early form had a mixed reception from the Conservative Opposition and from the Liberals. Some were plainly hostile. Others, acknowledging that the Labour Government was very likely to drive it through, were disposed to have its provisions modified as far as possible and to mitigate its perceived negative elements. Many Opposition MPs active in the debate represented constituencies with a marked interest in tourism and sought to ensure the Bill was shaped in the interests of their constituencies. Quotes from the debates are given in Appendix 1. They illustrate the adversarial style of British politics at the time and the strength of feeling on tourism. What were the most controversial issues? They are summarized below under separate headings.

The role of the state

Those most strongly opposed complained of the Government's failure to treat the tourism industry like any other. They held the view that the public financial support proposed would be less than the burdens imposed by an unfair fiscal regime, particularly SET. The debate was pursued with special vigour by several MPs with a strong belief in reducing taxation on all industries, minimizing government 'interference' and giving maximum opportunity to markets, that is, to the freest possible interplay of demand and supply, to stimulate growth. Some criticized the general land use planning framework and slow moving procedures as obstacles to adequate hotel development.

The ongoing conflict between free market thinking and intervention was clearly reflected in a statement made by the main spokesman for the Conservative Opposition, Sir Keith Joseph:

Like all industries in a developed economy the tourist industry should have its own momentum and balance. Provided the Government create a suitable economic context the industry should be able to look after itself. If demand changes or rises then supply too should change or rise. We now have the expectation that tourist demand, particularly from overseas, is rising but supply is not. Why is this? What has gone wrong with the market operation of this sensitive, sophisticated, complex industry? ... What has happened is that the Government have insensitively, probably not realising what they were doing, heaped on the tourist industry burden upon burden which has wrecked its capacity to respond to rising and changing demand. The Bill ... does not attempt to deal with the basic health of the industry. It deals with one specific tourist problem, and that is the question of increasing the supply of hotel rooms, because the supply and demand response was broken due to Government burdens. (Second Reading, 27 February 1969)

The role of the national tourism organization

A particular point of contention was the structure and role of the national (British) organization to replace the British Travel Association. Many Opposition MPs expressed admiration for the Association's past performance. They put great store by its large Board and extensive Committee and consultative network which was, in their view, essential to ensure close cooperation between the many and disparate components of a complex industry. No mention was made of the significance of this network as an amalgam of lobbies.

Conservatives put forward an amendment to increase the proposed number of appointees to the Board of the new British organization from 9 to 16. There was also an amendment to oblige all Boards to set up advisory Committees to:

> include persons with knowledge of the tourist industry and the members of each committee viewed collectively [to be] widely representative of those aspects of the tourist industry with which the particular committee is concerned.

The proposer of the amendment, the Member for Blackpool South, indicated that he and its supporters had in mind something similar to the existing British Travel Association, describing a list of members which included the Brewers Society and the British Hotels and Restaurants Association.

Coordination

A further issue which attracted attention was the coordinating role of the new national body, particularly its authority, if any, over the proposed new Tourist Boards for England, Scotland and Wales. It was envisaged by the Government that the British Board would have certain general duties such as that of advising government on matters affecting tourism in Britain as a whole but its main and exclusive function would be to promote Britain abroad while the exclusive functions of the Tourist Boards would be to administer schemes and to finance individual projects for capital development as well as undertake the registration and classification of tourist accommodation. The issue of coordination was particularly problematic bearing in mind that the Scottish and Wales Boards would receive their finance directly from government whereas their predecessor Boards had subsisted on very limited funds from the British Travel Association.

Another key issue allied to that of coordination was the input which

Scottish and Welsh interests would have into overseas promotion. They regarded their case as special and exceptional and felt that a London based organization could not represent them adequately.

Cooperation with parallel bodies

Cooperation with public bodies having potentially an interactive relationship with the tourism organization was discussed. The most obviously relevant body was the Countryside Commission, whose responsibilities included the provision of a wide range of facilities for recreation and tourism, both inland and along the coasts, as well as their protection. There were references to many other bodies. There was potential for conflict but also for complementarity and mutual reinforcement of policies and activities.

Areas within countries

MPs from many different parts of Britain spoke up for their own areas and in particular for the need to set up machinery to provide for and attract overseas visitors beyond London and a limited number of well-known centres such as Stratford-upon-Avon. The English MPs had already been approached by lobbies disturbed by the initial lack of provision for English regions, for some of which tourism was arguably more important than it was in Scotland and Wales. Pressure from these areas and from the English seaside resorts strengthened the case for the establishment of an English Tourist Board and for the Bill to enable this and the Scottish and Wales Boards to support and help finance area organizations within each country. There was very wide support for such organizations but divided views on how they should be financed and how their boundaries should be set.

Some held strongly that general administrative areas could not be treated as tourism areas.

Regulation

Proposals for the statutory (compulsory) registration and classification of hotels and other accommodation for tourists proved to be highly controversial. Speakers for the Opposition contended that existing guides produced, for example, by the motoring organizations provided for consumers' needs. It being assumed that the system would be used as a basis for a national list, some MPs poured scorn on the idea of an unwieldy government guidebook featuring all accommodation. The proposal was again presented by its opponents as unnecessary government intervention in an area in which they claimed markets were capable of operating satisfactorily and of supplying a need for information if there was a demand for it. In their submissions, several speakers cited the hotel and catering trade associations firmly opposed to the Bill in general and to this provision in particular.

Opposition to the Bill as a whole was epitomized by a fierce debate on the name of the proposed new British organization. The Member for Eastbourne (Sir Charles Taylor):

> I realise that the animal, as the Minister said must undergo some changes, but I still do not believe there is any need to change the name. … The British Travel Association had a considerable amount of private enterprise attached to it. … I think that we have too many authorities. I suggest that the word 'authority' stinks of Government control, Government interference, and bureaucracy (Third Reading, 24 June 1969).

The severest criticism was made by the right-wing member for Wolverhampton South West, Enoch Powell:

> It would be a pity if the Bill were to leave this House without at least one Member laying his curse upon it. … It has all the classic features of a Socialist Measure. It establishes bureaucratic boards in order to perceive commercial opportunities and promote commercial operations … (Third Reading, 24 June 1969).

The Government's will prevailed in the final version of the Act. The major interventionist element, an 'emergency measure' to bring quickly on stream a large number of new hotel rooms, was strengthened. Provision in principle for price display was confirmed. The Conservatives' proposed amendment to give BTA coordinating or 'overlord powers' failed. So also did a move to increase the size of the BTA Board and to prescribe by law an expanded Committee structure so as to make the whole organization 'representative' of the industry. The BTA and the Boards were instead required to have regard to the desirability of consulting others. They were to have discretion, by implication, to set up committees as they saw fit. The Act reflected strong support for area organizations expressed by all sides in the Parliamentary debates. The Boards for England, Scotland and Wales were given both encouragement and powers to support them.

Certain matters were left open, for example the division of responsibilities for research, strategic planning and domestic marketing. The Junior Minister during the debates expressed the hope that the new authority would, when established, 'cooperate at all levels with the boards, that the boards would work together and that there would be no useless duplication of activity ...'. The Minister had earlier pointed out in a House of Commons Committee, following the agreement to establish an English Tourist Board, that the Authority would be 'essentially a promotional authority with no more, perhaps, than rather vague advisory functions as far as development of tourism in the three countries [was] concerned' (Report of Standing Committee E, 13 March 1969, Column 33).

Members were appointed to the Boards of all the new organizations in the second half of 1969 and they came into full operation in January 1970. Labour appointed to the new 'compact and functional' BTA Board a Chairman who was a leading businessman with background and experience in the City (finance), shipping and tour operations. This was probably, *inter alia*, in recognition of concerns expressed in Parliament that the new body would be excessively bureaucratic. It is also clear from his memoirs that some other business leaders were brought in at his behest or with his approbation (Sir Alexander Glen, 1975). His Board took over the senior management and staff and the buildings of its predecessor. The tourist boards for the three countries started from zero or from low bases.

Within less than six months there was a change of government and the Conservatives were back in power. What happened next? The narrative continues in Chapter 7 to allow for further discussion of issues already mentioned and exploration of some new areas.

7

History introduces the policy issues: main developments, 1970–1992

This chapter summarizes the main developments in UK tourism policies, organization and programmes which were responses to worldwide trends affecting many countries from 1970 to 1992. The narrative gives insights into issues and opens the way for them to be explored in later chapters. Developments in the 1990s and in 2000 are addressed in Chapter 14.

There were two very different phases running respectively from 1970 to 1979, when Labour and Conservatives alternated in power, and from 1979 to the end of the period, namely, the 'Thatcher years' and the first two years in office of Margaret Thatcher's successor, John Major. Both phases may be divided into shorter tranches. They will be discussed as far as possible in chronological order.

First phase: 1970–1979

The Conservative Government lasted from June 1970 to March 1974 and Labour held office from then to May 1979. During this whole phase some common ground existed. There were similar views on the use of provisions in the Act for public spending on facilities and amenities to foster development in economically weak geographical areas. But Labour placed greater emphasis on this in the publication of its Guidelines in 1974. Both parties, when in power, strongly supported the British Tourist Authority's overseas promotion activity. Other non-contentious elements were the use of public funds to promote domestic markets and information services for tourists within Great Britain. Throughout, the establishment of area organizations within England, Scotland and Wales and the progressive devolution of functions to them was encouraged. Both Governments tended to stand back while the BTA and National Tourist Boards attempted to settle among themselves the demarcation of some functions left unclear in the Act.

The major divergences between the two parties during the decade of the 1970s were on the issues of (i) taxation and (ii) state regulation of standards, as symbolized by the prospect of compulsory registration of hotels and other forms of accommodation. The areas of broad consensus and disagreement are now discussed in turn.

Regional development

A Conservative Government made the decision to make grants and loans to new developments or improvements in plant in the most severely affected areas of economic decline in Scotland, Wales and in the extreme Northern and Western parts of England. In making use of its discretionary powers to use these funds selectively, the English Tourist Board favoured developments that would increase tourism flows and provide for specific types of tourism which were innovative in the context of these areas. The Board's early strategy was to give support to investments that were unlikely to be profitable in the medium term but had good long-term prospects for full profitability. They tended to be projects ahead of their market but not in need of permanent subsidy. This placed an obligation on the Board to develop skills in forecasting and to be highly sensitive to market trends. The function performed *vis-à-vis* the industry was analogous to that of the R and D

(Research and Development) function of a large industrial corporation, though not named as such. The sums deployed were relatively small.

In its Annual Report to March 1972 (1972, p. 22), ETB stated that:

To help in administering a scheme involving applications as varied and diverse as tourist projects, ETB has classified them under three broad headings – Non-Commercial Projects, Pace-Setters and Tourist Infrastructure. The first of these can be subdivided into 'loss leaders' and 'amenities'. 'Loss leaders' are projects which offer attractions designed to draw into the region substantial numbers of tourists whose expenditure on other facilities, such as accommodation and restaurants, would benefit the regional economy. This category might include museums, wild life sanctuaries, historic buildings and sites – particularly those with special character and appeal to tourists. ... 'Amenities' are those projects which in themselves do not have a high pulling power but will make the tourists' stay more satisfying or improve the organization of tourism in the regions, e.g. car parks, information services and signposting, countryside walks, picnic sites, parks and gardens, or sporting facilities.

'Pace-Setters' are projects which are essentially looking ahead to the needs of future tourism and include entirely new ideas where the pioneering risk is great, radically new designs of known types of tourist attractions or amenities that exist in roughly similar form. ...

Finally, there are schemes which create the basic structure upon which tourist facilities and services can develop. Such projects differ from 'amenity' projects because of their much greater cost and likely longer time scale. ...

In giving support to such a wide variety of projects, the Board's aim is not only to support existing facilities, but to assist exciting imaginative schemes that will break new ground in the tourism field, to make holidays, however short or long, more pleasant and, above all, to provide more employment.

The report gave concrete examples of each type of financed project.

During the last half of the decade, this funding was extended to include the whole of the North of England. National marketing was shaped in order to match and reinforce development. One example of an area opened up to tourism by this matching activity was the great port city of Liverpool.

The ETB's strategy anticipated the Policy Guidelines announced by the Labour Government soon after it returned to power in 1974. These applied to the ETB and BTA and were as follows:

> To give more emphasis to publicising the attractions of Britain outside the main tourist centres and outside the peak seasons so as to stem the growing pressure on congested centres, and bring economic benefits of tourism to areas that need them.
>
> To switch Government expenditure to develop untapped potential for tourism in those areas that can readily absorb and benefit from more visitors, particularly in certain parts of the Development [economically weak] Areas.
>
> To cut the heavy expenditure on generalised promotion both at home and overseas.
>
> To put more sponsored activities on a self-financing basis.

Overseas marketing

This was not fundamentally affected by the Development of Tourism Act. Although under a new and differently constituted Board of Management, senior executives and overseas staff were retained and they operated from the same headquarters buildings as before. The major marketing innovations of the 1960s were further developed. These included the renowned trade workshops in which the BTA played the role of broker between British suppliers and overseas buyers. New style British Travel Centres abroad, combining BTA's services with those of the national carriers, were opened from 1978/79 onwards, the first in Frankfurt, Germany.

Domestic marketing

This was an activity conceded to the National Tourist Boards. All undertook campaigns to present to the home public the case for holidays in Britain. The overall effect sought was import saving by attracting markets that would otherwise go abroad. Inevitably there was some incidental competition between England, Scotland and Wales. All cooperated in the creation of a Britain-wide network of Tourist Information Centres (TICs) in the service of domestic and overseas visitors.

Marketing strategies stressed that this network was to be promoted abroad as an extra reason for choosing Britain for a trip or vacation. A significant advance was in the new field of short break and weekend tourism (*source:* Annual published Statements of Marketing Intent during the 1970s).

Devolution to areas

The Annual Reports of the Boards indicate that this was given the highest priority in England. Small, under-funded voluntary organizations known as regional travel associations existed in some parts of England. They were strengthened and expanded while the rest of the country developed similar new organizations in a crash programme. In the first months of the ETB's existence it was conceded that the Directors of these Boards would not be on the central organization's payroll but would be answerable to regional boards and committees at which the ETB would have minority representation. Early tensions over regionalization were touched on in the autobiography (1981, p. 37) of ETB's first Chief Executive, F.P. Cook. During subsequent negotiations, regional organizations were structured on a pattern similar to that of the associations which pre-dated the 1969 Act and which, in fact, had been modelled on the old British Travel Association structure. They were each funded by grants from the ETB and local governments and private sector subscribers. By subscribing, the latter gained among other things the right to be consulted and to participate in decision making. Within a short time these organizations styled themselves Regional Tourist Boards. It was expected that they would both act as agents to implement national programmes and carry out their own autonomous operations on their own account. National programmes depended on a degree of discipline and standardization. This clearly called for skilled leadership and a sophisticated approach to financing during the annual rounds of negotiation when ETB's contributions to regional budgets were to be settled. The structure proved to be a difficult one from a national point of view. Thus some *ad hoc* solutions had to be invented. For example, when a national scheme for the voluntary registration and classification of hotels on a standard basis was introduced, the ETB was obliged to employ staff directly under its chain of command and to house them at its expense in Regional Board offices.

The process of devolution was much slower than might have been expected from a reading of statements made at the outset by the Chairman of ETB in Annual Reports. By the end of the period under review, substantially strengthened Regional Boards were beginning to agitate fiercely for the shedding of central budgets to their own level. This was to prepare the way for direct, open lobbying of the Minister in the early 1980s (Chairman's Introduction to the East Anglia Tourist Board Annual Report, 31 March 1983 and South East England Tourist Board Report, 31 March 1983).

Demarcation of national functions

In the political climate following the return to power of the Conservatives in 1970, the new BTA emerged as an organization very similar to the one it had replaced. This aligned with the wishes previously expressed in Parliament by many Conservatives in their years of opposition. As before, the Board was underpinned by a wide-ranging committee structure, some committees being reinstated with the same title, others with a change of name. Confirmation may be found in the sections on committees and their members which appear in the British Travel Association Annual Reports from 1967/68 and 1968/69, together with those of the British Tourist Authority for 1971/72 and 1973/74. A new, high-powered group called curiously the Infra-Structure Committee, chaired by a Board member and leading hotelier, had 'responsibility in all matters pertaining to the taxation, fiscal and operational background of tourism in Britain' (BTA Annual Report for year ended March 1971). Study of the trade press of the time shows that BTA's public relations activities and its line on fiscal and regulatory matters paralleled closely those of the key trade associations and lobbies (*Sources:* weekly issues of *Caterer and Hotelkeeper*, August 1970 to March 1972; BTA's Annual Reports for the period; extract from the 6 August 1970 issue of the trade paper in Appendix 2).

The autobiographies of BTA's first Chairman and the ETB's Chief Executive reflected the difficulties in working out distinctive roles for each organization and in securing inter-organizational cooperation (Glen, 1975; Cook, 1981) The underlying problem was that legislation driven through by one government was implemented under the aegis of another of a very different complexion. It should not be imagined that major moves were made without sounding out the Minister concerned and his advisers. This would have been normal practice but would have been behind the scenes.

It is quite clear that the overall picture by 1971 was very different from that which had been envisaged by the Labour Minister who had piloted the Act through Parliament, for he had envisaged the new BTA as very largely an overseas promotion agency. Under this dispensation, in all probability, the national tourist boards would have produced, after consultation, overall development and marketing strategies, the overseas element of which would have been implemented on their behalf by the BTA.

The overall strategic role allocated in practice to BTA paved the way for continuing high level dialogue between the organization and many institutions on development, as distinct from marketing, matters. These were at risk of running in parallel with dialogue between the English Tourist Board, responsible for financing development, with the same institutions. The Annual Reports of both organizations suggest considerable duplication of roles. Scotland and Wales were not affected in the same way. Their spheres were more restricted, as together they represented some 15% of British tourism. The BTA worked through these national boards rather than in parallel in accordance with long-standing convention based on political and practical considerations.

The BTA's Annual Report to March 1971 (1971, p. 10) referred to a new principle of co-equality which was claimed to have facilitated cooperation between the national boards and BTA, something which would not have been achieved otherwise as promotion demanded 'a totality of effort combining the services available at home and marketing of these overseas'. This was being achieved, the report claimed, by a sensible demarcation of effort, which had become increasingly clear by the autumn of 1970 when it was possible to agree formal definitions of responsibilities. One of the agreements, as later reports indicate, was that BTA would take the lead role in overall strategic planning and related research. An early outcome was a document entitled *Britain – the Broad Perspective* in 1974.

In its Annual Report to March 1974 (1974, p. 4), BTA pressed its case further to establish a role as the senior coordinating body. Under the heading 'Does Britain need a policy for Tourism?', the BTA's Chairman remarked:

> The report has traced some of the trends in 1973 and the problems which grew throughout the year. How far can a National Tourist Organisation influence trends of this kind? Certainly with limited resources BTA has shown that it can do much in marketing overseas, while at home Government does listen to its advice over policy. But BTA is not in charge of tourism, or of tourist services, or of the tourist trade. In a mixed economy the second and third should be responsible, as they are today, for their own profitability and their own development. But the first category poses questions to which the sombre outlook which Britain now faces makes an answer more pressing than previously.
>
> Over the last five years BTA has tried to follow loyally the pattern established by Parliament in the Development of Tourism Act, 1969, a pattern which very early on its Chairman described as one of constructive co-equality with the National Boards for England, Scotland, Wales and Northern Ireland. This policy has certainly encouraged local initiative and local responsibility and has been a valuable and interesting experiment in administrative devolution, particularly to Cardiff and Edinburgh. Certainly the marketplace must never be divorced from the product, as it could have been under this structure, and it is good to be able to report that much sensible progress has been made in ensuring that this danger did not develop.
>
> There are areas, however, where it may now be timely to ask whether co-equality can be pressed too far so as to exclude coordination.
>
> In saying this, BTA is in no way doubting that the development within Britain of amenities and services, and their informed and attractive presentation to the visitor, should be, as it is today, the responsibility of powerful National and Regional Boards. But there are activities in which effort must be united and sometimes in life leadership is needed.
>
> The criticisms to which reference has been made elsewhere in this report sometimes centre on the lack of policy for tourism in Britain. This merits examination. Certainly, as said above, those responsible for the marketing and development of tourism generally find them-

selves in agreement. But frequently, Britain does not seem to know what she wants from tourism. There are those who say 'forward' and others say 'back'. Together with the National Boards, the BTA has tried to build bridges with the conservationists, both nationally and locally. But efforts like these sometimes can be in a vacuum, and it would seem high time for Government to formulate a policy which it would be the responsibility of the BTA and the National Boards to execute.

A possible first step towards this might be for the Chairmen and the Chief Executives of BTA and the National Boards to have regular formal meetings with the Secretary of State for Trade. For the gap is real. Until it is filled and a mechanism providing some degree of co-ordination is established, current criticisms will continue to have quite a lot of point.

The remarks need to be considered in the light of the knowledge that they were addressed to a Conservative administration and against a background of previous pressure from Conservatives when in opposition to have the BTA cast as the top body. BTA was, in fact, to get a Policy, but from a Labour Government which was in power again that year.

This Policy launched the 1974 Guidelines, referred to earlier, which were widely understood to require the BTA, among others, to work towards the long term balance of tourism away from London towards other parts of the country.

The Guidelines did not settle the question of hierarchy. Sir Alexander Glen, writing a little later in 1975, said that he had been told on appointment as BTA Chairman that he was 'to be the Tourist boss' (p. 246). He felt that the Government should modify the structure so as to give BTA 'certain coordinating duties' (p. 253). He added that otherwise 'we may find these [Britain's tourism] earnings more fragile than is often thought' (p. 253). No government since has given the BTA such duties. The polemic was partially addressed ten years later when the Conservative Government appointed one person to be Chairman of BTA and ETB. Scotland and Wales were left out of the equation. In the meantime Britain's tourism earnings long term grew apace.

The fiscal regime

From 1970 the fiscal regime was transformed. One by one the burdens and 'discrimination' of which the hotel industry had long complained were removed or alleviated. These changes began almost immediately. It was announced that the Selective Employment Tax would be phased out. A new system of depreciation allowances to be set against tax was introduced (Minister's statement to the House of Commons, 8 April 1971, reported in Hansard). Referring to the short-term scheme to stimulate hotel development begun under Labour, the Minister said that the present government would not want to extend it. 'We think' he said 'that reduction of the tax burden is a better way to help the hotel industry than a general system of grants and loans.'

Registration and classification

Proposals to make these compulsory were fiercely resisted by the trade associations and the hotel industry, as reported in the trade press already quoted. The idea was condemned by the former Chairman of the British Travel Association, by now President of the British Hotels and Restaurants Association (*Caterer and Hotelkeeper*, July 1971). Many believed that a comprehensive system would provide governments with a tool for price control. The Scottish and Wales Boards expressed strong support for compulsion.

The English Tourist Board prepared detailed proposals for compulsory registration but voluntary classification. The latter implied ranking of establishments according to physical characteristics, for example, proportion of rooms with private bathrooms. Grading involved subjective judgement and taste and would inevitably require a system of inspection. The BTA coordinated consultations on the ETB scheme. Its Annual Reports reveal a neutral or obliquely negative stance. Eventually a limited scheme was put forward which would have required establishments by law to enter their names on a register and, if they wished, to fill in a form providing 'objective' information on their range of facilities. The proposal was hailed by the leading trade association as 'a triumph for common sense' (*Caterer and Hotelkeeper*, 18 May, 1972).

In due course, the Government refused to make registration compulsory. The national tourist boards then set out to develop an entirely voluntary system. This had some value as a basis for marketing. Guides were published and establishments displayed signs. There were obvious weaknesses. The information available to consumers was rudimentary and the number and range of establishments participating was far from comprehensive. It would take many years to expand and improve the scheme.

Second phase: 1979–1992

The fundamental transformation brought about by deregulation and privatization programmes, including privatization of telecommunications and the national airline, need no elaboration here. They were central to the policies of a succession of governments led by Margaret Thatcher. The purpose of this short section is not to give a comprehensive account of tourism during this long period. The aim rather is threefold. It is (i) to put briefly on record the main developments in tourism policy, organization and practice in this new political environment, (ii) to examine the extent to which issues already identified remained 'live' and (iii) to observe any significant changes in the way they were handled.

The first major ministerial review of policy since 1974 was completed in 1983 when the Secretary of Trade, Norman Lamont, indicated that the 1974 Guidelines (requiring a shifting of the balance of tourism away from London) were no longer relevant.

Under an outstanding Cabinet Minister (Lord Young), a coherent review of tourism and policy statement was presented in 1985 in the Cabinet Office document *Pleasure, Leisure and Jobs*, followed up in 1986 with a statement on steps taken in line with policy – *Action for Jobs*.

During this time responsibility for tourism was moved with the Minister for the Department of Trade and Industry to the larger Department of Employment. Exceptionally, the sector was the subject of consideration by a Cabinet Committee. The move was accompanied by an increase in the mainstream Civil Service team with oversight of tourism. The 'tourism and leisure industries' were given greater recognition as generators of jobs and small businesses.

Administrative barriers to enterprise were reduced. For example, regulations concerning road signs to tourist attractions were greatly eased with the development of a nationwide system of 'white on brown' signs.

In an apparent change of direction, policy once more favoured 'dispersal of visitors out of London'. New emphasis was placed on professionalism and training the workforce. This was coupled with increased interest in quality and competitiveness in this sector of the service industries.

Under the Department of Employment for the first time high level attention was given explicitly to the need for coordination of actions across all Ministries with a contribution to make to the development of tourism (Cabinet Office Enterprise Unit, *Pleasure, Leisure and Jobs*, 1985).

The BTA continued to be supported heavily on the overseas promotion front. Periodic reviews by Ministers required the ETB to devolve more and more activity and a growing share of its budget to increasingly powerful and influential Regional Tourist Boards. The latter, however, also gained an increasing share of their income from the private sector. The central ETB organization was severely reduced and increasingly specialized. All-England domestic marketing campaigns went into steep decline.

Budgets for discretionary deployment by National Tourist Boards to finance development of facilities and amenities were extended throughout England in 1982. They were then terminated abruptly in 1988 under a Minister who succeeded Lord Young. This followed a public relations campaign in which the English Tourist Board stressed the industry's dynamic record and potential and the Board's promise to 'back success' in its strategy for 1987 to 1991. ('A Vision for England', 1987). It is reasonable to suppose that one of the arguments for termination which might have appealed to the Minister was that a highly successful industry no longer needed grant or loan support.

New legislation permitted the Scottish Tourist Board to carry out its own direct promotion overseas in consultation with the BTA. The Wales Tourist Board was granted greater control over the promotion of Wales abroad. The English regions became heavily engaged in overseas promotion using a combination of local government and private sector funds strengthened by BTA resources. The three national boards diverged into very different organizations, that for England being much reduced while the Boards for Scotland and Wales had more wide-ranging portfolios and relatively much larger resources.

Following the lead of these Boards the accommodation registration and classification schemes were improved by the introduction of independent verification by inspectors of information provided by establishments. Scotland pioneered arrangements whereby all types of tourist accommodation could apply to be inspected with a view to receiving recognition for facilities and quality of service.

Finally, in the period 1979–1992 governments paid increasing attention to the impact of tourism on the environment. Their sponsorship of cooperation between the statutory tourist organizations, the Countryside Commission and other organizations is discussed in Chapter 9. The series of reports under the heading 'Tourism and the Environment: Maintaining the Balance' (1991) reflected the new importance attached to and wide experience gained in 'tourism management', a term which had hardly been respectable in the 1970s. (Note the BTA's doubts about the concept in its Annual Report for 1976/77, p. 9). Central government guidance to local government on land-use planning for tourism evolved from a rather flimsy circular in 1979 (Circular 13/79), issued by the Department of the Environment, to the more substantial Planning Policy Guidance (PPG 21), issued by the Department in November 1992.

The preceding chapter and the present one have introduced a number of major, issues:

- The role of the state: Why should governments intervene? How should they intervene?
- Organization, including organizational hierarchy, coordination and cooperation.
- National, regional and local levels of policy and action: regional and local boundaries.
- The seasonal and spatial redistribution, 'channelling' and management of tourism.
- National tourism programmes and their evaluation.

All the above were foreshadowed in the experience of a large number of developed countries in membership of the OECD, as recounted in the first part of Chapter 6. The OECD included the UK, and the same issues were explored in more detail with reference to this one country. But most of them are known to have been of concern to policymakers across a wide range of developed and developing countries, including many in membership of WTO, as the remainder of Part Two will demonstrate. Regional organization, understandably, is not documented as a key issue for smaller developing (Third World) countries.

8

The role of the state. Why should governments intervene? How should they intervene?

Introduction

Policy documents, high level reports and ministerial statements often refer to the economic development of tourism as 'largely a matter for the private sector'. But the context will as often reveal that the involvement of state and government is indispensable. The Foreword to WTO's *Towards New Forms* of *Public–Private Sector Partnership* (1996c) states:

> Although tourism is an activity sustained mainly by private initiative, governments have traditionally played a key role in its development …

Both the public sector and private enterprise have to be heavily engaged if the sound long-term development of tourism is to be secured. This is the overwhelming consensus of the numerous sources to be quoted in this chapter.

A number of detailed explanations may be advanced for the state's involvement, but they can be reduced to two: (1) states and their governments are drawn by actual or proposed general legislation and policies, such as those governing taxation, into considering their specific effects on tourism; (2) legislation, policies, institutions and programmes may be initiated and supported by government with tourism as their central focus.

Almost every aspect of the life of a host community has a bearing on internal and incoming tourism and is potentially affected by it. Tourists are temporary members of the community. A large body of law making at every tier – national, regional and local – has implications for this activity. A report on legislation affecting tourism in Britain was drawn up in early 1982. It identified over seventy relevant Acts of Parliament. Drawn up by BTA and the National Tourist Boards, it was an aid to the continuous monitoring of possible changes in a large body of legislation that could conceivably have positive or negative impacts on tourism.

Some legislation had a clear, direct relevance to tourism, which provided a framework within which an identifiable core of government departments and agencies formulated and implemented policies for leisure, recreation and tourism. The core, however, could still be very large, as confirmed by a chart drawn up in 1979 by Travis. The chart identified seven UK Ministries whose policy advice to Ministers and programmes could affect tourism. They were the Departments of Trade, of Transport and of the Environment, the Ministry of Agriculture, Fisheries and Food, the Department of Education and Science, the Home Office and the Department of Social Security. Each Ministry was responsible for one or more relevant specialized agencies, ranging from four National Tourist Organizations (under Trade) through the Directorate of Ancient Monuments and Historic Buildings and Countryside Commission (under Environment) to the Forestry Commission (under Agriculture). The complete list extended to 16 major national agencies.

The two relevant kinds of legislation, referred to above, are worth identifying in more detail. The first covers general areas that may have significant consequences for tourism, positive or negative, such as legislation concerned with immigration, consumer protection, road safety and liquor licensing. The second kind is that which is concerned directly with the development and regulation of the leisure, recreation and tourism industries. It also covers protection of the built and natural environments and other assets that have special significance in the context of tourism. The first kind of legislation draws governments and public authorities willy-nilly into considering its impacts on tourism and into debate with interested lobbies, pressure groups and individuals. The second is directly entered into with tourism in mind either in its own right or as an element within the wider field of leisure, recreation and tourism.

A further illustration of the wide interaction between general legislation and tourism is to be found in *Europe's Tourism. How Important Is It?*, published by the European Tourism Action Group and others in 1999. Under the heading 'Tourism: the bigger picture', the document states that:

> the work done by the tourism team in the [European]) Commission's new Directorate-General for Enterprise is only part of the picture.

The authors name many policy areas which are claimed to have clear links with the tourism industry and its customers. They are:

> culture; consumer policy; competition policy; employment policy; environment and sustainability; GATS; information society; internal market; regional policy/structural funds; SMEs; social policy; taxation/VAT; the Euro; training; transport and VISAS.

According to Brewton and Withiam (1998), in the United States, in the context of a 'first attempt at a comprehensive US Tourism Policy', the US Department of Commerce published a report, *Tourism: Putting the Pieces Together*, which reflected the efforts of 13 federal agencies to head off the trend of the nation's declining international market share. According to the report, more than 170 programmes affecting tourism were managed by 30 departments and agencies.

Another example is provided by the record of negotiations conducted under GATS regarding the worldwide liberalization of trade in services. The record of the WTO Seminar on 'GATS. Implications for Tourism'

(1994a) addressed Tourism and Travel as one of 12 service sectors to be the subjects for multilateral agreements between governments. It observed that agreements on many of the remaining 11 sectors would have implications for tourism. These included, for example, 'Recreational, Cultural and Sporting Services', 'Communication Services' and 'Transport Services'.

Chapter 2 indicated that modern legislators and governments have strong motives for intervening in tourism. The economic and social significance of tourism, as an industry, is recognized. The contribution of recreation, leisure and tourism to the quality of life of citizens is widely acknowledged.

However, does the state's clear interest in tourism require massive investment and *dirigisme*? If this is largely a matter for private initiative, should not the state confine its involvement as far as possible to the provision of an appropriate physical, regulatory and fiscal framework? Why should not the state leave development funding to private enterprise competing for business in a large, dynamic and free marketplace? The considerable resources and significance of private capital will be reflected in later chapters. In the meantime it will be the contention of this book that its role should be viewed in context. There is a strong case for active state supervision and, in some instances, direct intervention as well as public funding. The main elements of the case are now outlined.

Wider objectives

Tourism may have the potential to contribute more than alternative industries to the achievement of wider objectives established by governments as priorities in the general interest of the community. These may range widely from general social and political engineering to foreign exchange earnings and on to the improvement of incomes and living conditions for women (especially in poor countries). Here are some examples of prioritized wider objectives:

■ According to Valenzuela (in Williams and Shaw, 1998, p. 43) the dictatorial regime of General Franco prioritized tourism in Spain, regarding it not only as a valuable economic sector but also as a means of legitimization in respect of other

European states, or at least of large elements of their populations.

- Cadieu (1999, p. 5) refers to the initiatives taken by the French state from the 1930s onwards to use tourism as an instrument of social change and to promote Social Tourism as a concept which embraced public subsidy of holidays away from home for low income groups. This was an integral part of 'welfare'.

- Cooper et al. (1993, p. 151) reported that the Wales Tourist Board sought to develop and market tourism in ways that would yield the optimum social and economic benefit to the people of Wales. Implicit in this was the need to sustain and promote the culture of Wales and the Welsh language as well as to safeguard the natural and built environment.

- The British Government recognized the potential for job creation, especially through the stimulation of small and medium sized businesses, in an era of nationwide high unemployment (Pleasure, Leisure and Jobs, Cabinet Office Enterprise Unit, 1985 and its sequel, Action for Jobs, Department of Employment, 1986).

- A joint Financing Proposal agreed by the European Commission and the Government of Syria in 1996 recognized the sector's contribution to the building of links between the European Union and Syria and its significance in spearheading moves towards a mixed economy and, ultimately, privatization (unpublished Syria Case Study by D.J. Jeffries, 2000).

- In many countries, regional development has high priority in public funding and it has been the key to the 'development of poorer regions which might not survive economically without tourism' (OECD, 1993, p. 13). Several academic writers have commented on this, notably Pearce (1988) and Swarbrooke (1997).

- In very poor developing countries governments are encouraged by aid programmes to use tourism not only as a tool to combat poverty but as a means for encouraging and financing biodiversity and nature conservation, a matter of considerable interest in donor communities. See, for example Changing the Nature of Tourism, produced by the Environment Policy Department of the UK's Department for International Development (1999). Support for ecotourism, so fashionable in the 1990s, was indicative, inter alia, of the very high priority given to nature and wildlife conservation among multilateral and bilateral aid agencies.

Transport policy, infrastructure and regulation

Governments usually provide the basic physical infrastructure necessary for tourism – such as roads, airports and communications – as well as creating the legal framework within which the transport industry operates (Foreword to *Towards New Forms of Public–Private Sector Partnership,* WTO, 1996c).

Increases in disposable income and free time coupled with the urge to escape briefly from the home environment have spurred the demand for tourism since its beginnings in the first industrialized societies. But it was made possible, driven and shaped by developments in transport, making travel faster, cheaper, more comfortable and safer. The history of transport improvements worldwide from 1840 to 1979 has been ably summarized by Burkart and Medlik (1982, Part I). In the British context, Cooper *et al.* have stated (1993, p. 16), in a chapter on transportation, that:

Adequate transportation infrastructure and access to generating markets is one of the most important prerequisites for the development of any destination.

Governments have continued to influence tourism fundamentally through control of and heavy investment in transport infrastructure. Pearce, in *Tourist Development* (1989), described massive government underpinning of major developments in France (Languedoc Roussillon), Mexico (Cancún) and Spain (the coast south of Alicante, among others).

Numerous instances are given in the volume edited by Williams and Shaw (1998) of the bearing of transport on tourism. Post-war investment in road, rail and air transport in France are summarized by Tuppen (1998, pp. 243–68). The impact of nationwide improvements in Spain's transport infrastructure is reviewed by Valenzuela, (pp. 51 and 52). The dramatic effects of transport and airports deregulation on Irish tourism are detailed by Gillmor (p. 229).

Deregulation, especially of aviation, has been used expressly as an instrument of change to shape tourism anew in a number of countries. In his seminal work *Aviation and Tourism Policies* (1994), Wheatcroft points out that countries may earn more from tourism as a result of liberalized aviation than they may lose by exposing their national airlines to free competition. He cites Australia and Mexico (p. 6) as typifying:

> those countries which have adopted liberalised aviation policies in the belief that the tourism benefits will be greater.

Commenting (pp. 61–2) further on Australia he writes:

> New policies recently adopted in Australia are extremely interesting to this study because they rest on a quite explicit political decision that the potential gains from expanding tourism are greater than the benefits to be derived from protecting a national airline. The tourism industry, through its organisation, the Australian Tourism Industry Association, campaigned for several years to persuade the government to introduce more competition into the air transport market ... These pressures ... led to sweeping changes in transport policies. ... The key point is that all these changes reflect the very high priority which Australia is now giving to the development of tourism [which is] Australia's biggest export earner and, in the optimistic scenario, the number of tourist visitors is targeted almost to treble from 2.4 million in 1991 to 6.5 million in 2000.

The conclusion of this section is that the state's major role in transport development provides it with an important instrument for promoting and managing tourism in the national interest. This, together with the power of the state in land-use planning and the fiscal regime are the three most important instruments at its disposal.

The complexity of tourism

The great complexity of tourism, of the industry and of its products, calls for coordination and cooperation, which arguably only governments have the authority and apparatus to organize.

Quoted in WTO (1998a, p. 13), Dr Harsh Varma, addressing an Asian audience, said:

> We are all very aware that tourism is a very wide, sophisticated, multisectoral industry. No other industry covers a group of associated sectors as wide as tourism ranging from accommodation, sight-

seeing and travel services, to transportation ... and the retail trade. It is a complex combination of industries of the world's largest order with an extremely sophisticated structure ...

If we trace the origin of modern tourism, after the Second World War, we would find that in the early stages of development, the government's involvement in the tourism sector was complete or total in all aspects. The government created basic infrastructure like roads, water supply, electricity, telecommunications. The government also provided the superstructure like hotels, restaurants and other tourist facilities and services. Over the period of time, as the industry matured, the government's role has undergone a major change. In most of the developed countries, it is the private sector which has adopted the role of a major or a senior partner while the government's role has been confined to that of a policy maker and the one which is really involved in the regulation of the industry. I must say that recognizing the industry's enormity and its structural complexity, one of the essential conditions for the successful development and promotion of tourism in any country is the active involvement of all players of the industry at all levels. In the public sector, the involvement is needed not only at the national or central level, but also at the regional, local and community levels. In the private sector, a vast number of companies and organizations of diverse types are more and more involved in the development of the tourism industry.

It has been argued that the need for coordination increases in countries where the industry is highly fragmented into small enterprises. Such fragmentation has already been discussed in Chapter 2. Without assistance the industry is very weak in terms of its ability to convey coherent information to the marketplace. Keller and Smeral (1997, p. 21) have remarked that:

Since tourism is a sector dominated by small-scale operations which, unlike industry, have no research and development, this task must be taken on by government.

It has been affirmed that these tasks (information and R and D) cannot be left entirely to the larger enterprises. Nor is it always practical to raise the necessary funds directly from small enterprises, the only realistic means being the taxation system whose use is justified provided the results achieved yield general economic benefit (Jeffries, *Selling Britain – a Case for Privatisation?*, 1989, p. 79).

Market failure

The full interplay of suppliers and markets alone may not work satisfactorily. For instance, failure in some sub-sectors may affect the success of the industry in general. Weakness in one area – for instance local taxi services or seasonal closures of attractions – may have a disproportionate effect on the destination's overall reputation.

More importantly, completely unrestricted operation of markets may not be compatible with the achievement of wider purposes such as the protection of the environment and the safeguarding of public goods for which the industry and its customers do not pay.

Bodlender, in WTO's *Privatization Papers* (1994b, Theme II, pp. 15–16), observed that:

> in areas where a tourist industry is developing the unfettered operation of the market may lead to results contrary to what are desired. What often happens is that a combination of real estate speculation and the prospect of a rapid pay-back on invested capital, causes the accommodation sector to outpace the capacity of the resources required to support a balanced tourism development programme.

He quoted Wanhill (in WTO, 1994b, p. 16), who had put the matter lucidly as follows:

> poor development comes about because the market mechanism fails to allocate resources correctly. This is due to the fact that many of the products that tourists seek are in the domain of public goods. These are goods we can all enjoy in common, and are equally available to us all. In tourism, public goods are gifts of nature, the consequences of history and culture, and are also provided by the state in response to a public obligation requirement.

> The principal feature of most public provision is that it is non-excludable. If the goods or service is to be provided at all, it may be consumed by everyone without exception and usually without charge

at the point of use. Public goods form no part of the private costs facing the tourism developer and are therefore open to abuse through overuse.

Who but the state, acting in the collective interest, can step in with measures to prevent or correct such abuse? The question is central to the debate on sustainability.

Public sector provision for leisure, recreation and tourism

Governments and the public sector are heavily engaged operationally, even in countries where privatization has been maximized. They are producers, often on a large scale, of the tourist product as part of free or subsidized provision. This may be available where no distinction can be made between users in the host community and tourists or 'outsiders'. The public sector therefore is involved directly in tourism production and has to cooperate with private sector producers of sub-components of the tourist product. This observation is particularly applicable to the attractions and events sub-sectors. Outstanding examples are major historic monuments such as the royal palaces open to visitors in Britain and events such as the 1989 celebrations in France marking the 200th anniversary of the French Revolution. Provision has to be made for tourists in terms of space and associated services, that is, components of basic tourist products. Such elements are in the public domain and are bound to remain so in view of their cultural and social significance. Most countries offer a huge range of publicly owned attractions and official events and ceremonies which have meaning for a much wider public than recreationists and tourists, important as these may be. The best of these are extremely important contributors to the pulling power of tourist destinations. The opportunity to experience them is part of the 'core benefit' derived from the basic tourist product which gives people access to them.

Resolution of conflict

Tourism, despite all its rich benefits, is a potential source of conflict within host communities, as a reading of Chapter 3 will have confirmed. Such conflicts are multifarious, varying in intensity from one community to another and growing worldwide as tourism expands faster than any other activity or industry. The state and governments are called upon to resolve conflict. That is their *métier*. Tourism is increasingly political.

Concluding remarks

Governments are passively and actively involved. Much of what they do, although not focused on tourism, has side effects. They also actively intervene.

The discussion so far has identified two basic explanations for governments' deliberate intervention. First, governments may have strong *motives* (e.g. strong interest in resolving key problems such as political and social issues, chronic national unemployment or severe regional imbalances threatening national stability). Second, governments have to intervene and contribute due to the *intrinsic character* of tourism. It is characterized by the following:

- Dependence on heavy public investment in transport infrastructure and well-regulated, safe transport services.
- Market failure in some sub-sectors and fragmentation into small, heterogeneous businesses.
- Dependence to some extent on the public sector's direct operational involvement in tourism production.

Pro-tourism lobbyists would do well to consider stressing to governments that the industry can make an *exceptional* contribution to the achievement of its overriding, key objectives (where this is justified by the facts). Advocacy may be weak where it does no more than highlight the character of the industry as a reason for public sector support or for industry-favouring measures. The two propositions should be linked: the potential for exceptional rewards and the unique nature of tourism.

But the case for government support is likely to vary considerably from country to country. Tourism in mature destinations has less need of public involvement than elsewhere, although even in these cases there exist new fields for development, for example, particular regions or new sectors. There are also several categories of countries which do not yet have a mature industry in the sense of having a large and well-developed private sector. These include former Communist countries in Eastern Europe, countries gearing up for international tourism for the first time, such as Libya, and developing countries which continue to depend on international aid channelled through their governments.

Much international debate in recent years has focused on an alleged worldwide disengagement of the state. There has certainly been massive disengagement since the 1980s in formerly Socialist command-and-control economies throughout the world. Here the central producers of tourism, particularly in hotels, catering and transport, have been widely, often comprehensively, privatized. They are now increasingly on a par with their opposite numbers in Western economies. In the latter the state was always, relatively speaking, disengaged. The belief that there has been even further disengagement in the West may be exaggerated. The issue has been clouded by the debate on the role of NTAs and NTOs. Decline in support for the latter is not necessarily symptomatic of further general public sector disengagement from tourism. It may only mean that the typical NTA and NTO are seen as less important in the scheme of things than in the past. The relevance and impact of public sector actions continues to be massive. However, governments appear to be articulating them and coordinating them in new ways.

The changing role of the NTA/NTO was well under way from the late 1980s and was symptomatic of shifts in the whole worldwide tourism scenario. This was debated at a high-level WTO international seminar which took place in Budapest in 1993: the theme was 'Tourism Development and the Responsibility of the State'. Opening remarks made by WTO's Deputy Secretary General (p. 16) are worth quoting at this point:

Tourism is profoundly multidisciplinary; in terms of governmental organisation, I would say, interministerial ... If one takes from around the world the countries which have constructed an efficient tourism during the 70s and 80s ... one observes that ... they constitute almost integrally countries which endowed themselves with strong, structured tourism administrations. ... the great difficulty with which we are confronted is that, for tourism, the State must know at once how to be present when necessary and how to withdraw when it's obligatory.

9

Interorganizational relationships, coordination, cooperation and hierarchy

Introduction

International tourism on today's scale would be quite impossible without international cooperation. The contribution of international organizations over the whole of the latter half of the twentieth century is beyond the scope of this book. The best reference sources on this vast subject are the series of Annual Reports of the OECD Tourism Committee, the publications of the World Tourism Organization and, in the purely European context, the published output of DG XXIII of the European Commission. The present chapter is confined to reflections on systems within sovereign states.

Governments intervene in and encourage tourism through a complex structure of governmental and officially recognized organizations which it is convenient to visualize as existing at different levels within a pyramid, the national executive at the apex and the local level at the base. The structure should not be taken literally as corresponding to the distribution of real power and influence as the base may have considerable resources and powers to act independently and strongly to influence 'upwards' the development of policy. The whole structure is of course subject to continual pressure from electorates, business interests and lobbies.

Between the apex and the base there is now in most countries an intermediate level of tourism organization which is described in many instances as 'regional'. The term should be treated with caution as it applies to spatial scales that are quite different. The regions in major European countries are roughly of the same order of magnitude while in the USA regions are much larger. The Rocky Mountain regional tourism organization, for instance, covers Idaho, Montana, Wyoming and South Dakota – an area as large as France, Belgium, Germany and Austria combined. In practice European regions equate to 'countries', within US states, for example, the Gold West country of Montana. In operational terms states in the USA are comparable to nations elsewhere in many ways. They have created an intermediate level of organization, at least in part for the same practical reasons as. have the European countries (to be discussed below).

The coordination of different parts of the structure is taken by the author to occur when one organization exercises authority over two or more others in order to get them to work together in pursuit of a common policy or objective. Cooperation is taken to refer to voluntary agreements or joint actions across the same levels in the structure or between levels.

An example of policy coordination is embodied in the US National Tourism Policy Act (1981), which set up a Tourism Policy Council (TPC) to bring together high-level agency officials with direct programme operating responsibilities to consult and discuss needed improvements, to examine specific tourism-related programmes and to assist in resolving inter-agency conflicts should such arise. The TPC key function is to:

coordinate the policies and programs of federal agencies that have a significant effect on tourism, recreation, and national heritage preservation. (Edgell, 1990, p. 101)

An example of coordination of a different order (that is, purely operational) is the ongoing programme directed by England's central tourist organization which for many years has required all officially recognized local Tourist Information Centres to operate to common standards and to provide, mostly for the sake of mobile tourists, information and itineraries covering the whole country.

Notions of authority, hierarchy and coordination are linked.

The national level

Discussion conveniently starts with the NTA and NTO, which are a part of the structure but always somewhat below its apex.

The WTO definitions were quoted in Chapter 1. Here are some examples of NTAs:

- The French NTA consists of the Tourism Directorate, concerned with policy, finance and internal matters and Maison de la France, charged with external marketing. Both are the responsibility of a Minister of Tourism within the giant Ministry of Public Works, Transport and Housing. The Maison de la France is effectively the NTO.
- The Spanish NTA is Turespaña, which, although 'autonomous', is chaired by the Secretary of State for Commerce, Tourism and Small Enterprises within the major Ministry of Economy and Finance. Turespaña is also the NTO.
- The Fijian NTA is the Department of Tourism. The NTO is the Fiji Visitors Bureau. Its Board, responsible for policy and management, is chaired by the Minister for Tourism and Civil Aviation.

Many academic texts tend to view NTAs and NTOs in isolation but they are subject to the coordinating activities of senior Ministries. These in turn cooperate (and can at times be in conflict) with other Ministries, including the normally most senior Ministry of Finance or Economic Planning.

During the first 15 years following the 1969 Act, Britain's NTA was the Department of Trade (and Industry), the sponsoring Ministry for both the BTA and the ETB which, together, performed the functions of NTO for England. (There were separate structures for Scotland, Wales and Northern Ireland.) The President of the Board of Trade (the Minister) might seek the cooperation of the Home Office (on, for example, visas) and the Foreign Office (on, for example, cooperation between British Embassies and the NTO's offices abroad).

There exist in some countries standing arrangements for all Ministries to consult with one another regularly on matters affecting tourism. They have a chequered history and their internal workings or the results achieved have rarely been subject to external scrutiny or published studies.

The work of the US Tourism Policy Council is relatively well documented. See, for example, *United States Tourism Policy – Alive But Not Well,* by Brewton and Withiam (1998).

In the UK the best documented strategy for interministerial cooperation was presented in Lord Young's report *Pleasure, Leisure and Jobs* (Cabinet Office Enterprise Unit, 1985) and its sequel, *Action for Jobs* (Department of Employment, 1986). The strategy called for action across a wide front, demanding inputs from a large number of Ministries (Departments). Progress was monitored and results made public. There were substantial positive achievements. In a section headed Co-ordinating Government Interests (para. 73), the original report stated:

> The discussions between Departments which led to this report have illustrated the value of a broad review in ensuring that the significance of this sector is fully reflected in individual Government policies. Accordingly it has been decided to arrange for the Departments concerned with tourism and tourism-related policies to keep under coordinated and regular review the range of Government policies which impinge on tourism and leisure and any obstacles to the industry's development which may stem from these policies.

Beyond the first year, systematic checking of all the action points seems to have died out. The Minister moved on. Little more was heard of the fundamental proposals with long-range implications concerned, for example, with the adjustment of road building programmes to favour tourism and the development of regional airports to spread tourism in the context of a policy to relieve pressure on London. Questioned by a House of Commons Committee during the 1989/90 session, a civil servant said:

I am satisfied that we within the Department of Employment [by then the tourism sponsoring Ministry] have the mechanism for influencing other departments. We have, for example, the Tourism Coordinating Committee chaired by the Secretary of State which has all the Ministers on it … it meets … about twice a year I believe.

The above was quoted by Elliott (1997, p. 86) in a critical assessment of the UK's coordinating arrangements.

The history of interministerial coordination in the field of tourism hardly inspires excitement, either in the UK or elsewhere. For example, Michaud (1995, pp. 38–9), while accepting that the need for such coordination was generally acknowledged in France, also noted that 'curiously' the Interministerial Committee for Tourism – presided by the Prime Minister – had not met since 1983.

In the second half of the 1990s, the Fiji Government established a Tourism High Level Consultative Forum. Meeting several times a year, its members include senior officials from relevant Ministries, the main trade associations, the national airline and others. The ultimate success of this forum will depend on the implementation of a Fiji Tourism Development Plan which was prepared and published in 1997 with finance from the European Development Fund. Implementation of the plan was dependent on there being available further finance for a technical assistance project to:

assist the Department of Tourism to develop its capabilities including in implementing proposed Tourist Development Areas, and to work with the Ministry, the Fiji Trade and Investment Board, the Fiji Visitors Bureau, other Ministries and the Public Service Commission in developing a more suitable investment climate for investors in the tourism sector, both domestic and foreign.

The project was designed to strengthen the Department so that its focus would be on:

representing the interests of the industry to the rest of government.

The source was a number of internal documents made available to the author by the Department of Tourism. At the time of writing it was not clear whether the technical assistance would be forthcoming. The

Cabinet was reported to be enthusiastic about the plan. However, optimism had to be tempered by the fact that two previous national plans in 1973 and 1989 were never implemented, according to Burns (1997, p. 164). (Subsequent political events in 2000 have obviously put in further doubt the future of the coordinating and planning process.)

So far discussion has addressed briefly the higher levels of government as well as the NTA/NTO place therein. An important consideration is the need for horizontal cooperation between them and other agencies. There may be several whose role involves them in tourism and who are the agencies or executive arms of Ministries other than the tourism sponsoring Ministries. In England in the 1970s and 1980s such agencies included the Arts Council, the Sports Council, the Directorate of Ancient Monuments and Historic Buildings and the Countryside Commission. There has been a long history of cooperation between the NTO and these agencies. To the extent that the sponsoring Ministries required the agencies to work together there was coordination as well as cooperation, usually envisaged in Memoranda of Understanding between agencies. A typical example (1978) featuring the Countryside Commission is given in Appendix 4. Another more recent example (1998) is the Memorandum drawn up by the BTA and the British Council governing cooperation abroad in tourism and in cultural affairs (Appendix 5).

Cooperation between the NTO and the Countryside Commission has been the subject of numerous reports and agreements over the years, though receiving far more attention under Conservative than Labour administrations. (The rural constituency is the traditional power base of the Conservatives.) Titles of studies and conferences, mounted chiefly by the ETB and Countryside Commission, speak for themselves: 'Visitors in the Countryside', proceedings of a Rural Tourism Conference (1988a); 'Visitors in the Countryside – a Development Strategy' (1988b); 'Shades of Green – Working Towards Green Tourism in the Countryside', Conference Proceedings (1990), and so on.

Such activity tended to focus throughout on the formulation of general principles which would be applied in detail at local level by local representatives of national agencies or would be commended to others, notably local governments. At a relatively early stage, the 1978 Memorandum referred to above embodies the 'Sandford principle', which established that where tourism and countryside conservation (in National Parks) was in conflict conservation should have priority.

Again in the UK, a series of four reports entitled 'Tourism and the Environment: Maintaining the Balance' (English Tourist Board and Employment Department Group, 1991) reflected the striving for consensus among a very wide range of national organizations on the conservation of England's patrimony in three key sectors: historic towns, heritage sites and countryside. Working Groups drawn from a wide spectrum of organizations were established by the government to 'look at visitor management issues in three different types of environment'. Their reports were examined by a 20-strong 'task force' which produced a consolidated report for submission to a national conference in April 1991. The report set out general principles and gave agreed guidance on 'practical management tools' such as assessment of capacity, transport management, marketing and information, conservation and adaptation, design and control of development, and involving the local community. The presentation was illustrated by numerous 'best practice' case studies illustrating the translation of approved principles and techniques into concrete action in specific places. The case studies were brief and could not convey fully the challenge of cooperation at local level involving, usually, the complex interactions of numerous interests, including the local representatives of national agencies. Others have explored the issue in greater depth (see, for example, Bramwell and Sharman on 'Collaboration in Local Tourism Policymaking', 1999, pp. 392–415). National agencies can go little further than providing a framework for such interactions, carrying out research and giving technical advice.

Structure 'beneath' the national level

Some academic texts present the local tourism organization as belonging neatly at the base of an apparent command structure with the NTA/NTO at the apex. This can be misleading. In many countries they belong to different pyramids. In England, the Regional Tourist Boards have received core finance from the tourism sponsoring Ministry via the NTO while local OTAs have been financed by the Department of Environment and its successor the DETR, responsible for local government.

A correct, though simplified, representation would be as shown in Figure 9.1.

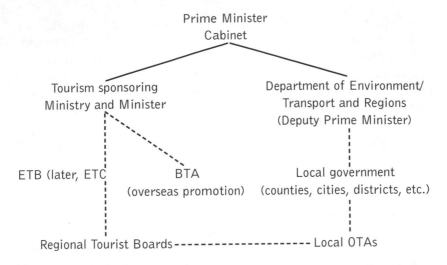

Figure 9.1 Simplified structure of tourism organizations in the UK

At a Local Government Association Conference in Liverpool in 1999, the DETR was described as 'ten times as large' as the previous tourism sponsoring Ministry, the DCMS. The DETR also housed many parallel agencies, such as the Countryside Commission, now the Countryside Agency.

Regional Tourist Boards in England are and always have been partnerships between the NTO, local government and the private sector, depending increasingly on voluntary contributions from local government for core finance. Local government is not a junior partner. Within England and Wales its annual expenditure on tourism marketing alone is nearly double that of the BTA and the NTOs combined. Its overall expenditure on leisure, recreation and tourism is around 25 times their budgets.

Of the government departments that shape tourism supply fundamentally in the UK, those concerned with transport and local government are by far the most significant.

More on the regional level

The longest tradition of official sponsorship of tourism is municipal, going back to the middle of the nineteenth century. NTAs developed slowly from the turn of the century. After the Second World War they multiplied and expanded rapidly, pressed into service by governments to boost foreign currency earnings. Regional tourism organizations are more recent. They have their origins in many developed countries in the mid-1960s and later, coinciding with steep growth in mass motor-car ownership. But a number of other factors have contributed to their growth and strengthening. Devolution of central government powers from the early 1980s has heightened the importance of the regional (and local) dimension in tourism. Regionalism has been especially strong in Europe and has gained momentum under the aegis of the European Union and its institutions. The European Regional Development Fund has been a powerful instrument in this respect. Europe's two leading tourist destinations, France and Spain, now have highly developed regional tourism structures. In 1995 the Maison de la France national budget was US$86.61 million, while the combined budgets of the Regional Tourism Committees was US$40 million (WTO, 1996c, pp. 29, 31). The ERDF's influence on regionalization has been well covered by Pearce (1988).

Some NTAs in many other parts of the world laid the practical foundations for the strengthening of the regional level. For example, Pearce (1992, p. 185) describes initiatives taken in New Zealand.

In England, regional strengthening was for five reasons:

1 In the 1970s the new involvement of the NTO in the financing and development of supply led the ETB to conceive a regional network as a more efficient structure than a central one for managing tourism. (An early emphasis on *supply* and *management* was made clear in the English Tourist Board Chairman's statement of November 1971 at a Conference on Tourism and the Environment. See Appendix 3.)

2 National marketing operations required detailed knowledge of tourist facilities and services and this could be more efficiently gathered via regional branch offices by personnel close to them.

3 The growth of mobile tourism had already led to the development of scattered clusters and units of tourism in towns, villages and countryside throughout the land. Policy dialogue could not continue to be conducted exclusively through the well-organized lobbies in the traditional resorts and spas.

4 There was a need to encourage cooperation between resorts and the new growth points in anticipation of further growth in the potential for mobile tourism. This was made clear in the ETB's earliest Annual Reports.

5 It was recognized that one overall national programme could not fit all. Some variations and supplementary activities might have to be exclusive to particular regions, for instance, the unique Lake District and London.

Thus both political change and shifts in the patterns of tourism combined to bring on stream a new type of tourism organization. However, this has not been an unqualified success, either in England or elsewhere.

The European Travel Commission, in a 1999 Survey of 22 member NTOs in Europe (West and ex-Communist bloc) found 11 or 50% expected that the growing regionalization of Europe would make their relationships with regional tourist boards more difficult.

One major weakness of regional OTOs, noted by observers in several different countries, is that the general administrative boundaries which define them as tourism destinations are at odds with the realities of the sector. In particular, they are generally held not to be suitable as marketing entities while, paradoxically, many give marketing a high priority. Bieger, calling for a change in Swiss tourism structures, refers to organizations at state, regional and local level and remarks (1998, p. 7) that:

All these tourism organizations work for areas within political borders. On the other hand, in most cases, the area that the tourist regards as a product and in which he [sic] consumes his services during his stay, is independent of political borders. Therefore an efficient coordination of the tourist product can't be guaranteed by these political organizations.

With regard to the Netherlands, Ashworth and Voogd (1990, p. 89) observed that a survey of entrepreneurs, the targets for 'place promotion', revealed that:

the regions as perceived did not correspond to the actual existing political and statistical collection regions.

Airey and Butler, in a paper for AIEST on Tourism at the Regional Level, examined the issue in detail. The key theme, the authors stated (1999, p. 86), was that:

> although the regional dimension has been an important element of tourism, at least since 1945, the regional level is not one that relates well to either tourist demand or to the suppliers of tourist services. … In all of this the regional dimension is one that is, above all, linked to public policy and expenditure … Tourists do not normally visit tourist regions and the industry does not organize itself on a regional basis … Above all, tourism has to be understood at the local, destination level.

Airey and Butler's paper was 'strongly influenced by the UK in particular and Europe in general', although the issues raised had a more general applicability. In the UK regionalism has indeed become increasingly controversial. Airey and Butler cited two statements from the professional body, the Tourism Society, at the time of the new Labour Government's 1998 review of tourism as follows:

> Promotion should be undertaken at the national level AND at the destination level but never at the regional level.

> Tourism destinations do not follow administrative boundaries. In England, in particular, most regions are too large and highly inappropriate as areas to be developed and promoted for tourism. This is perhaps one of the main reasons why regional tourist boards have performed very patchily. For example, while some regions, such as Cumbria, coincide with destinations (in this case, the Lake District), others bring together highly incompatible destinations such as Great Yarmouth and Cambridge in the East of England.

Research in depth by Meethan (1998, p. 586) has explored the reasons for widespread dissatisfaction with the West Country Tourist Board, one of them being that:

> whatever and wherever the West Country is, it is not a coherent and discreet entity to which residents feel a sense of attachment.

Whitehead, speaking at a Tourism Society meeting in 1998, said that the boundaries of the Regional Tourist Boards and Regional Development Agencies made no sense, the West Country, which stretched from Swindon to Bournemouth and on to Cornwall, being cited as a particular example (reported in *Tourism*, Issue 98, Autumn 1998, p. 21).

Heeley (2000, p. 17) has stated:

> The regions the RTBs represent provide insufficient marketing focus and are themselves not brands ... They are coherent destination areas neither in name nor reality.

Heeley's paper is highly instructive in tracing the origins and development of RTBs. He states (pp. 9–10) that:

> Administrative decentralization was embodied in ETB's initial intention to appoint and fund each of the RTB's chief executives. ... the RTBs became 'independent' (but in reality local authority dominated) regional marketing consortia, thanks to a combination of the power and influence of the local authorities, of sales and marketing-minded chief executives, and of minimalist private sector funding. ... there is a prima facie case to conclude that the operating of regional tourist boards in England from 1972–1999 has been by and large unsuccessful in attracting tourists and industry support.

The full text of Heeley's paper, delivered to a conference at the University of Surrey in January 2000, is unpublished but a summary is to be included in a conference report to be published by Butterworth-Heinemann.

The accuracy of his external analysis is confirmed by ETB's internal papers, the subject of a Personal Memoir by Jeffries (1999). Although Heeley is right about the heavyweight influence of the local authorities on the expansionist ambitions of the Regional Tourist Boards, it must also be noted that the system that evolved gave considerable material advantages to an unrepresentative element of the private sector who became 'partners'. Local authorities may not have intended this but it happened, largely without being noticed. The problem has not been entirely resolved. While over many years funds from the centre to the boards were subject to increasingly tight conditions to ensure they would be used for national purposes and for the benefit of the sector as a whole, some doubts must remain about the deployment of local government funds which underpin the present structure.

The Tourism Society published its view in 1998 in response to a consultative document issued in the name of the new Labour Cabinet Minister responsible for Culture, Media and Sport (and Tourism), Chris Smith. The Society stated:

> There is a fundamental issue for DCMS to address here. The trend towards regionalization from central Government is clear and incontrovertible. The problem is that tourism, as stated earlier, does not follow the pattern of other sectors. Indeed the absolute reverse is true – whereas greater regional focus might well be appropriate for the majority of UK interests, not only within the DCM's portfolio, the future prosperity of England's tourism requires a move *away* from regional focus. It is hardly surprising that RTBs have faced a barrage of criticism. Their remit, in so far as it relates to geographically specific marketing, is no longer appropriate to the needs of modern tourism. Faced with a diminishing rationale and limited funds for such enormous geographic areas, RTBs have sought to raise revenue through membership schemes. But these schemes have been largely inappropriate for individual tourism businesses, due to the lack of homogeneity in the regional tourism product and the large distances required to attend meetings. No wonder that active membership (as opposed to membership induced by discounts on accommodation schemes and advertising costs) has achieved low penetration of potential catchments. No wonder also that these adverse conditions have led to RTBs becoming exaggeratedly self-interested, sometimes at the expense of national interests.

From the mid-1980s, the progressive weakening of the coordinating role of the central organization in the face of increasingly autonomous regional bodies within inappropriate boundaries had its consequences. (See Mutch, 1996 on the English Tourist Network Automation project, a case study in interorganizational system failure.)

The European Travel Commission report quoted earlier suggests that regionalization within Europe is seen as problematical. In Europe in some quarters regionalism is seen by some as part of a long-term political agenda to break up the nation state in favour of a European superstate. (See, for example, *A Parliament for England* by Teresa Gorman

MP, addressing 'the EU's plan to destroy the United Kingdom by breaking it up into 12 separate regions ruled by Brussels'.)

It will remain that tourists visiting particular countries – above all those touring the country widely – will expect coherence in the chain of services on offer. Autonomous regions do not seem to be the best way of delivering such coherence. Many believe that there is a place for a regional tier but there is continuing debate on what its precise role should be.

10

The local dimension

Introduction

From the earliest times tourists converged on and congregated in special places. For example, centuries before the birth of Christ people gathered for health and recuperation at Epidaurus in Ancient Greece and on the island of Cos, where Hippocrates ministered at the famous Medical School.

In the early Christian era St Paul on a visit to Ephesus:

> had some uneasy moments because a certain Demetrius, a silversmith who specialized in 'silver temples of Artemis' called upon his fellow artisans to protest at the way Christianity was hurting their business; his 'silver temples' were miniature models intended for the throngs who came to see the temple of Artemis at Ephesus, which ranked among the 'Seven Wonders' ... (Cassen, 1994, pp. 131, 287)

For thousands of years pilgrims have flocked to the holy places of the world's great religions: Jews, Christians and Muslims to

Jerusalem; Christians to Rome; Muslims to Mecca; Buddhists to Kandy in Sri Lanka; Hindus to Varanasi on the Ganges; Sikhs to Amritsar and the followers of Shinto and Buddhism to Kyoto.

The seventeenth and eighteenth century Grand Tour for the landed classes of Northern Europe took them to Paris and to the fountainheads of the Renaissance in Florence, Venice and Rome. During that time inland spas such as Bath and Wiesbaden flourished and then were overtaken by the new coastal watering places of Brighton and Nice. The railways of the nineteenth century took tourists to railheads in hundreds of cities, spas and seaside resorts. Pimlott (1947) and Walton (1983) tell of the railways' impact on particular places in England, where passenger services were first developed. Quoting a wide range of sources, Judd (1995, p. 175) describes how railroad building and city development and, by implication, tourism went hand-in-hand in the United States. In his paper 'Promoting tourism in US cities', Judd writes:

In fighting for railroad connections in the nineteenth century, cities gave away land, purchased railroad bonds and sometimes helped finance construction. Up to 1861 cities supplied $300 million in railroad subsidies compared with $229 million from the states and $65 million from the federal government. In the years 1866 to 1873, the legislatures of 29 states granted authorization for aid by local governments to railroad projects.

Even after the advent of mass motor-car ownership, bringing with it greater potential for dispersal in the second half of the twentieth century, the world's tourism is still concentrated in large cities and resorts. Heeley (2000) quotes Sir George Young's view that in modern times tourism is still essentially a local phenomenon and tends to a high degree of spatial concentration.

Most movement is between and within the most developed, most urbanized countries. The locations of the most popular forms of secular tourism have shifted. In Europe, for example, they have shifted to the large concentrations of tourist development in the Mediterranean, particularly along the southern coasts of France and Spain. The leading cities in Europe are said to have a major share of international and, particularly, intercontinental tourism. J. Moreu, Director of Amsterdam Tourism, said at a WTO Conference (1999b, p. 60) that:

The larger more metropolitan cities, capital cities I prefer to call them – whether they are a capital or not – possess most of Europe's culture both for the past and present ... these destinations are so called European 'musts' for the visitor. Capital cities are therefore in most cases visited first and can be considered as teasers for the country.

Though one might not agree with the remark about their near monopoly of culture, the quote reflects the reality of large localized concentrations of international sightseeing tourism. Of overseas visitors to Britain, around 50% visit London.

The dispersal of tourism is facilitated by the motor car and motor coach, but where this occurs the scattering is often into clusters, including satellite clusters around the big metropolitan and coastal centres. Wherever circuits for cultural tourism have developed, historic and heritage towns have become new tourism growth points. They include hundreds of cathedral and castle cities in Europe alone.

That tourism is widespread yet locally focused may seem a paradox. The dispersal of tourism into small units in rural areas – and its growing importance to rural economies – may seem contradictory. Yet even rural tourism gravitates to particular types of countryside – those which are scenically outstanding, for example – while it is absent from others. National Parks in many countries are magnets for tourism and are commonly faced with severe visitor management problems. Cadieu (1999, p. 62) notes that there are:

three Frances: the France of mass tourism, the France of more diffuse tourism and the France of little or no tourism.

Efforts to spread tourism have been an important feature of policy in many countries since the 1970s (see Chapter 11). They have been in part a response to the tendency of tourism to concentrate spontaneously and to expand outwards from nodes of development, once established.

The distinctive character and special problems of tourism-intensive locations

According to Wanhill (1987, p. 55):

> In the UK, to compensate for any need to increase the provision of public services, local authorities in resort areas are deemed to have an enhanced population and accordingly receive extra resources through the Rate Support Grant provided by central (UK) government.

In France a highly developed body of law recognizes and ranks communities as *stations classées* for a number of purposes: to recognize their special needs, to underpin local administration and to allow them to raise local funds through *'taxes de séjour'* on tourist accommodation. Supplementary grants from the central state and funds raised locally pay for tourism development and events as well as specialized activities such as external promotion and information for visitors. A portion of the proceeds from casinos – a major source of revenue – may also be used for resort development. The law recognizes the heterogeneity of destinations, allowing the Ministries of Tourism and of Health to place resorts in well-defined classes. The first two were recognized in 1919 as the tourism (or touring) class of resorts and the climatic class. Other classes were added, the last two in the middle of the Second World War as follows: thermal or hydromineral; wine-growing or wine centres; seaside; and finally the winter sports and mountaineering class. Resorts may also have tourist offices which are officially classified from four to one star plus an additional, more basic office known as a Syndicat d'Initiative (Cadieu, 1999, pp. 146, 147).

There is de facto recognition, too, of the existence of considerable variations between destinations within categories in that devolved power allows resorts to handle issues flexibly in line with local needs. Further, local distinctiveness is cultivated as destinations compete for the tourist's favour. (A word of caution here: the French word *station* equates to the traditional British usage of the term *resort*. Both terms apply to settlements that may often include a large number of medium to small enterprises. In American usage a *resort* may often be one large hotel with supporting leisure facilities. See Chon and Singh, 1995.)

131

Local and municipal enterprise

There is a long history of impressive enterprise at local level. Heeley (2000) has summarized this usefully with references for further reading. Ashworth and Voogd in *Selling the City* (1990) as well as Gold and Ward in *Place Promotion* (1994) have critically examined recent municipal enterprise in a wide range of countries. Kotler, Haider and Rein (1993) have written in *Marketing Places* about recent explosions of civic energy in the field of tourism, mainly in North America.

Most of this literature serves as a reminder that tourism is more and more integrated into wider strategies to boost cities. Tourism and leisure are subsumed into a more general story about the city's merits as a place to relocate company headquarters, as a suitable venue for sporting and cultural events, conventions and meetings and as a site for new investment. Massive developments of infrastructure and super-structure, effectively changing the physical reality of places, have been carefully engineered and their impacts have been reinforced (in theory and perhaps in practice) by image promotion. The tourism and leisure industries have played an important part in the regeneration of many of the world's waterfronts in decaying port cities, according to Judd (1995, p. 178). To ask whether such changes have been successful, positive or commendable, is to open up a debate which is beyond the scope of the present book. It is pursued by the authors of the works cited.

The point to retain is that it is at the local level that material action can be organized coherently, for better or for worse, and where tourism policy is at its most specific. The term local, incidentally, has to be treated with some latitude. In the English context, for example, it must embrace the County, which may include areas such as Devon or Cornwall, as well as the Unitary Authority and District. Counties have land-use planning responsibilities for the Districts within their boundaries.

From the beginning localities worldwide have tended to specialize as destinations for tourists. By the end of the nineteenth century the most important groupings were cities, spas, coastal resorts and winter sports resorts. The mention of cities may need some explanation in parentheses. Important cities specialize in the sense that they are the seats of national or regional governments, the main sites for major buildings and monuments and the venues for significant events and ceremonies.

They bring together business and shopping centres and are the locations for theatre, nightlife and entertainment. They are specialized in that they offer a comprehensive range of urban attractions and services conveniently in a relatively restricted area. Arguably, the most attractive of them – cities like Bruges, Copenhagen and Edinburgh – bring all these things together within walking distance of one another. They are 'special' in that they offer a *combination* of experiences not available in other types of 'resort'.

Judd, writing on the renewal of downtown areas of large numbers of US cities in the past three decades, quotes (1995, p. 178) Frieden and Segalyn's reference to the new downtowns as:

> every mayor's trophy collection made up of an atrium hotel, festival mall, a convention center, a restored historic neighbourhood, a domed stadium, an aquarium, new office towers and a redeveloped waterfront.

Judd observes (1995, p. 179) that:

> Cities must, usually, invest in all or most of the components making up tourist space. One or two pieces are not likely to be sufficient. Agglomeration economies apply to tourist districts not principally because concentration lowers costs or increases the efficiency of business attractions, but because a full panoply of services and businesses is necessary to make the space maximally attractive to consumers of the tourist space.

But cities do not have a monopoly of tourism. As tourism has diversified so it has given rise to a greater range of specialized destinations answering to the needs of individual market segments. New segments with new motives and interests congregate in specific locations – for ocean surfing, for scuba diving, for the observation of wildlife, for industrial archaeology and so on. Hay-on-Wye in England has a remarkable concentration of bookshops and is a choice venue for 'bookworms'.

In countries that have a large number of different types of destination, policy debate and formulation at the national level tend to excessive generalization and 'statements of the obvious'. The phrase was used in 1985 by a British Parliamentary Committee (Trade and

Industry) critical of national tourism policy, quoted and discussed in Elliott (1997, p. 87). The greater the focus on local affairs the more it is possible, as the French say, to *concrétiser* the issues. Coherence of action is facilitated by:

- the relatively small scale of the actions;
- the physical proximity of the main players;
- the literal visibility of the main opportunities and problems; and
- the relative ease with which people with a common interest may be brought together to address them.

In the UK context, a good illustration of local cooperation between a large and heterogeneous number of local interests has been presented by Bramwell and Sharman (1999).

It is at the local level that families and individuals rooted in place (and perhaps property) can be expected to have regard for the long term and for the well-being of future generations. It is at this level that the interlocking sub-components of the overall destination component may be identified with relative ease and faults corrected. Here too there may be the best opportunity for collective action to welcome tourists. Civic pride may play a part in this.

Because of spatial concentration and specialization, there exist local areas where the industry is dominant and is even the exclusive economic activity. It is such places that have been, and are, among the pioneers. This degree of specialization does not characterize whole nations, with the exception of a number of very small countries, notably some tropical island states. In large highly developed countries devolution of tourism development and marketing as far as possible to the local level is imperative.

What makes a destination?

This is a difficult question to which perfect answers have not yet been found. The key to the answer, it is suggested, is the geographical dimension of the tourist product. For Northern European tourists travelling by charter plane to a typical stay-put resort holiday, spending all of their time away in, say, Calvia, Majorca, this town is the destination. As thousands of tourists do this, tourist enterprises and interests within

Calvia can have little difficulty in recognizing themselves as part of one destination. Calvia has been in fact an outstanding example of resort renewal and regeneration in the 1990s, as reported by Wright in the Winter 1999 issue of *Tourism*. Mobile tourism poses the most difficult problems in this context. Places linked together on the typical itineraries of a significant number of tourists also constitute a destination. How 'significant' is defined is the difficulty. Significant may mean that the volume and value of tourism effectively shared by the places on the itinerary are important enough to warrant cooperation between them in terms of production and marketing. They have a shared interest in providing the interlocking sub-components of an overall destination component just as the enterprises and residents of Calvia have. Such interest may be fairly clear in some cases. The stock Scottish package coach tour described in Chapter 4 illustrates the point. So significant is the volume of such tours that the consumers and the producers probably have little difficulty in recognizing Scotland as a whole as a complete scenic tour destination. Such tours feature strongly in the brochures of members of the British Incoming Tour Operators' Association.

There are, however, more complex situations that cannot be so readily observed and evaluated. Individual locations may provide the sub-components of many different destination components, each appealing to different market segments. The City of Winchester, in South Central England, is a destination in its own right for weekenders and for conference visitors. They will tend to explore Winchester and the surrounding areas during their time away. Winchester is also an overnight stop for coach parties touring England's cathedral cities, for motorists travelling to and from the West of England and, possibly, as a stop for motorists travelling between the central Channel ports, the English Midlands and the North. Winchester therefore is part of several distinct destinations. Its co-producers are numerous. Full cooperation with all of them would call for alliances with a wide range of interests at local, regional and national levels. Policy formulation may rest on a consideration of the importance to Winchester of the different streams of tourism which cross its boundaries (in other words, the different destination components to which it contributes).

Methods for deciding how to group locations into coherent destinations, meaningful for both producers and consumers, are still in their infancy. The debate in England on regions, discussed in Chapter 9, supports this view. Critics of present arrangements for defining regional boundaries – which implicitly set the parameters for cooperation between partners – have said that some of them are 'not destinations'. This, in the author's submission, implies that locations within their boundaries do not contribute significantly to the same set of destination components.

Chapter 9 reveals that England is not unique in the questioning of the relevance of traditional administrative boundaries. In France there is an ongoing debate on the new concept of *pays* and on the evolution of laws governing intercommunal cooperation. The notion of *pays* ('country') is said to be 'more linked to the past, tradition and folklore …' (Cadieu, 1999, p. 77). Cadieu quotes (p. 78) an official text dated 1995 written as part of the preparatory work for a new national land-use planning outline (schema). This recorded the need for a new territorial division (*redécoupage*) into *pays*. The document commented:

> Dispersal in tourism matters is the source of duplication notably as regards promotion. The mobilisation of tourism potential depends a great deal on the ability in each territory to articulate between the base [*commune*] levels and the needs of the wider level of country [*pays*] for reservation and promotion services.

This thinking has already been translated into proposals (Cadieu, 1999, p. 79). According to these, the Maine et Loire *département*, for example, would be divided into five *pays*. Michaud (1995, pp. 18–19) reports on the growing trend, notably in rural areas, towards intercommunal cooperation to promote the *labellisation* or branding of distinctive *pays*. The Economic and Social Council of the Provence–Alpes–Côtes d'Azur–Corse region (the country's leading tourist region) has defined 54 *bassins d'acceuil touristiques* or 'areas for welcoming/hosting tourists'. Further information on the concept is given in a *Mémento* produced by the chamber of commerce for the region (Chambre régionale de commerce …, 1997).

In England, new terms 'the natural destination' and 'destination branding' are increasingly part of the professional's vocabulary and are highly relevant. Branding, which is not necessarily based on administrative boundaries, has followed the emergence from the mid-1980s of a new force in British tourism, the public–private sector partnership at local level.

Public–private sector tourism partnerships

In the UK, pioneering work began with the formation in 1978 of the Plymouth Marketing Bureau, which was established as a company limited by guarantee, governed by a Board of Directors, of whom six were nominated by the local authority and nine elected from local trader interests (R. Mathews quoted by Heeley, 2000). Similar initiatives were followed in the early 1980s by a number of leading cities. Local partnerships were established in a wide range of very different locations throughout England in the context of Tourism Development Area Action Programmes (TDAPs), grant-aided and technically assisted by the English Tourist Board in their start-up years. Often starting as informal gatherings of public and private interests, many of these emerged as companies with full-time staff. There were 21 TDAP partnerships by 1989/90. Pooled funds were used for integrated activities, which included pump-priming of capital developments such as tourist attractions, training, environmental improvements, marketing and visitor servicing (Broom, 1990, internal documents provided by the author; see also Bramwell and Broom, 'TDAPs', *Insights*, 1989, pp. 6–17).

Public–private sector partnerships have arisen in a general political climate favouring privatization and rolling back the frontiers of the state. They are a result too of pressures to achieve greater efficiency, it being assumed that greater private sector involvement will lead in this direction. This assumption is plausible in that the tourism industry is complex. Its marketing is sophisticated and not easily understood by the generalist official in the public sector. Bramwell and Rawding (1994, p. 428) consider that partnership may also facilitate marketing across local authority boundaries. A leading British organization in the new mould is Coventry and Warwickshire Promotions. This is a company limited by guarantee but it is a not-for-profit company. Its Board of 13 encompasses two from the local authority, three from universities, one from the chamber of commerce and seven from trader interests, two of whom are elected from a 150-strong membership. Formed as recently as 1997 it has a staff of 28 and had a budget of 220 000 (US$ 350,000) by the year 2000.

In the UK every type of tourist destination is served by such partnerships – major cities, historic towns, seaside resorts and rural areas. Many local authorities still prefer an older system entirely controlled by elected politicians, advised and supported by mainstream public servants. The principal role of local OTOs, whatever the formula, is marketing. Partnership budgets grew rapidly from their inception in the early 1980s.

In France three types of local OTO provide in different ways for combined public private sector cooperation, according to Michaud (1995, pp. 13–18). These are, first, the Syndicats d'Initiative or local tourism offices – associations of locally elected councillors and private individuals (hotelkeepers, caterers, cultural and sporting associations, traders etc.). The earliest was founded in 1889 and such associations are by far the most common form of local organization. Two other categories exist in smaller numbers and are more recent in origin: municipal tourism offices and mixed economy companies. The scope and functions of all three types of organization are defined by statute.

The United States experience

Judd (1995, p. 176) has summarized the trends in the past three decades, which confirm the relatively weak role of states in tourism compared with the highly focused energies of cities. Over this period, this author states, cities have been engaged in a competitive struggle that parallels the railroad wars of a century ago. Officials have thrown themselves into it by initiating a major round of public spending. Cities are more aggressive in the fight for tourists than either the states or federal government. According to Judd (p. 178):

In just three decades downtowns have been transformed from centers of wholesale and retail trade to centers of high-level corporate services and recreation. Tourist and entertainment facilities coexist in symbiotic relationship with the corporate towers, and there is some overlap: shopping malls, restaurants and bars cater to daytime professionals who work downtown as well as to visitors. The transformation of downtown economies has been supported by and produced an expensive infrastructure, virtually all of it constructed over the last two to three decades by governments or supported with an array of public subsidies.

Central to city development has been the construction and promotion of convention and meetings centres. Morrison, Bruen and Andersen (1998, p. 1) have indicated that:

> One of the major trends in North American tourism in the past 25 to 30 years has been the increasing emphasis on marketing cities and other local communities as tourism destinations. Convention and visitor bureaus (CVBs), an organizational concept which originated in the USA, have been the central force in the growing power and influence of local destination marketing organizations. Fueled mainly by the introduction of local hotel room taxes, several US CVBs now have tourism marketing budgets greater than their respective state governments and that of the US Travel and Tourism Administration.

The roles the CVBs play in their local economies, the authors state, is often misunderstood and under-appreciated. Bureaus play a number of roles, but it could be said that 'their primary reason for being is to act as a destination marketing organization'. In the USA they have become the principal means for marketing by attracting large and small meeting and pleasure travel groups and independent travellers. According to Morrison *et al.*, however (p. 5):

> the CVB often acts as an advocate for the local tourism industry with respect to its citizens and elected officials. In this role, the CVB provides information and raises the awareness of tourism business levels, economic impact and current industry issues. Other CVB roles include visitor services (local information, accommodation booking, merchandise sales, etc.); research collection and distribution; support of local tourism education and training programs; and associated special services required by its industry-members. Of increasing importance, CVBs are becoming more prominent as 'destination developers' by acting as catalysts and facilitators for the realization of tourism developments and events.

The same source (p. 5) quotes the IACVB (International Association of Convention and Visitor Bureaus) as reporting that 77% of member bureaus receive funding through room taxes. These taxes represented approximately 53% of total bureau funding of US$585 million in 1993 for the 278 responding IACVB members. The remaining bureau revenues come from government matching grants (24%), membership dues (5%), restaurant taxes (2%) and other non-dues sources (16%).

The disengagement of the state is something of myth as far as the USA is concerned. Substantial public funding is used for infrastructure development. The most significant marketing activities are supported by taxation, which cannot be imposed without government involvement, and by government grant-in-aid.

National and international cooperation

Local OTAs cooperate with others when they recognize a common interest in the act of producing services for a shared stream of tourists. They are often, but not always, neighbouring OTAs. They also cooperate with other OTAs having common problems. Cooperation can be in lobbying, research and marketing. A few of very many possible examples of organizations with a tourism interest within sectors are at national level:

- the Historic Towns Forum in Britain
- the Club des Grandes Villes de France
- the Groupe de Travail des Villages de Vacances
- France Golf International

and at international level:

- the International Association of Convention and Visitor Bureaus
- the Federation of European City Tourist Offices
- the European Council for the Village and Small Town (grouping members in 28 countries in East and West Europe).

Joint marketing of particular types of location is often organized sectorally by NTOs. The French clubs mentioned above are three of eight clubs which are the basis of joint public–private sector financed tourism marketing abroad, coordinated by Maison de la France. The idea has been taken up in several other countries. There is an assumption, presumably reasonable in view of the continuing French use of the club concept, that some tourists contemplating a trip wish to consider a range of choices within a sector before opting for one or a small number of destinations. In addition to the NTO's clubs, there are other groupings which are organized and presented sectorally but which enable each customer to opt finally for one specific location and type of holiday. For example, some 40 000 country properties or *gîtes* are marketed by their own national federation.

The worldwide view

This chapter has drawn very largely on British, French and US sources to demonstrate the importance of the local level and to discern some significant trends. Growing local involvement is, however, a worldwide phenomenon. In November 1999 WTO held in Brazil its 3rd International Forum under the slogan: Parliamentarians and Local Authorities – Tourism Policy Makers. WTO stated in a 1998 promotional leaflet that:

> Local authorities responsible for counties, districts, cities, towns, villages, rural areas and attraction sites are increasingly becoming more involved in developing and managing many aspects of tourism. This is in line with the trend in many countries toward decentralisation of government to give more responsibility to local authorities. These authorities often know better what is in their own best interest and will strive to achieve local development objectives. It also reflects the emphasis now being given to community involvement in tourism, with local communities participating in the tourism planning and development process of their areas.

Growth in local public–private sector partnerships is also a worldwide trend (see Lane, *Tourism Collaboration and Partnership: Politics, Practice and Sustainability*, 2000).

11

Seasonal and spatial redistribution

Introduction

A trend away from boosterism and towards 'managed' tourism was noted in Chapters 2 and 7. Public management implies action to shape or constrain tourism. Such action clearly runs counter to purely spontaneous development in response to market forces.

The issue of spatial redistribution is potentially controversial. Less so is the issue of spreading the season, which receives only a brief acknowledgement here. Disagreement within host communities on the desirability of spreading the season is rare. Governments and the industry generally agree that success in this respect is constructive – relieving overcrowding at the peak and contributing to higher occupancies and profitability. Host communities have had relatively little control, anyway, over the key factors that influence seasonal patterns of departures from their source markets, for example, the dates of school, factory and public holidays, deep-seated traditions and, in some cases, the most important factor of all – seasonal changes in climate. Tropical islands cannot do much about the hurricane season nor winter sports resorts about the effect of summer on the ski-slopes. Destinations have been able to overcome problems of seasonality by means of mostly non-controversial measures. They have included, for example, successful efforts by London interests to attract intercontinental markets – including conventions and cultural tourism – which traditionally travel at times other than the European peak summertime. Elsewhere in the UK there have been developments of 'weather indifferent' tourism and climatically controlled leisure environments, such as those of Center Parcs.

An important contribution to spreading the season has been made by the new mass phenomenon of weekends away, short breaks and additional holidays. People who have several trips away every year by definition cannot have them all at once at the peak; they must spread them out in time. The long-term promise of extended paid leave entitlements, growing disposable income and faster, cheaper transport was foreseen by the English Tourist Board as early as 1971, when a document entitled *Towards a National Tourism Marketing and Development Strategy* announced the Board's intention to major on the promotion of weekends and additional holidays off-season. Indeed, the promotion was the keystone of ETB's national market building activities for the following 15 years. The Wales Tourist Board cooperated closely with ETB.

The initial promotion of weekending was seen as the first step in the expansion of the short break market. Following research and test marketing and looking to the long term, ETB's Annual Report for 1973/1974 stated (1974, p. 7):

Average holiday entitlement will be around four weeks and many will enjoy more. Many people will have two holidays away from home and several will have three but they will not necessarily be taking the same type of holiday each time. They will do *what only a privileged few do now* [emphasis added] and may take three quite different holidays each year: for example, one active (sailing, riding, walking, climbing, ski-ing); one cultural (a music or arts festival, learning to paint or sculpt, assisting an archaelogical dig); and on recuperative holiday perhaps by the sea or at a health farm.

As the market changed, the profound implications not only for seasonality but for the future character and geographical patterns of tourism were debated. *Travel Trade Gazette*, in September 1983, described the

ETB strategy as having created a 'revolution in British holiday habits'. (See the following: ETB Annual Reports; *Britain, Extra Holiday Break Survey 1974* by Taylor Nelson for ETB; ETB Statements of Marketing Intent, 1977/78; Dataplan Survey, 1986, in BTA/ETB archives; Jeffries, 1978, 1985.)

By 1986 the industry as a whole and virtually all regions and resorts had followed ETB's lead. Its own campaigns were greatly reduced. The number of short trips (1 to 3 nights away) taken by the British within the UK in serviced accommodation increased from 4.6 million in 1973 to 6.0 million in 1985 and 10.8 million in 1998. (Differences in research techniques mean these give orders of magnitude only.) Figures in *Digest of Tourist Statistics*, No.22 (BTA, 1999) indicate that by 1997 more than two-thirds of all holidays of 4 nights or more by British people were *additional* holidays (p. 73).

A number of contributions in Williams and Shaw (1998) bear witness to the importance of the short break market as an agent of substantial change in other European countries. They recognize also its significance as a factor in spreading tourism spatially.

ETB's earliest marketing strategy, in 1971, anticipated that within England tourists on weekends, short breaks and additional holidays would wish to travel to a much wider range of locations than the traditional spas and seaside resorts. Its published weekend/short break guide covered also many other locations, including industrial cities, historic towns and rural hideaways. Positive effects on the future 'mix' of business in new locations and on profitability were anticipated. ETB's strategy was formally to 'engender new growth points'.

Strategic geographical redistribution

This section deals with ambitious, centrally orchestrated programmes to open up new tourist regions and to shift the whole balance of tourism strategically within countries.

France

The earliest and perhaps the best known as well as the largest of these was the French Languedoc Roussillon development of an area of coast between just south of Montpellier to the Spanish border – an area 180 kilometres long and extending some 20 kilometres inland. The project had the powerful backing of the President of France, General de Gaulle. In 1963 the Government set up an Inter-Ministerial Mission sponsored by the Ministries of Economy, Interior, Equipment, Agriculture and Tourism to initiate the development (*source:* French Government Tourist Office).

The following account is based on Clarke (1981, pp. 448–53). Advantages put forward for tourism development included the fact that it would use regional resources that otherwise would remain unused, and that tourist spending provided a direct injection of money into a regional economy and could create an additional source of employment. The French authorities were mindful of the fact that the creation of a tourist industry promised to strengthen the economy of the region, which was traditionally dependent on wine growing, whose income had trailed the national average, and was characterized by a high rate of out migration and high level of unemployment and under-employment.

The launching of the coastal development scheme required administration at two levels. First, the Mission was responsible for overall planning and supervision of the project, for the acquisition of land and for the carrying out of basic infrastructural work – main roads, ports, forestry, mosquito control. Second, preparation of sites and installation of resort infrastructure, such as installation of services and preparation of car parks, was carried out at the local level by mixed economy companies. Once prepared, the serviced sites were leased by the companies to private developers for building. An overall plan was presented in 1964 and updated in 1972. This plan identified five tourist units, each with an estimated reception capacity of 150 000 beds and based on a beach capacity of 600 persons per hectare and a construction density of 100 beds per hectare. The tourist units, laid out along the coastline at distances of 25 to 35 kilometres from each other, were to be separated by mature conservation zones, strictly protected to preserve their appeal to visitors. Afforestation zones, tourist protection zones, possible extension zones for the resorts and industrial zones were also defined in the plan.

According to Clarke, by 1980 this whole stretch of coast had been completely transformed and had been provided with a range of modern tourist facilities, including some 17 pleasure ports and seven new towns. A major new road system connecting the new resort towns with each other and with national roads and motorways was in place.

Ferras *et al.* (1979, p. 197) note that visitors to the region – half a million in 1964 before the implementation of the project – nearly quadrupled in 12 years. By 1975 gross receipts of the region's tourist industry equalled those of the region's agriculture. From then on, say the authors, tourism was the motor of the Languedoc economy.

The declared objectives of the French Government went well beyond revitalization of an ailing economy. The aims were *inter alia* to serve social needs by providing a recreational outlet for the French in the context of 'social tourism' and to draw tourism away from the Côte d'Azur, *considered as saturated* [emphasis added] (Ferras *et al.*, p. 204).

An interesting update on the region was published by Klemm in *Tourism Management* (1996), showing how its tourism, once almost non-existent in the region, has matured.

Mexico

A similarly ambitious project began in Mexico in the mid-1970s in the Caribbean coastal strip of Cancún, at that time an extremely remote rural area on the other side of Mexico from the famous international resort on the Pacific, Acapulco. Land tenure problems in Acapulco meant that little further expansion of Mexico's sun-and-sea tourism potential could be achieved there. The timing of the initiative was opportune, as US tourism to Cuba was severely constrained by relationships between the two countries. Airport infrastructure developments and the introductions of direct flights from Miami opened the way for new inflows of tourism. Cancún was developed with massive aid from the Banco Inter-Americano de Desarrollo (Inter-American Development Bank). By 1991 the hotel capacity of Cancún exceeded that of Acapulco, the next largest resort, and approached closely that of Mexico City. The initiative was led by the President of the Bank, Antonio Ortiz Mena, former Minister of Finance for Mexico (*source:* Mexican Ministry of Tourism, London).

Another large-scale, long-term project is currently being undertaken in the richly historic and scenic southern region of Mexico, Oaxaca. The project is the subject of a formal agreement between the Federal

Government and the state of Oaxaca. The published plan for 1997–2002 foresees substantial public–private sector investment in infrastructure, superstructure, historic building conservation, cultural programmes and promotion. The full title is 'Action Plan for the *Priority* Tourist Development Zone of the City of Oaxaca and its Valleys'.

Korea

In South Korea, the Chungmun Tourist Complex in Cheju Island began its first stage of development in 1978 and was scheduled for completion in 1996 (WTO, 1998a, pp. 43–4). The second stage began in 1996 and was scheduled to be completed in 2001. The total amount of investment in the first stage of the Chungmun complex project was US$424 million. The Central Government and the NTA invested altogether 12% of the total investment. Cheju Provincial Government invested a mere 0.07%, while the private sector invested 88%.

In the second stage, the NTA invested 73% (US$58 million) to purchase the site and prepare the complex, and private organizations invested 27%. In total, about US$504 million was invested in the two stages, with the public sector having invested 22% and the private sector, 78%.

This project has been recognized for revitalizing the local economy by creating jobs as well as increasing the level of income. The complex employed 1488 employees and 78% of them were local residents in 1996. Total income in 1996 was US$33 million and US$ 1.2 million was paid in local taxes. Now the Chungmun Tourist Complex is a world-class facility which attracted almost 3 million tourists in 1996. More than 130 000 foreign tourists visited the complex (WTO, *Asian Tourism Experiences*, 1998a).

South Pacific

A very different illustration of strategic re-distribution policies is the record of the long-term series of programmes undertaken for eight ACP island states of the South Pacific served by the intercontinental aviation gateway and hub of Fiji. The programmes were coordinated by the Tourism Council of the South Pacific (TCSP) in Suva through the mid-1980s to late in the 1990s, with substantial assistance from the

European Union's European Development Fund. A dominant share of the region's tourism was held by Fiji, and indeed by a cluster of internationally owned or managed resorts within two hours' drive of its international airport in Nadi. A critique of the programmes was made by the author for the European Commission in 1996. While this is confidential and may not be published, it is possible to make some observations using widely available material.

The Tourism Council of the South Pacific, the bulk of whose funds were provided by the EDF, began the first of a series of three-year programmes in 1986. The Council's Annual Report for 1993 revealed that by far the largest single element in the budget was for marketing and promotion. Other activities included small pilot development projects, education, training and research. One study of transport links was reported. Eight island countries benefited from this aid and there are indications that the smaller countries received funding disproportionate to the small scale of their tourism.

The implied intention of the programmers was over a ten-year period to increase the region's share of world markets and to spread tourism more widely beyond the centres of high concentration in Fiji. Neither of these objectives was achieved.

According to WTO figures, between 1985 and 1992 international tourist arrivals grew by 102% to Australia and New Zealand, by 90% to South and Central Pacific and by 25% to the eight countries. In a competitive situation, the more concentrated elements in the private sector were bound to fight to retain market share. The marketing budgets of the four leading four/five star hotels in Fiji exceeded that of the whole TCSP programme (*source: Hoteliers*).

The basic inter-island pattern remained little changed, as revealed in Table 11.1.

Numerous reports have confirmed the key weakness in Fiji's and the region's tourism: insufficient and relatively high priced and infrequent air access to and within the islands (Economic Intelligence Unit, *International Tourism Reports*, No. 2, 1994; No. 1, 1996; No. 1, 1998; CHL Consulting, *Regional Air Travel Review*, 1998). Lack of air access is one of the seemingly intractable problems of the Solomon Islands – a country benefiting from as much promotion as the other countries and recipient of aid for a development plan. According to TCSP's periodic

Table 11.1 Tourism arrivals in the eight countries

	1985		1990		1995	
	No.	%	No.	%	No.	%
Fiji	118175	64	278996	64	318495	63
Kiribati	3028	*	3332	*	3857	1
Papua New Guinea	30391	9	40742	9	32578	6
Solomon Islands	11974	3	9195	2	11795	2
Tonga	14216	4	20919	5	29520	6
Tuvalu	684	*	671	*	922	*
Vanuatu	24521	7	35042	8	43554	9
W. Samoa	43919	12	47642	11	57954	13
Total	356908	100	436539	100	508675	100

*Less than 1%.

Visitor Surveys this country had less holiday visitors at the end of the promotion period than at the beginning.

It is of interest that the 1997 Fiji Tourism Development Plan mentioned in Chapter 9 revolves around radical proposals to raise public and private sector capital for new Tourism Development Areas. The aim will be to increase capacity and to spread tourism away from centres of concentration to other areas, including smaller islands in the Fiji groups. Success, as the authors make plain, will depend among other things on the adequacy of air services.

Great Britain

Another instructive case is the long history of programmes following the British Labour Government's 1974 Guidelines which required the NTA and NTOs to spread tourism away from congested centres (referred to in Chapter 7). The main purpose was clearly to relieve pressure on London by developing and publicizing other parts of the country. The development fund available was modest. The policy was announced after a period of extraordinary growth in London's tourism, which met with wide criticism. Sir George Young's seminal book *Tourism: Blessing or Blight?* (1973) was eventually borne of the debate at that time. An open-ended scheme to grant-aid new hotel rooms cost the Government over £60 million as against the forecast of £8 million, such was the demand from developers. Half the funding was claimed by London interests and the capital's bedroom stock increased by 23 000 in a little over three years in the first half of the 1970s. (*Source:* London Tourist Board Annual Report for 1974/75). A 'feverish burst of hotel construction' was noted in the House of Commons on 8 April 1971 by an MP who claimed that the London projects were producing an over-saturation of expensive luxury accommodation in London. Another MP, in the same debate, said 'at the rate we are going London will be literally flooded with tourists in the next two years'.

The Annual Reports of the BTA and the ETB are testimony to the formal acceptance by the Boards of the requirement to spread tourism away from London. This presented particular problems for the BTA. Promoting lesser-known areas to international markets might mean lower volumes of tourism overall, which would run counter to BTA's overall objective of increasing foreign currency earnings. The difficulty of implementing the policy was exacerbated by the fact that the Labour Guidelines, developed no doubt behind the scenes during a tourism boom, were launched after the first oil shock of 1973 – just as a period of severe recession was beginning in international tourism. Much of the new capacity was for a time critically under-utilized, as the trade press of the time (*Caterer and Hotelkeeper*) reveals. This was a period during which pressure from London interests to promote the capital vigorously could be expected. When the Conservatives announced their first review some time after returning to power, the Minister, Norman Lamont, asserted in November 1983 that the bias of previous government policies in favour of the less well-known tourist areas had led to 'under-selling London overseas' and 'were wrong' (Heeley, 1989, p. 372). British governments have subsequently blown hot and cold over the London question. Lord Young's *Pleasure, Leisure and Jobs* (Cabinet Office Enterprise Unit) in July 1985 (that is less than two years after his colleague's statement in the House of Commons), announced (item 35):

More generally, growing pressure on accommodation and attractions in London and the time taken for new developments to come into operation emphasises the need to encourage a wider dispersal of tourists – and foreign tourists in particular – out of the capital while recognising that for many of them it is the point of arrival and the main single attraction.

Later governments reinstated London, as it were. In the 1990s extra funds were made available to promote London.

During the longest period in which policy placed emphasis on strategic redistribution, the capital's share of tourism from overseas showed a decrease in nights spent in the capital from 47.2% in 1973 to 39.2% in 1982. Share of overseas visitor nights, not measured in the early years, increased from 1980 to 1982. During the following decade to 1997, when policy fluctuated, the capital's share fell back to the 1980 level and share of nights fell slightly below the 1982 peak. Later trends showed little change (Table 11.2). Source: BTA.

Table 11.2 London's share of overseas visits to Britain, 1973–1997

	Visits %	Nights %
1973	—	47.2
1980	59.9	38.7
1982	61.4	39.2
1992	53.8	36.9
1997	52.8	38.4

The numbers to which these percentages apply grew very considerably. Arrivals grew from 7.4 million in 1973 to 23.3 million in 1997. Visitor nights grew from 137.9 million in 1980 to 205.9 million in 1997. This meant that places outside London received many more visitors – spending around 85 million nights in 1980 and 127 million nights there in 1997. Certainly overseas tourists were present in localities where previously their numbers were not significant. But this does not mean that London's *share* declined significantly or that changes in share relieved pressures in London. Insofar as pressure was eased or accommodated, this was due to improved management within London and extension of tourism development away from its epicentre. Improved management was in fact part of Lord Young's strategy.

Not surprisingly, powerful organizations and enterprises with a stake in London have repeatedly resisted moves seen as undermining its pre-eminent position. Most of the larger tourism companies have a share in the capital city. Flagship hotels of the largest groups are to be found there. Lobbies have made their presence known from the time when the capital's position, in the tourism context, became seriously controversial. A move by the Greater London Council (GLC = local government) to impose a bed tax on inner London hotels was fiercely resisted and defeated by a combination of hoteliers, the trade association, BTA and the London Tourist Board during 1971 and 1972. The promoters of the tax had wished to use it to encourage the spread of development away from the centre (*Caterer and Hotelkeeper*, 25 March and 18 November 1971; BTA Annual Report 1971/72).

The GLC continued for some time to pursue policies aimed at conserving the quality of life for the residential community and protecting the housing stock. *A Plan for Management*, dated April 1974, stated (p. 10):

Nationally, it will continue to be the policy of the Tourist Boards to work for a more even distribution of tourism throughout the country. This will not mean a reduction in the present numbers of tourists staying in London; to a very large extent this is governed by existing hotel capacity. But in the longer term, combined with a strict control over additional capacity, it could lead to tourists spending more of their time outside London and help to keep in check the volume of tourism from overseas and other parts of this country that might otherwise have to be provided for in London.

In the long term, interests coalesced into the influential public–private sector organization London First (formed in 1992),which merged with the London Forum, a private sector body established (in 1993) by John Major's Government in fulfilment of a manifesto pledge to convene a new body to promote London. Both bodies, chaired by Sir Allen Sheppard, Chairman of Grand Metropolitan, joined forces with other groups, including local authority interests, to promote London vigorously for tourism and inward investment. This was rather on the lines of approaches pioneered by the great American cities described in Chapter 10. A key aim of the Forum was:

to build on London's position as a World Class Capital for the benefit of the United Kingdom.

The amalgamation of organizations involved had (and have) on their boards and committees a formidable list of leading industrialists and politicians (*source:* papers provided by Robert Chenery of the London Tourist Board).

Conclusion

The cases cited in this section are not in sufficient numbers to permit clear-cut conclusions about tourism in general but they do offer some pointers. Efforts to spread tourism strategically will probably require long-term backing and commitment from the top. Massive capital development and fundamental changes in transport access will be essential to success. Official marketing and pilot development projects on the scale usually available to NTAs will be most unlikely to carry sufficient weight. Private sector interests in established concentrations are likely to use their superior resources and commercial muscle to ensure that spatial patterns do not change to their detriment.

Spatial redistribution – the local dimension

Spatial redistribution is usually a feature of local management plans, although there are other important considerations: limiting numbers, crowd control, techniques to influence behaviour and spreading tourism in time. There is now a large body of documented experience. UK examples include management schemes for highly sensitive areas such as Canterbury, Chester, Hadrian's Wall and Fountains Abbey in England – all the subject of reports to a joint Tourism Society/ICOMOS Seminar in March 1999 (reported in the Society's journal, *Tourism*, Issue 101, Summer, 1999). *Getting it Right – A Guide to Visitor Management in Historic Towns* (1994), published by the English Historic Towns Forum, is an excellent contribution to the subject. Visitor management in a rural area – the Hope Valley in England's Peak District, is analysed in depth in Bramwell and Sharman (1999). A range of World Heritage sites in many countries is addressed in Shackley's *Visitor Management* (1998). More wide-ranging, though less focused on individual cases, is WTO's *Guide for Local Authorities on Developing Sustainable Tourism* (1998b).

NTAs and NTOs: programme planning, evaluation and measurement

Introduction – keeping a sense of proportion

This chapter is about financial 'aid' to the tourism industry as represented by the budgets of NTAs and NTOs. They are by a number of standards extremely modest. The French delegate to a WTO Seminar (1993, p. 103) stated:

> Tourist development is most often realized on the ground in collaboration between enterprises and local collectivities. This is what explains the largely 'microcephalic' character of the tourism administration: a Ministry bringing together a little over 400 staff (110 000 in the Ministry of Public Works) with a budget of 400 million francs (1/3000th of the state budget) while the mass of local administrations (Departmental, Regional Committees and

local offices) have much greater resources. The budgets of the Regional Committees were 196 million francs in 1989. The budget of the town of Metz alone was 74 million francs or 7% of the communal [local government] budget.

Cadieu (1999, p. 33) says that the national tourism budget is one-third of that of the Meteorological Office, and quotes a French Deputy:

France, the number one country in the world in terms of the number of tourists welcomed, devotes three times less to exploiting the fine weather than to announcing it.

In 1980/81, when British Government spending via the NTA/NTO was close to a peak, the combined grants to the BTA and the three National Tourist Boards for all purposes – marketing, capital financing and research etc. – were £26 million or 1/3000th of public spending (*source:* Government Expenditure Plans 1980–81 to 1983, HMSO, London). In the 1985–7 period, Districts in England and Wales, the lowest level of public spending, injected £521 million into tourism while the combined national budgets for capital developments was £35 million (Association of District Councils, *It's the District Councils who Deliver*, 1988; Tourist Board Annual Reports).

Long before the United States Government abolished its NTO, the USTTA, in 1996, its *raison d'être* was repeatedly challenged by Congress and in the media but, even when the organization maintained a network of offices abroad and a marketing activity along classic NTO lines, its budget was extremely modest. According to Richter (1985, p. 164), the proposed budget was:

less than 5% of the size of the US Defense Department's budget for military bands, or roughly the equivalent of the money budgeted for using enlisted personnel as maids, cooks and servants for top military officers.

WTO has made efforts to monitor national spending, as indicated in WTO (1996a). Marketing (promotion) made heavy claims on NTO budgets in 1995. The top ten spenders were, in order, Australia, UK, Spain, France, Singapore, Thailand, Netherlands, Austria, Ireland and Portugal. In several countries – Spain, Singapore, Thailand and

Portugal – the public sector funded 100% or very nearly all of promotional budgets while in others the private sector made substantial contributions.

The top four promotional spenders (US$) were:

Australia	88 million
United Kingdom	79 million
Spain	79 million
France	73 million

As the WTO (p. 36) observes:

> France would seem to be the country with the most effective NTA/NTO as it only spends US$1.20 to attract one tourist arrival, or US$2.70 to generate US$1000 in tourism receipts. In other words, for every US$1 investment in promotion abroad, it sees a return of US$375.
>
> Second in the ranking is Spain, followed by the United Kingdom and Portugal. Australia, which is considered to have one of the most efficient NTAs around the world, comes out worse than its competitors among NTAs and NTOs with the biggest promotional budgets. But the country which would certainly have come out well on top, if details of its budget had been incorporated in the WTO survey, is the USA, which has always spent far less in terms of national tourism promotion in ratio to the receipts it generates.

The remarks must have been written by an official with a sense of humour. There can be no correlation between the promotional budget and tourism spending *in total*. Large numbers of 'tourists' travel on business or to visit friends and relations for whom the blandishments of the NTOs play little part in the choice of destination. The overwhelming influence of tour operators on some destinations was noted in Chapter 5. Other sources – the media, commercial guidebooks – have an important role although they are commonly assisted by NTOs. Marked short-term changes in a country's fortunes can usually be correlated with major changes in the market environment.

Examples include the massive cancellations of US travel to Europe in 1985 following a series of terrorist incidents (Chon and Olsen,

1990, p. 211) and the sudden downturn in 1986 following the Libyan bombing crisis. Currency fluctuations also have important short-term effects. A TIA report (1997) on Market Share Indicators observed that:

> We have recognized that the local economy, world events and the relative value of another country's currency compared to the dollar can influence travel trends much more dramatically than any promotional campaign.

In 1998 the Scottish tourism industry's overall revenue declined significantly below target. This was attributed by the STB in its Annual Report for the period to the competitive influence of the Football World Cup, the poor weather that year and the strength of the pound sterling (Scottish Tourist Board, 1999a, p. 8).

Even the largest NTO budgets are too small to be a dominant factor in the short to medium term. New Labour's publicity splash *Tomorrow's Tourism* (DCMS, 1999a, p. 38) reported that:

> BTA estimates that tourism expenditure in Britain influenced by its marketing activity has risen from around £750 million in 1994–95 to £1 billion in 1997/98.

These estimates represent a yield of £27 for every £1 of BTA spend. However, Britain's earnings (BTA, *Digest of Tourist Statistics*, No. 22, 1999) in 1994 were £9786 millions and in 1997 £12 244 millions. So BTA 'influenced' 8% of receipts.

What NTAs/NTOs do: strategies and programmes

Every organization is different. Generalizations should be treated with caution as there can be major exceptions. Individual NTAs/NTOs may go through phases which are atypical in the context of their history generally.

The NTO as the executive arm concentrates on marketing. As this is the main focus, useful reference may be made to Jefferson and Lickorish (1991) on internal organization and methods. Some very common functions of NTAs/NTOs are as follows:

- operation of services regulating the most obvious producers of the basic product such as hotels and incoming tour operators;
- education and training of the workforce with, again, emphasis on the providers of the basic product;
- research, statistics, forecasting;
- preparation of strategic plans – often advisory documents rather than true plans;
- marketing;
- development, with an emphasis on the pioneering of new products (the R and D function).

All of the above may be confirmed by reference to the WTO publications in the Bibliography. The OECD Tourism Committee 1990–91 review of government involvement in tourism promotion (OECD, 1993) is another useful source.

An important NTA/NTO role is to advise policymakers on the likely effects on tourism of upcoming legislation or proposed government action. Very little research has been done to evaluate the advisory function.

NTAs and NTOs undertake activities designed to encourage expansion or improvement in the supply and quality of the industry's products. As pointed out earlier, few now have substantial funds to assist in capital investment. But programmes aimed at 'educating' the industry, its managers and its workers are commonplace, whether they take the form of public relations exercises or formal training schemes. Very little information exists on systems regularly in use for evaluating such activities. Evaluation may be arranged in a hierarchy starting with tests of efficiency by asking such questions as the following. Could this activity (say, a series of training seminars) have been carried out at a lower cost? But full evaluation extends beyond this level in order to assess:

- results achieved in terms of the volume or quality of supply;
- achievement of immediate objectives in terms, for example, of the industry's profit performance or growth;
- contribution of improved industry performance to the achievement of wider objectives, e.g. increased foreign currency earnings, more and better jobs created, etc.

There is no evidence of the application of advanced, comprehensive evaluation techniques to typical official tourism programmes in the more developed countries, though the technique known as Logical Framework pcm (project cycle management) has been used by aid agencies in the context of international cooperation in tourism. (An unpublished case study produced by the present author in 2000 for the EU and the Republic of Syria demonstrates the technique. It is available by e-mail. See Bibliography.)

In the author's view, insufficient published information exists to allow generalizations to be made about the performance of the whole range of functions for which NTAs/NTOs are commonly responsible.

The two functions on which it is possible to offer further comment applicable across a wide field are (a) long range planning and (b) marketing.

Long range strategies

These have been and are produced by NTAs and NTOs. Long range strategies may only be fairly judged after the lapse of many years. Those of the 1970s and 1980s were seldom implemented. If implemented, they were not sustained. While they were usually launched very publicly they were seldom revisited when they should have been, that is, during and after the period they were intended to cover. Launched under one administration, they were forgotten by the next. Cadieu (1999, p. 285) comments somewhat sourly in the French context:

Numerous [official] reports on tourism have never been referenced by Ministries or by *la Documentation Française*. It is obviously regrettable ... This often avoids having to question their effective [long-term] impact. Beyond the effect of their announcement, linked most often to a good press conference accompanied by a good press kit, the reports are often quickly forgotten. One report chases after another. Paradoxically, the objective is less to anticipate than to buy time on the political agenda ... The [National, State] Plan is often preceded by numerous reports. The Ninth Plan was the occasion for two important reports [produced in 1982 and 1983 respectively by an interministerial mission and a working group called by the Ministry responsible for economic planning and town and country planning] … In the same way the Ministry of Tourism regularly commissions reports. It is often the opportunity to recompense or raise the profile of a Member of Parliament … so many reports to fill out the archives of the Ministry …

Choy (1991, p. 326) reported that half of a large number of tourism plans in a WTO study had not been implemented and noted that there had been little follow-up research on actual accomplishment of tourism plans.

Esmond Devas, a consultant whose clients have included the European Commission, Development Banks for Africa, Asia and the Caribbean as well as the World Bank, has advised that a large number of NTA/NTO plans in different parts of the world were not implemented or were not successful. He gives as one of the main reasons for failure the fact that most such strategies and plans originated too low down in the system and carried little weight with the major departments and ministries (personal communication).

A further weakness is that strategies at this level were often in reality sets of proposals for action dependent on the agreement of a wide range of organizations other than the sponsoring NTA or NTO. They were not expressions of commitment on the part of the organizations concerned. BTA produced two 'Strategies for Growth' for the periods 1984–1988 and 1989–1993 but, with the exception of BTA's own commitment to its marketing projections, the document consisted of 'guidelines' for a wide range of organizations and enterprises over which the BTA had no control. Inevitably, many of the guidelines were extremely generalized, for example, this extract from the 1984–1988 'Strategy' (p. 19):

- A concerted national effort on a much larger scale will be needed to conserve heritage assets as a basis for expanding tourism revenue, and their own income.
- Tourism development needs support from, and where appropriate action by, those state agencies, such as the Countryside Commission, the Arts Council etc. Like local authorities, the agencies should have their own tourism policy. Some already do.
- Greater attention will need to be paid to the product/market match. As specialized travel grows a more precise identification of market needs and sophisticated efforts to meet them will be essential to compete at a time of rising international standards.

- Generally speaking, capacity and services in sea and surface transport are adequate. Improvements should be sought at ports and termini, access routes, interchange facilities and tourist fares.
- In the transport field more efforts should be made to use regional airports for incoming tourists. There is a need for the relaxation of restrictive regulations on certain air routes. More competition and greater flexibility for tourism fares should be sought for routes where tourism potential is substantial.

Why some strategies or plans succeeded and others did not has received very little attention from analysts in the tourism industry. A large enough body of empirical knowledge does not exist. But this is an important question, assuming the current trend towards more 'managed' and 'sustainable tourism' will continue. The author puts forward a set of conditions which should be met by strategies or plans to enhance their prospects for success. These are based on experience, some of which has been reported in Chapter 11, and on common sense. The conditions to be met are that the strategy/plan should be:

- relevant to the country's priority, wider objectives;
- influenced by a thorough knowledge of market potential and the special characteristics of tourism as an industry;
- fully supported by all who have the resources and authority to ensure implementation;
- fully understood and supported by the host communities whose lives and livelihood will be affected;
- consistent with transport strategy in recognition that transport and tourism developments are interactive and that the ultimate product always has a transport access and a destination component.

Strategies should also:

- take account of the events which are going to happen anyway, stating their likely effect on the outcome;
- identify separately new actions to be undertaken by the sponsors to achieve the aims of the strategy, their costs, the results expected and how they will be measured and evaluated.

The overall British strategy that has best fitted (though far from completely) these conditions, was that launched by Lord Young in 1985. Some of the changes brought about were retained by successive governments, but as a whole the strategy was not sustained over a long period. Comprehensive national strategies requiring the long-term commitment and inputs from all possible partners would seem to be unrealistically ambitious. Planning with a narrower focus – geographical or sectoral – would seem to be more achievable.

Some more recent strategies have been more focused and have been subject to systematic, well publicized and periodic review.

Scotland's share of overall tourism expenditure in the UK in 1997 was 9%. In 1994 the high level Scottish Tourism Co-ordinating Group (STCG) published a strategic plan. Progress in implementing the plan, which presents targets for future arrivals and expenditure as well as qualitative targets, has been regularly reported. The STCG was chaired by the Minister with responsibility for tourism in the Scottish Office and brought together the agencies involved in supporting the Scottish Tourism Industry together with the Scottish Tourism Forum, which represented the private sector. An Interim Review, published in March 1999 (Scottish Tourist Board, 1999b), promised a further strategic plan to 2005.This document noted that the future structure of ministerial responsibilities and, therefore, the location of the tourism portfolio, would be a matter for the (new) Scottish Parliament to decide. Strategic planning so far conforms to the conditions for success suggested above except the last two, which require a causal link to be established between new actions to be taken and the achievement of the targets set. Therefore, post hoc evaluation of the effects of the strategy will be difficult. This is a common problem and presents special difficulties in the light of the fact that tourism tends to grow spontaneously anyway. But it is a problem that must be addressed if strategies are to be made more effective and credible. The awkward questions are these. What would happen without the strategy? What will happen with the strategy? How much does the strategy cost? Is there a leading organization with the resources and authority to drive it through? How far will this organization be accountable if the strategy is not implemented or does not succeed?

Marketing

There is space here only to make a number of basic points which must be preceded by the briefest possible outline of the typical activities of NTAs/NTOs. This summary draws on more than 40 years of experience of such activities in a large number of countries. Ample descriptive material is available from other sources. Recommended are the works of Middleton (1994, 1996), Mill and Morrison (1992) and Seaton and Bennett (1999).

Essentially these activities:

■ bring tourist products to the attention of intermediaries, e.g. travel agents, and would-be-tourists, and
■ facilitate their booking and purchase.

They can be focused to bring specific products to the notice of market segments (precisely defined groups of potential customers) most likely to purchase. In international marketing the appeal is often made to the tour operator, travel agent or other intermediary who has the financial motivation to pass the message on to the public. In domestic marketing the appeal is more likely to be direct.

Although some NTOs may operate booking services, in the main they act as brokers and communication links between suppliers and buyers. In the simplest possible illustration, they produce and distribute hotel guides for travel agents and consumers. These then select the hotel(s) meeting their requirements, make direct contact with them and a sale is closed.

The media used by NTOs are of great variety: paid for television, press, radio, outdoors poster and, increasingly, internet advertising; 'free' coverage obtained in the same media from programme producers and travel writers; printed matter and direct promotion by personal call or telephone. At numerous professional workshops, travel marts, road-shows and travel trade fares NTOs act as brokers between, typically, international tour wholesalers (buyers) and incoming tour operators, hotel chains and tourist attractions (suppliers). The buyers may book space in advance in bulk for the future use of their customers.

The media mentioned may be combined. Typically, NTO press advertising offers to post a brochure to consumers – effectively a shopping list that can be used to make a direct purchase. Advertising jointly financed with private sector partners will mention the names and products of the partners, their prices and where they may be booked. Much promotion contains or leads to the making of specific, priced product offers and effectively puts these visibly 'on the shelf' so that customers can take their pick. The image content of the promotion will usually be a beautiful but cliché representation of the NTO's destination, to trigger instant recognition. Marketers try to build on what is already liked and known about the destination unless they have exceptionally large budgets at their disposal. When they claim that the destination is a 'strong destination brand', they are usually saying that it has a history and is well known – e.g. Egypt with its Pyramids and Sphinx.

As indicated in Chapter 5, some activity is 'pure' image promotion, which is extremely difficult to monitor and evaluate. Clearly product specific promotions can be monitored by means of simple techniques to check the volume and value of purchases made. It is not difficult or uncommon to devise marketing activities which lend themselves to measuring gross receipts earned per dollar, pound or euro of outlay. This is valuable in many ways – not least in assessing the relative cost efficiency of alternative communications media and their reach in terms of specific market segments. The closer NTOs get to joint public–private sector marketing, the more the product-specific type of promotion is likely to be pursued.

A number of generalizations are possible:
1 Evaluation methods are well known within the tourism marketing profession but the results are seldom released. They are commercially valuable and are concealed from competitors.
2 Close partnership and joint financing with the private sector leads to an emphasis on short-term returns.
3 Where the NTO's performance is assessed on the value or proportion of finance it attracts from the private sector there will be a tendency to promote the products of the most developed regions and sectors, that is, those with the greatest resources.
4 Unless very great care is taken, there is a risk that the main effect will be to assist some enterprises to gain market share at the expense of non-participating enterprises at the same destination.
5 Where the survival of the NTO depends on the amount of commercial support, the private sector may be tempted to use it as a channel for lobbying on wider issues than marketing. This may be why, in some countries, there has been a trend towards separation

of policy making and promotion within the structures of NTAs/NTOs (noted in WTO, 1996c, p. 37).

6 The long-term R and D function of NTAs/NTOs to develop new areas, new sectors and new products currently receives low priority.

It is arguable that, short term, the largest and most prosperous enterprises should pay a high proportion of the costs of promotion which delivers direct, measurable benefits, though there is a case for some public contribution even then (see Jeffries, 1989). It is also arguable that, long term, R and D is the true and indispensable vocation of the NTA and its executive arm, the NTO. In the mid-1960s, BTA was alone in promoting English language learning holidays in cooperation with a few small, embryonic language schools. Its promotions over many years were backed up by its renowned Youth Workshops, bringing together overseas educational organizations and the growing list of English language schools in Britain. After 30 years this sector is now a staple of the British tourism industry and vital to the economies of many resort towns. The Let's Go weekend promotion described earlier was at its inception fully financed by ETB (public sector) funds. Twenty years later short breaks had become a mainstay of the industry, which was bearing the full marketing cost.

The development of the weekend market helped to compensate in part for the substantial long-term loss of long holidays (4+ nights) to Mediterranean and other sun destinations (see Table 12.1).

Table 12.1 Nights (millions) spent in commercial accommodation in the UK by domestic holidaymakers, 1973–1998

	Short breaks	4+ nights
1973	9.5	114.0
1985	12.4	58.0
1998	20.9	38.6

Source: British Home Tourism Survey and UKTS. Owing to changes in sampling methods, figures indicate orders of magnitude of change (*source:* Ian Rickson, Head of Evaluation, BTA)

In his monumental study for EIU International Tourism Forecasts to 2005, Anthony Edwards (1992, p. 270) put tourism promotion among factors influencing countries' market shares slowly in a process 'spread sometimes over decades'. Edwards used sophisticated multiple regression techniques in his analysis of world destinations and past performance.

At a WTO Seminar (1999b), Martin Sandbach of BTA said (pp. 120–1):

I don't believe we have been honest enough with ourselves in recognising that our commercial, industrial partner stakeholders have a short-term view of the world and we as NTOs are charged by government to have a medium-term or long-term outlook. Most of our trade partners have a 9-month long-term perspective and I know of at least some companies with 95 per cent of their budget in tactical marketing. These are not partners with whom it is easy to create strategic programmes.

A community as a whole – and hence the public sector – must have regard for both the short and long term. That is why the R and D function and the evaluation of its contribution over very long periods merit a higher place in policymaking.

Part Three

Recent Trends in a Selection of Countries, Regions and Localities

13

The United States, France, the United Kingdom and the European Union at the turn of the century: an overview

Useful descriptions of the main tourism resources in each of the three countries are given in Boniface and Cooper (1995). Together these countries offer every type of tourist product available at the beginning of the twenty-first century. Their combined shares of all international tourist arrivals and receipts were 23% and 28% respectively in 1997 (see Table 13.1)

The three countries do not compile comparable data on domestic tourism. The available figures show the following:

- 1997: US resident travel within the USA on 'trips' (broadly synonymous with tourism elsewhere but restricted to trips of 100 miles or more away from home) amounted to 1256 millions, spending US$408 billion (source: TIA, 1998a).

Table 13.1 Tourist arrivals and receipts of France, the UK and the USA, 1997

	International tourist arrivals (thousands)	Receipts ($US million)
USA	47 754	73 268
France	67 310	28 009
UK	25 515	20 439
Total	140 579	121 716
World total	610 763	435 981

Source: WTO, 1999c

- 1998: French 'tourist stays' of 4 nights or more away in France totalled 153 million, spending around US$60 billion (source: Direction du Tourisme, 1999).
- 1997: The number of tourist trips of 1 night or more away from home by UK residents within the UK was 134 million, spending around US$25 billion (source: BTA, Digest of Tourist Statistics, No. 22, 1999).

On the basis of fuller data given in the three national sources quoted, the author estimates that the proportions of total spending on tourism attributable to *domestic* tourism are at least 75% in the USA, 60% in France and 50% in the UK. However, these are certainly conservative estimates, which do not take fully into account shorter overnight trips and day tripping. In Britain 1.2 billion 'tourism leisure day trips' were taken by the British in 1996 (*source:* Countryside Commission, 1997).

Some brief notes on similarities and differences

Degree of economic liberalization

All three countries are broadly speaking liberal market economies, but the French formal economic planning system leans towards command-and-control. It has not pursued liberalization and privatization as far as the other two. In France there is a greater use of subsidy and fiscal incentives, according to the World Tourism Organization Business Council (1998, pp. 66, 69).

Hypothecated taxation to finance tourism

There are significant differences. In both the USA and France hypothecated or dedicated bed taxes, sales taxes and other levies are used to help finance tourism development and marketing while in the UK such taxes have always been opposed.

Degree of centralization

At first sight the US Government's interest in tourism would appear to be more devolved (to the state and city level). The country has a very small NTA and no NTO while the other countries have larger NTAs and active NTOs. But account should be taken of the part played by federal authorities, which control huge resources for recreation and tourism: for example, the National Park Service, the US Fish and Wildlife Service, the US Forest Service and the Bureau of Land Management. They own and manage a major share of the vast lands available for tourism and recreation. They operate jointly, for example, a Federal Passport Program, which enables holders, in return for a single fee, to benefit from reduced fees charged for camp grounds and many other facilities. While the international marketing activities of some states and cities give them a high profile outside the United States, there may be a tendency for outside observers to forget these (national) federal agencies which support and engage heavily in tourism development and marketing, notably in the domestic context. In the three states closely associated with one of the country's best known recreational resources, the Yellowstone Park, much of the land is federal land: 68% of Idaho, 48% of Wyoming and 39% of Montana (this latter 39% covering an area as large as England).

Private sector associations

Within all three countries there exists a multiplicity of national private sector associations which bring together and represent the interests of separate sub-sectors. There is no equivalent in France and the UK of the Travel Industry Association of America, which brings virtually all sub-sectors into a powerful, influential, high profile private sector organization whose mission is to:

represent the whole of the US travel industry to promote and facilitate increased travel to and within the United States. TIA fulfils this mission by accomplishing these objectives:

- To promote a wider understanding of travel and tourism as a major US industry that contributes substantially to the economic and social well-being of the nation;
- To bring cohesion to the travel industry and provide communications forums for industry leaders;
- To serve as the authoritative source for travel industry research, analysis and forecasting;
- To initiate and to cooperate with governmental entities in the development and implementation of programs, policies and legislation that are responsive to the needs of the industry, and to intervene in those issues and initiatives that would directly affect the facilitation and promotion of travel to and within the United States;
- To develop and implement programs beneficial to the travel supplier and consumer. (http://www.tia/whatstia/missionstm)

Chambers of Commerce operate quite differently in English-speaking countries from their counterparts in French-speaking countries. The AFCI (Assemblée des chambres françaises de commerce et d'industrie) links 181 regional and local chambers. These organizations often run major installations such as ports, airports and large convention centres as well as being significant sources of policy and technical advice, according to Cadieu (1999, pp. 286, 287). The Assemblée has a respected research unit.

National consultative systems
All three governments have evolved elaborate consultative networks and committee structures with the declared aim of facilitating dialogue between the national public authorities and all stakeholders. The industry is strongly represented. There is further reference to present consultative networks in Chapter 14.

Consumer protection
France has a stronger tradition of state sponsored consumer protection. (See for example AFCI, 1989 on 50 years of hotel classification as an aid to consumer choice.) A high degree of centralization is manifest in the retention and continuing refinement of long-established national,

legal provisions for recognizing and classifying all the major types of tourist accommodation (lodging) as well as giving official star ratings to hotels and to sites for camping and caravanning. *Restaurants de tourisme* may also be legally classified. Classification takes into account the quantity and character of facilities and services as well as the state-certified professional standing of operating personnel, in some cases. The system is under the tutelage of the Ministry of Tourism (in conjunction with other Ministries) and is administered via Departmental Prefects. Participation confers the right to official listing and to the use of approved plaques and signs as well as the opportunity to participate in regional and local schemes designed to assist the industry financially and in other ways. It is virtually obligatory in practice for establishments to obtain official recognition, notably those in the following categories 'overseen' by the Ministry of Tourism (the date of the Decree or latest amendment to the law covering each category is indicated):

- Hotels and tourism residences   14 February 1986
- Furnished tourism accommodation   3 February 1993
- Camping and caravanning sites   11 January 1993
- Maisons familiales   23 November 1990
- Holiday villages   8 December 1982

Note: *maisons familiales* are non-profit-making establishments of a 'social, family or cultural character', mainly for holiday use and open as a matter of priority to families with modest incomes.

Social tourism

France is also different in that the state has long been more closely associated with the encouragement of subsidised tourism development and marketing for the benefit of low income groups with the support, for example, of trade unions. An important indicator that this tradition is very much alive is the recent development of the *chèques vacances* system, administered by the NTA, which has been given fresh impetus by a Minister of Tourism who is a Communist member of the Jospin coalition. Some 1.5 million wage-earners annually use *chèques vacances*, or vouchers, to purchase subsidized holidays for workers on low incomes. Under a July 1999 amendment to the law, the scheme has been extended to 7.5 million more wage-earners, although the numbers who will actually participate remains to be seen.

The European Union

To understand contemporary tourism in France and the UK (and in other European countries for that matter), it is essential to comprehend the increasingly pervasive role of the European Union and its institutions. Swarbrooke (1997, pp. A–145) notes that over the 20-odd years since the UK joined, the influence of the EU in tourism has grown dramatically in two ways, namely:

- through the development of policies on tourism specifically;
- through the application of a range of other policies to the tourist industry, including those relating to employment, regional development, transport, consumer protection, education and the environment.

The total range of policy areas affected were discussed by Downes (1997) and fuller descriptions are given in the EU's own 'Practical Guide' (see European Commission, *Tourism and the European Union*, 1995a).

There exists a paradox. Superficial examination would suggest that the EU's involvement has been almost negligible if the focus is exclusively on the work of the Tourism Directorate within DG XXIII of the European Commission (the nearest equivalent to an NTA for Europe). More careful scrutiny leads to a very different conclusion.

The EU has no formal *competence* in tourism. In other words, it does not have the legal right to pursue and develop a tourism policy of its own or to issue related laws and directives. The reason for this is simple. The EU can normally act only in those policy areas in which it has been assigned powers by the various European treaties, such as Rome (1957), the Treaty on European Union (signed in Maastricht in 1992) and Amsterdam (1997). There are treaty provisions on agriculture (giving us the Common Agricultural Policy), transport, environment, economic and monetary union, the single market and many more areas besides, but nothing on tourism.

The Maastricht Treaty did *mention* tourism, but all the relevant treaty article did was to commit the EU to look at the subject again during the next inter-governmental conference (IGC). This next conference was the one that led to the Treaty of Amsterdam in 1997, but, in spite of the Maastricht commitment and a 1995 Commission Green Paper (consultation document) on the role of the EU in tourism, it took the debate no further forward.

All of which means that if the Commission's Tourism Directorate wishes to carry out a programme of specific tourism activities, it has to propose a programme under article 235 of the treaties. Article 235 allows the EU to take action in areas for which it has no formal competence – but on condition that its proposed programme has the unanimous support of all member states.

Under this dispensation, the European Commission executed over the past decade a series of action plans and activities which amounted to a combination of research, education, reflection and public relations. The debate about what the EU should do *expressly for tourism* continued into the year 2000. Presumably a formal *competence* in tourism would lead to a granting of greater powers to its central tourism organization in this field and to more direct operational involvement. Briefing papers supplied by Nick Markson, EU Policy Manager for BTA in Brussels, indicate that three issues need to be addressed for this to happen:

- the subsidiarity question and the insistence on the part of some national authorities that tourism is their 'patch';
- the national view that member states compete against each other in tourism markets and do not form part of one large European tourism 'product'; or
- apprehensions among many in the industry that more EU involvement means more legislation.

The part played by DG XXIII, now and in the foreseeable future, is relatively slight. Of far greater importance are the EU's considerable powers and resources to decide policies and authorize funding designed *primarily* to shape development in a particular area – say freedom of movement across frontiers or transport – but which are bound also to shape tourism, indeed, to use tourism as a major motor of change in some areas.

The 'Practical Guide' introduces the topic 'EU Policy which Impacts Tourism' (pp. 247–66) with the remark that:

One of today's realities is that policy and legislation developed at European level is one of the more important factors influencing the world in which we live. European policy and regulation has a fundamental impact on the environment in which businesses operate or, indeed, the way in which local affairs are run. Many of the important economic decisions that affect all EU citizens are now taken *collectively* by the Member States of the European Union and are no longer the independent competence of national governments. Many of the rules and regulations implemented by national governments are thus of Community origin even if they appear as national legislation.

The document then sets out to provide an overview of the broad range of policy measures initiated at EU level which have direct or indirect impacts upon the tourism sector. These are listed below:

- Completion of the Single Market in Europe.
- Economic and Monetary Union: a single currency.
- Transport policy.
- Liberalization of transport services.
- Company law.
- Direct taxation.
- External relations and development policy.
- Regional and social development.
- Employment and social policy.
- Research and development.
- Free movement: making life easier for tourists.
- Free movement: the operational impact for tourism.
- Competition policy.
- Value Added Tax (VAT).
- VAT on passenger transport.
- VAT, travel agents and tour operators.
- Rights of tourists and consumer protection.
- Excise duty and 'duty free'.
- Environmental protection and tourism.
- Architectural and cultural heritage.
- Agricultural policy.

Discussion under each heading leaves no doubt as to the profound implications for tourism. The policies are of two kinds: those whose emphasis is on the fiscal and regulatory framework for the tourism industry and those that determine, *inter alia*, the redistribution of centrally pooled funds to individual countries, programmes and projects.

For example, with regard to the fiscal framework and on the specific subject of VAT, the document (p. 259) notes that:

Member States can introduce one or two rates of at least 5% [lower than the standard rate] to cover products or services of social or cultural character. In the tourism sector the following are included:

- passenger transport
- tourist accommodation provided by hotels and similar including camping sites and caravan parks
- thermal spa services
- use of sporting facilities
- admission to amusement parks, sporting events, shows, theatres, cinemas, fairs, circuses, museums, zoos, concerts and exhibitions.

One of the most important regulatory measures is the Package Travel Directive (p. 262), which obliges operators to supply tourists with detailed and comprehensive information before departure, sets certain other conditions and also requires compensation to be made available where the package tour has not met the operator's claims.

Under 'Regional and social development' (p. 253) it is observed that:

There are varied levels of economic and social development between the Member States of the EU and, indeed, within many Member States there are significant disparities. The European Union's Regional and Social policies aim to reduce those disparities in order to promote equal opportunities throughout the territory. The Community Structural Funds provide grant aid to this end.

In order to stimulate economic development in the less developed regions, the EU encourages actions and activities which are economic generators, preferably with multiplier effects. Tourism is recognised as a sector with a great potential to generate both economic development and employment. Accordingly, the sector benefits from considerable support from the Structural Funds.

(This policy field is reviewed in detail elsewhere in the Guide.)

The section on 'Architectural and cultural heritage' (p. 265) explores specific use of these resources:

One of the key factors that the European tourism sector can exploit is the cultural heritage which is available in abundance in Europe. Indeed, along with the tourism sector, the cultural sector is increasingly seen as an area of potential future employment and growth. In the policy field, therefore, the interests of both sectors often coincide.

Tourism operational programmes under the Structural Funds in the Member States often include significant support for architectural, industrial or rural heritage, for example. Actions range from support for museums to conversion of historic buildings into hotels or other accommodation.

Elsewhere Structural Fund support often covers aid for culture centres such as concert halls, theatres, libraries and others. Urban regeneration programmes which are funded often feature conservation of historic town centres. The most direct beneficiary of all such support is the tourism sector.

The early use of Structural Funds for tourism was evaluated by Pearce (1988). Since then there has been considerable growth in their importance and in their extension to many more regions, notably in the UK. However, care should be taken not to overestimate the importance of these funds. According to a communication from the European Commission to the author, the 1994–9 allocation for the UK from all Structural Funds was 599.42 million euro for tourism measures (11.43% of total Structural Funds allocated to these programmes) or around US$600 million. The separate sources were:

European Regional Development Fund (ERDF)
European Social Fund (ESF)
European Agricultural Guidance and Guarantee Fund (EAGGF)
Financial Instrument for Fisheries Guidance (FIFG)

The purpose of the allocations was to fulfil objectives 1, 2 and 5b (respectively concerned with promoting the development of the less developed regions, regenerating regions seriously affected by industrial decline and developing rural areas).

This rate of spending was of the same order of magnitude as had been available within Britain in the 1980s under Section 4 of the Development of Tourism Act. Swarbrooke (1997) was perhaps optimistic in implying that the replacement of the one by the other was significant for the industry as a whole. The sums involved were and are small in the context of a total *annual* capital investment by the UK travel and tourism industry of £11.1 billion, or around US$17 billion, according to WTTC (1994b). Arguably it is the EU's influence on fiscal and regulatory policies which is likely to have the greatest impact on the industry as a whole.

The tone and content of the European Commission's Green Paper (1995b) on 'The Role of the Union in the Field of Tourism' suggests a determination to extend further its influence. But the document leaves no doubt that one of the most formidable problems facing the Commission is that of coordination between the different policy areas.

14

The United States, France and the United Kingdom at the turn of the century: trends in policy and organization

Introduction

The following narrative covers issues that have been debated between governments and the industry within each country as well as highlighting some major reported changes that have occurred in the final decade of the twentieth century and on the threshold of the twenty-first. The picture is uneven, the more radical policy development having occurred in the two European countries – and particularly in the UK – where there have been major upheavals. Taken as a whole, the account tends to confirm the view, expressed in earlier chapters, that governments have continually to monitor the implications for tourism of broader policies and may also deliberately use tourism in pursuit of wider objectives. The chapter also bears witness to the tendency of governemts to keep under continual review their organizational structures for the sector and change them frequently.

The USA

One of the most important factors affecting the country's share of international markets during the decade of the 1990s was the Visa Waiver Pilot Program. This had been created by Congress in 1986 and its first purpose was to 'encourage and facilitate travel to the United States by tourists considered to be little risk for immigration purposes'. Step by step the USA extended the number of countries where tourists benefiting from this facility originated, but the scheme remained theoretically experimental. Towards the end of 1999 the TIA declared that, during the 106th Congress, it would 'work aggressively to establish broad support for making the Visa Waiver Pilot Program a permanent program'. The campaign succeeded. Permanency was confirmed in October 2000. The issue had featured continuously at the head of all TIA's lobbying activities over several years.

The whole range of issues highlighted by and through TIA was covered in the historic first White House Conference on Travel and Tourism. The record of the 1995 proceedings and follow-up (TIA, 1998b) permit an in-depth understanding of this sector in the world's only superstate.

Delegates from the travel and tourism industry – some 1700 – met for the Conference in Washington, DC in 1995. According to the TIA, the event was 'fueled by a pledge of support' from President Clinton and Vice-President Gore, senior members of the Government and a bipartisan cadre of Republican and Democrat supporters from the House and Senate. It was claimed that every aspect of the travel and tourism community was represented – industry trade associations, travel agents, tour operators, entertainment and attractions, transportation, lodging, food service, retailers, and others – as well as federal, state and local elected officials from around the country. Participants coalesced around a strategy to improve coordination of the public–private partnership, invest in better approaches to generate growth and meet global competition; and unify the industry's ability to work together in addressing key issues.

In 'From Strategy to Success', published three years later, the TIA addressed the status of many of the 41 actions and 10 priorities under-taken at the meeting to 'position the industry for a healthy future'. It was recalled that a task force of more than 25 industry leaders had been established with responsibility for planning and assigning follow-up on all recommendations. 'From Strategy to Success' (TIA, 1998b) pre-sented in outline, progress on actions grouped into four major subject clusters:

- Customer Service
- Education and Communications
- Research and Technology
- Government/Legislative Action.

Under the last of these headings, TIA reported:

> While legislative efforts to obtain long-term funding were unsuc-cessful in the 105th Congress, the US National Tourism Organization (USNTO) Board and TIA and its consultants are assessing the possibility of another legislative effort in the 106th Congress in 1999. TIA contributed staff support, adminis-tration and funding for the USNTO, an innovative public/private partnership to promote and increase travel to the US. In the aftermath of the conference, TIA on behalf of the travel industry stepped up its efforts to obtain long-term funding for the USNTO by enlisting the assistance of leading US communications and public affairs consultants. These efforts were rewarded in 1996 when the US Congress passed, and the President signed, legislation [the United States National Tourism Organization Act] that formally des-ignated the USNTO as the official national tourism organization responsible for growing the $94 billion inbound international travel market.

'From Strategy to Success' also announced that a survey of state tourism offices had shown that, in 24 states of 39 responding, travel and tourism qualified for grants, loans or incentive programs when they were linked with scenic or historic highways and $140 million had been authorized for state and local infrastructure improvement along the US borders with Canada and Mexico, which would help encourage more travel from two of the country's largest inbound tourism markets by lessening delays at border points of entry.

Another implied outcome of the TIA's successful lobbying was the Transport and Efficiency Act. The legislation provided approximately $216 billion for highway and transit upgrades, repairs and improvements. In addition state tourism information centres would now be eligible for enhancements.

'From Strategy to Success' was imbued with a mood of high optimism. It remained discreet about the rather awkward fact that the USTTA, America's NTO, had been abolished in 1996 and private sector funds had had to be used in an attempt to fill the gap in overseas promotion left by its demise.

The introductory text to the United States National Tourism Act 1996 stated:

- Because the United States Travel and Tourism Administration had insufficient resources and effectiveness to reverse the recent decline in the United States' share of international travel and tourism, Congress discontinued USTTA's funding.
- Promotion of the United States' international travel and tourism interests can be more effectively managed by a private organization at less cost to the taxpayers.

The Act then set out the purposes of the new body as follows:

1 seek and work for an increase in the share of the United States in the global tourism market;
2 work in conjunction with Federal, State, and local agencies to develop and implement a coordinated United States travel and tourism policy;
3 advise the President, the Congress, and the domestic travel and tourism industry on the implementation of the national travel and tourism strategy and on other matters affecting travel and tourism;
4 operate travel and tourism promotion programs outside the United States in partnership with the travel and tourism industry in the United States;
5 establish a travel and tourism data bank to gather and disseminate travel and tourism market data;
6 conduct market research necessary for effective promotion of the travel and tourism market; and

7 promote United States travel and tourism, including international trade shows and conferences.

The Act also made this stipulation, however: if within 2 years after the date of the enactment of the Act the Board had not developed and implemented a comprehensive plan for the long-term financing of the organization, the main provisions for and relating to its establishment would be repealed. Activity in Congress in late 1999 designed to facilitate the formulation of such a plan was not successful. At the beginning of the twenty-first century overall US destination promotion is pursued on a modest scale by the private sector under the aegis of the TIA, concentrating on cooperation with carriers and tour operators in source markets.

It is evidently extremely difficult to make a strong case for federal funding of promotion outside the United States. It would have to be very large indeed to add significant weight to the combined efforts of the private sector, states and cities in the export market. According to the US National Tourism Organization, Inc. (1998, pp. 4–5), 556 travel organizations, including private companies, state travel offices and city visitor bureaux, reported they spent US$1.03 billion 'promoting travel to the United States in 1996'. The numbers involved represented a 33% response rate. So the spending figure is conservative (Cooper and Lybrand Survey). This compares with the $17 million budget of the USTTA in 1995, its last full year of operation, according to Brewton and Witham (1998, p. 51).

Looked at from the American point of view, the nearest official competitor of the foreign NTO is the individual state. Both can maintain offices within and outside the USA in main source markets. They do compete with one another for shares of the US domestic and international markets. US states were expected to spend some $524 million in 1998–9 on tourism 'development' (mainly promotion). The average state budget had increased by 30% over the previous 5 years, according to TIA's *Newsline*, April 1999.

It is accepted that states within the USA compete with one another both for domestic and international tourists. Individual states can set great store by their ability to attract 'non-resident visitation' against that of other states (see comments on Rocky Mountain International and Montana in Chapter 15).

Although effectively without an official, overall NTO, the USA retains an NTA, the Department of Commerce, and one major element of the 1996 Act, the Tourism Policy Council. Within the NTA there is a small Tourism Industries Unit whose mission and goals are respectively:

To foster an environment in which the US travel and tourism industry can generate jobs through tourism exports, and

To assist travel and tourism exporters by providing research data and services by advocating policies that strengthen economic development opportunities for tourism.

The role of the Council, which has existed in various forms since the International Travel Act of 1961, is to ensure that the United States' national interest in tourism is fully considered in federal decision making. Chaired by the Department of Commerce, it has in its membership representatives of all the relevant, key federal agencies. The context in which the Council has developed suggests that its main focus is on coordination of federal actions which would be favourable to the *exporting* sector.

France

The principal event was the new law strengthening the regional contribution to tourism administration, development and marketing, known as the Loi Mouly. This was passed on 23 December 1992. Before this is addressed below, it is essential to emphasize that there remains a strong, clearly delineated role for the national authorities. This is manifest in a number of ways, examples of which are:

- tightly controlled national systems for registering and classifying resorts as well as the accommodation (lodging) and catering (restaurant) sub-sectors, as mentioned in earlier chapters;
- the marketing approach of the Maison de la France, the NTO, which places strong emphasis on public–private sector partnerships to promote national product sectors or brands (not however to the exclusion of regional and local brands);
- the existence of vertically organized national federations and

associations as well as the National Tourism Council – a 'Parliament of Tourism' administered by the NTA – which bear witness to the demand for dialogue between 'the industry' and 'the centre'.

Significantly, the Loi Mouly provides a framework for coordination from the centre as well as decentralization of some decision making to regions, departments and communes.

Laws relating to the regionalism of tourism were passed as early as 1942 and 1943 but presumably had little practical effect after the war. General decentralization and the creation of a new regional tier of government began in the early 1980s. It was in this context that a new law of 31 January 1987 established regional tourism organizations and this may be regarded as the first step. According to Pecqueux, (1998, p. 24), it was not until the Loi Mouly was passed that decentralization 'applied to the totality of tourist activity' [within each region]. This law provided a structure for the administration of tourism to be grafted on to, and form an integral part of, the new elected tier of regional government. The region was seen as taking the lead role as *chef de file* below the level of central government and, in a sense, senior to *départements* and *communes*.

The 1987 law permitted regional governments to create regional tourism committees. Among the tasks which could be delegated to them was the elaboration of outline plans (schemas) for the development of tourism in consultation with departments and others. They could be given charge of other functions such as schemes for the accommodation sector or professional training. They might be authorized to carry out promotions at home and abroad. Committees were to consist of a mix of elected representatives from the regional, departmental and local levels plus representatives of the 'tourism and leisure professions' and associations.

The law of 1992 builds on and considerably strengthens that of 1987. The role and authority of *l'Etat*, the central state, are specified and the importance of coordination and cohesion at and between all levels is stressed. The text protects the position of the established, classified resorts covered under a separate legal provision, the 'Code des Communes'. The central state's main *compétences* are briefly defined and include:

- the determination and initiation of procedures to recognize and classify 'tourist equipment, institutions and activities' in accordance with provisions fixed by decree;
- the rules and orientations of international cooperation in the field of tourism;
- the conduct of national tourism promotions in cooperation with local governments ('territorial collectivities') and other partners;
- support for local actions to develop tourism, notably by the signing of planning contracts (contrats de plan) in accordance with a law of 29 July 1982 which reformed the formal land-use and economic planning system.

A more detailed commentary on the Loi Mouly and of the respective, interlocking roles of the central State, regions, *départements* and *communes* is given by Pecqueux (1998, Part 1 Chapters III to VII).

The *contrats de plan* require further explanation. These are contracts negotiated between central and regional government which provide both a land-use and financial guideline for economic and social development, over the medium term, for each region within a coordinated national framework. They are developed under the aegis of a Comité Interministériel d'Aménagement et de Développement du Territoire. The current contracts cover the period 2000 to 2006. When, at the end of lengthy negotiations, they were published in July 1999, it was stated that they established a partnership between regions, *chefs de file*, in town and country planning, and the central state. Further, it was proclaimed that 'this contractualization commits the public authorities – all ministries – and local collectivities in long term planning and town and country planning'. The total contribution of the central state to implementation was revealed at a meeting of the Interministerial Committee under the presidency of the Prime Minister, also in July 1999. This indicated the budget available per region and per sector, of which 0.57% was allocated to tourism (*source:* Handout supplied by the Direction de Tourisme). Regional tourism committees played a part in negotiating the tourism element of their overall regional *contrats de plan*.

The French planning system is not only seen as a basis for partnership within the country. It sets the scene also for negotiations with the institutions of the European Union. A key circular of 31 July 1998, signed by Prime Minister Jospin, gave directions to Regional Prefects and Ministers of the Government on the conduct of negotiations which were to lead to the plan for 2000–2006. In this document, quoted by Pecqueux (1998, pp. 347–53), the Prime Minister specifically requires that the authorities pursue a strategy with the aim of 'benefiting totally from the support of the next generation of European Structural Funds'.

The United Kingdom

Under the Government led by John Major, responsibility for tourism was allocated in 1992 to the new Department of National Heritage which also became responsible for Media and Broadcasting, Royal Parks Agency, Historic Royal Palaces Agency, Sports, Arts, Museums and Galleries, Libraries and Heritage (Historic Buildings and Ancient Monuments). Tourism was allocated around 5% of the budget. The Department was then the sponsoring Ministry for a number of key agencies, all having a contribution to make to tourism. The Department was presented with a new opportunity to ensure that the policies and actions of these agencies were mutually reinforcing. The Countryside Commission was not brought under this umbrella. The tradition of cooperation under earlier Ministries was continued, for example, by means of a joint report produced by the Commission and the ETB on 'Sustainable Rural Tourism'.

The ideological, cultural and political significance of 'the Heritage' in the Conservative era has been the subject of an interesting critique by Hewison in *The Heritage Industry* (1987). It was towards the end of this era, in September 1994, that the DETR and the Department of National Heritage issued PPG15, that is, *Planning Policy Guidance: Planning and the Historic Environment*, which local authorities were required to take into account in preparing their development plans. The document provided

> a full statement of Government policies for the identification and protection of historic buildings ... of immense importance for leisure and recreation.

The National Heritage Department's record in the tourism field during the five years of its existence to 1997 is dominated by continuing efforts to improve the efficiency of the BTA and the ETB, notably through the introduction of medium-term Corporate Plans. Various pilot and exemplary schemes were sponsored to encourage the industry to improve the quality of facilities and services. The voluntary scheme for classifying and grading tourist accommodation was greatly improved. The foundations were laid for a new scheme to be implemented by the authorities and the motoring organizations which did not come to fruition until Labour was in power again. But efforts to persuade a comprehensive range of establishments to participate met with limited success. The Chairman of the London Tourist Board, David Batts, stated as late as 1999 that of 1000 or so reasonably sized hotels in London, only 30% were classified under ETB's voluntary scheme and the proportion of other units covered was even lower (ETB, 1999).

The Department strengthened its consultative network, creating a consultative Industry Forum of public and private sector representatives and experts. There was a strengthening of its role in liaising with other government departments, as indicated in a House of Commons National Heritage Committee report on tourism (1997, pp. viii, ix). In this way the mainstream Civil Service would appear to have taken over gradually much of the role of the BTA, whose old committee structure had once been the main conduit for dialogue between government and industry as a whole.

The greatest legislative innovation from 1992 to 1997 was the National Lotteries Act, 1993, with far-reaching implications for tourism. Under the Act, communities throughout the United Kingdom could apply for substantial partial funding for 'good causes'. Applications were assessed by a range of public agencies: the Millennium Commission, the Arts Council, the Sports Council, the Heritage Lottery Fund and the Charities Board. Several of these were concerned with England only but were matched by parallel bodies in Scotland, Wales and Northern Ireland.

The Millennium Commission assisted communities 'in marking the close of the second millennium and celebrating the start of the third'. The Commission used money (Annual Report and Accounts, 1998–99) raised by the National Lottery to encourage projects throughout the nation which:

enjoyed public support and which would be lasting monuments to the achievements and aspirations of the people of the United Kingdom.

The 'flagship' of the Commission was the Millennium Dome at Greenwich.

The prime and initial purpose of the funds was not to develop the country as a tourist destination, but large numbers of projects, designed to improve the environment and quality of life of communities, also promised to enhance the quality of the visitor's or tourist's experience. Thus, in London, Millennium City (1999, p. 3), the London Tourist Board proclaimed:

> London, more than any other city in the world, has seized a unique opportunity to reinvent itself for the 21st century and beyond. Funding from the National Lottery and commercial sources has resulted in a massive £6 billion investment in London's tourism and leisure facilities.
>
> Across the capital you will see new and improved cultural attractions, new exhibitions, improved infrastructure and new hotels and meetings facilities. These developments are creating a legacy for the city – making it a greater place to live in, work in and visit.
>
> Some examples of London's Millennium projects are: the Tate Gallery of Modern Art, housed in the former Bankside Power Station; the Millennium Bridge, which will link the new Tate with St Paul's Cathedral; the British Museum's two-acre Great Court, which will be opened to the public for the first time in 200 years; the British Airways London Eye, the world's highest observation wheel … and the jewel in the crown … the Dome at Greenwich.

The Millennium Commission will have disbursed around £2 billion (US$ 3.5 billion) between 1995 and 2001, underpinning a total expenditure of around £4 billion. The grants were allocated to:

> nearly 3000 sites, 62 Award schemes, 381 large Festival events and thousands of community Festival activities across the UK. (Annual Report, 1998–99, p. 11)

The Commission handled only a part, though an important part of overall funds. By the summer of 1998, Lottery distribution bodies in the UK had awarded nearly £5 billion in grants to recipient organizations for 'good causes'. This represented just under half of the total project values of funded schemes. In the case of the capital grant distributors, over 2900 projects had been awarded Lottery grants; 1141 sports, 772 arts, 801 heritage and 189 Millennium projects (*The Economic and Social Impact of the National Lottery*, University of North London, September 1998, p. 5).

Initiated under the Conservatives, much of the funding was effectively to increase the supply of leisure, recreation and tourism attractions. Many of these were well under way when 'New Labour' under Tony Blair won office with a landslide victory in 1997. The new government introduced policy changes in tourism which are best studied against the background of constitutional and institutional reforms avowedly designed to have profound long-term effects on the United Kingdom and its place in the twenty-first century (see The Economist, *Undoing Britain?*, 6–12 November 1999). The first of these was decentralization. Devolution of powers to the constituent parts of the UK – to a Scottish Parliament, to Assemblies for Wales and Northern Ireland, to appointed Regional Development Agencies in England and to a Mayor and Assembly in London – created a political and administrative structure which would determine eventually the shape of sub-structures serving tourism. Regionalization was also compatible with Labour's declared intention to seek greater rapprochement with the European Union. Another extremely important factor was ideological – manifest in the so-called 'Blairite project' to modernize the country, its self-image and its image abroad. Two main factors – devolution and cultural engineering – informed the conversion of the old Department of National Heritage into the new Department for Culture, Media and Sport, and the placing of tourism as a minor branch of 'the creative industries'. In December 1998, following lengthy consultations, the Department issued a 'New Cultural Framework' (DCMS, 1999b), which explained the new approach and summarized funding allocations for the years 1999 to 2002. The document noted that the DCMS was at the centre of a complex structure which delivered money and supported activities all of which fell under the broad definition of culture. The statement presented organizational and funding reforms affecting support for the following: Arts and Crafts, Museums and Galleries, Libraries and Archives, Film, the Built Heritage, Architecture, Sport and Tourism.

At the same time, a new strategic body for culture in its widest sense would be created in each region, while the DCMS would be represented in the Government Office for each region. Provision was made for increased support for BTA's overseas promotions. Of the total budget of £1 billion envisaged for 2001–2, some 4% would be allocated to tourism.

The full tourism strategy (for England) was announced by the Secretary of State, Chris Smith, in February 1999 at the same time as the DCMS publication *Tomorrow's Tourism* (1999a). This replaced the English Tourist Board with a new English Tourism Council, a smaller organization which was given certain advisory, research and secretarial functions as well as acting as a channel for funding of England's Regional Tourist Boards, whose share of the resources available was to be further increased. The Council had no marketing capability. It was to be expected that the English Regional Tourist Boards would move closer to the new Regional Development Agencies. By the late 1990s most of the Boards had become companies limited by guarantee. How they would fit into the new structure long term and whether they would receive funding from the RDAs rather than from central government were questions that remained open for the time being. Further discussion would be premature.

While the English situation remained fluid, the Scottish, Wales and Northern Ireland Boards moved from strength to strength. In the Autumn 1999 issue of *Tourism* (No. 102), the Tourism Society stated (p. 3) that spend per visitor, as measured by national tourist board budgets divided by the number of tourists, was as follows:

England	£0.20 per visitor
Scotland	£3.76 per visitor
Wales	£4.99 per visitor

In parallel with organizational reforms, the new government also reviewed the workings of the National Lottery. Following a 1997 White Paper to Parliament on 'The People's Lottery', the Lottery Act 1998 prepared the way for some new approaches to the distribution of funds; but they were to remain potentially highly relevant to tourism. There are, however, disturbing signs that they have been allowed to generate excess capacity in the attractions sub-sector (*The Times*, 4 February 2000, p. 31). Many attractions can only continue operating if they achieve targets for paying visitors. Although there have been some successes, for example, in Edinburgh, there have already been a number of bankruptcies. The Millennium Dome, started as a project under the Conservatives but developed in detail under Labour, has been the subject of growing controversy from the point at which it was seen as the key symbol of the 'Blairite project'. Government Ministers were seen as interfering with the content and style of this attraction for ideological and political ends. Inaugurated on New Year's Eve 1999, it was severely criticized, particularly in the 'quality' press. Within weeks of opening it was clear that visitor and revenue targets were unlikely to be met. By 23 May 2000 the Millennium Commission, under the Chairmanship of the Secretary of State for Culture, Chris Smith, had authorized massive extra grants and loans on top of the original Lottery grant (see Leaders in *The Times* of 29 January and 22 February 2000, in the *Daily Telegraph* of 23 and 24 May 2000 and an article by Boris Johnson in the *Daily Telegraph* of 25 May 2000, p. 30). According to M.V. Weyer in the *Sunday Telegraph* of 10 September 2000 (p. 38), the project had had a budget of £758 million, of which £628 million had come from the National Lottery. The article also commented on a variety of other failed Lottery-aided attractions as well as some successes. The writer considered that:

> the bigger the Lottery grant, the less likely the project is to be underpinned by genuine demand and more likely it is to overrun its construction budget, undershoot its visitor target and come back begging for more cash.

The initial hopes for the Dome were not to be realized. The Bulletin of the government's Tourism Forum of March 1998 (DCMS, 1998d, p. 21) had reported on a meeting the previous month in the presence of the Prime Minister and had stated:

> A spectacular ceremony on 31 December 1999 will herald the beginning of a year-long celebration of British ideas and technology. Exhibits and attractions designed by Britain's best talents will open up the choices facing humankind in the 21st century and beyond: how we might work, rest and play, what our bodies and minds can do and how beliefs are formed; and opportunities to improve our local, national and global environment. New Millennium Experience Company Chief Executive Jennie Page [managing the Dome] said:
>
> The company is on course to make the Dome the most talked about and successful event in the world in 2000. The project is on

time and within budget and we are on track to hit – and even beat – all the targets for visitor numbers, income and construction.

At the time of writing, the revised forecast of 4.5 million paying visitors compares with the original target of 12 millions.

According to claims made by DCMS, considerable progress was made in the development of its consultative machinery during the late 1990s and into 2000. In October 1997 the Culture Secretary announced the expansion of the Tourism Forum which had been inaugurated by the preceding Conservative administration (Appendix 6). The Department maintained at previous levels its support team of 21 mainstream Civil Servants plus an outside adviser (Appendix 7). Higher level consultation under New Labour was secured by the institution of annual summits graced by Junior Ministers from major Departments who reported on their recent and expected contributions to the development of the sector. A document issued by DCMS (April 2000) subsequently stated:

> The Tourism Summit was a meeting of Government Ministers to review progress in achieving the aims of the Government's tourism strategy, *Tomorrow's Tourism*, which was published on 26 February 1999. *Tomorrow's Tourism* is the first comprehensive national tourism strategy. It sets a challenging target for the tourism industry – to match the global rate of tourism growth by 2010 – and three overriding objectives –to provide the right framework for tourism to flourish; to develop and spread quality; and to encourage wise growth.
>
> *Tomorrow's Tourism* sets out 15 key action points. [An Annex] to this report summarises progress so far in these areas, including holding annual Summits to monitor progress and plan future action. The focus of the first Summit was the need for Government to operate in a joined-up way in its approach to tourism and to take account of the effects on tourism when making policy decisions.

The document presents the government's positive view of its own actions 'in favour of' tourism. More critical material is to be found in the deliberations of the House of Commons Culture, Media and Sport Committee's Fourth and Sixth Special Reports for the sessions 1997–98 and 1998–99. Full evaluation of the government's attempts to improve interministerial coordination and of the results achieved will only be possible after a lapse of several years and on the basis of a series of annual summits. Shortly after the first summit, the new English Tourism Council issued in May 2000 its first Annual Report based on its first nine months of operation. The ETC's programmes and initiatives were in close accordance with the government's strategy. They revealed an innovative approach to NTO management and to the funding of regional organizations. Evaluation, in the context of the present book, would be premature.

15

Rocky Mountain International and Montana

Rocky Mountain International

This is a consortium formed by the OTOs for Idaho, Montana, South Dakota and Wyoming. Its main task is to promote the region in markets outside the United States. Currently it has offices or points of contact for information in five European countries with separate services for the travel trade (tour operators, travel agents and travel press) and public. The consortium distributes a main (general) brochure, a list of tour operators based abroad which sell the region and a map showing the numerous locations served by a major hotel brand, Best Western.

The brochure is well oriented to serve the needs of independent travellers who will cross or tour the region by car. A range of simply mapped itineraries to take varying lengths of time – one week to one month – is presented. Each takes the tourist through all four states and summarizes what is to be seen and experienced en route.

The itineraries and some suggestions for stay-put or centre-based vacations give an indication of the main categories of destination components the region 'produces':

An American Indian tour, a museums and attractions tour, a golf tour, a palaeontology tour, tracks and trains across the Rockies, white water and high adventure, fishing, Northern Rockies and a National Parks Tour.

The offerings also include camping, ranch holidays, skiing and snow-mobiling. The itineraries are linked to gateway cities: Denver, Salt Lake, Chicago and Minneapolis.

The most obvious area for cooperation between the four states is international marketing. Each has a distinctive and separate strategy for internal development and domestic marketing. In line with practice throughout the USA, all hold highly participative annual Governor's Conferences at which policy issues, progress in implementing past strategies and proposals for the future are debated. Central to debates are the funding, roles, programmes and performance of each state's OTO.

Six documents have been studied in an attempt to gain insights into policy and practice:

- Idaho Travel Council, Strategic Marketing Plan 2000
- Travel Montana 1998–99 Tourism and Film Marketing Plan
- Montana 1998–2002 Strategic Plan for Travel and Tourism
- South Dakota Tourism 2000
- South Dakota Winter Games Strategy
- Wyoming Business Council Division of Tourism and Travel Marketing Plan 1998/99

Each features a mission statement or declaration of objectives which places a heavy premium on increasing 'non-resident visitation' and spending, which clearly implies vigorous competition between states in the region as well as a drive to attract tourists from outside the region.

The bedrock of funding is dedicated taxation except in Wyoming, whose state tourism office is financed from General Funds. Montana's statement mentions a dedicated accommodation tax and South Dakota's 1% tourism tax and a share of Deadwood's gaming revenues, which 'together provide an independent source of funding to promote South Dakota's visitor industry'. Several of the statements regard growth in tax revenues generally as an important measure of success. Indeed, targets are set for the future tax take. Building Idaho's economy by increasing visitor expenditures throughout the state is the goal of the Idaho Department of Commerce's Travel Development Division. Idaho's tourism development and travel promotion activities are funded by a 2% lodging tax, paid by travellers and collected by the state's hotel, motel and private campground owners. Collections exceed $4 million annually. Half the funds are used for statewide tourism development and travel promotion programmes targeted to consumers, tour operators and travel agents (international and domestic) and travel journalists. The remaining half is distributed to non-profit chambers of commerce, convention and visitor bureaux and regional tourism development organizations through the Idaho Regional Travel and Convention Grant Program. Private sector oversight is through the Idaho Travel Council, an eight-member, private sector advisory board appointed by the governor. According to an economic impact study commissioned in 1997, Idaho's $1.7 billion tourism industry created jobs for Idahoans and generated $134 million in local, state and federal tax revenues.

All states generate comprehensive information, for prospective customers, on their tourist products, on their accommodation, attractions and transport services and on how to make bookings conveniently.

Conventional public relations techniques are used to project an overall destination image. An unusual feature (at least through European eyes) is the operation of a Film Office within each OTO. Activity promoting the state as a location for film and television productions is seen both as valuable in its own right and as a powerful means of projecting an image. Some strategies set revenue targets for this activity.

The Wyoming Plan sets a target of $3 million annually in economic impact from film and video production and states that the Wyoming Film Office

> works with the film, television and advertising industries to interest them in Wyoming locations and production resources, and then to provide production companies shooting in Wyoming with a positive production experience. This section has two goals; first when film or

ad companies work in Wyoming, the production company contributes significantly to the local economy through local crew hires, rentals and purchases, sometimes as much as $100 000/day. Second, Wyoming locations/tourism destinations that are visible on the motion picture or television screen, have a significant impact on the potential tourist deciding to visit Wyoming. The state can still measure renewed interest in Wyoming whenever *Close Encounters of the Third Kind* is broadcast on TV.

The filming of movies and commercials in Montana generated $18 million in 1997. Montana scored an international success with the 1997 film *The Horse Whisperer*.

All of the statements vigorously promote and celebrate year on year expansion through tourism and its contribution to general economic growth. Competition between states is assumed to be ultimately beneficial for the consumer, driving up the standard of service and providing value for money, thereby encouraging further growth. There are caveats, however, about the presence or risk of over-development in some areas, notably in the Yellowstone Park in which three of the states have an interest. Entrances to this famous park are through Idaho, Montana and Wyoming. The Marketing Plan for Wyoming observes that:

> There are continued attacks on the use of Yellowstone, and to a smaller extent Teton Park. A coalition of environmental groups has filed suit to stop all snowmachine use in Yellowstone and a similar suit to stop all snowmachine use on the National Forests is anticipated. The Yellowstone Park Superintendent is giving mixed signals about future use of Yellowstone, with threats of shorter seasons and closed facilities.
>
> Overcrowding in the national parks is assumed, and the Division's phone receptionists continue to get asked whether reservations are required or even if the park is closed to visitors.
>
> While Yellowstone is a wildlife paradise, continued questions about grizzly bears, wolf reintroduction and brucellosis can only be seen as negative publicity. The parks are our magnets to attract visitors, and the negative publicity is not to our advantage.

This introductory section has offered a sketch of a huge region. Its tourism is explored further by focusing on one of the four states in the region – Montana.

Montana

Overall impression

The introduction to the general brochure, *Montana – Vacation Guide 1999/2000*, summarizes its self-image in these terms:

Montana's nickname is 'Big Sky Country'. And once you've visited, you'll know why. Whether it's mountains in the west or rolling plains in the east, high above you'll find a bright expanse of big, beautiful sky. But don't just look overhead for beautiful sights. Look all around you. Montana is filled with scenic wonders to see, fun things to do and friendly people to meet. Hike, bike, raft, watch wildlife, take photos, ride horses or spend time in our great indoors (shopping, museums, galleries and more). … Jagged mountains of granite. Rolling green plains. Crystal-clear lakes and refreshing streams. They are all here in Montana. Add teeming populations of wildlife and you complete the picture of Big Sky Country, a landscape rich in scenes of natural wonder.

Montana is home to two national parks: Glacier and Yellowstone. Glacier Park is known for its inspiring peaks, backcountry hikes and the aptly-named Going-to-the-Sun Road, a 52-mile excursion across the crest of the Continental Divide. Yellowstone, the world's first national park, features erupting geysers like Old Faithful, majestic waterfalls, petrified forests and roaming bison, elk and other wildlife.

But national parks aren't the only scenic treasures in the Treasure State. For every spectacular acre in Glacier or Yellowstone, there are millions more in our other public lands: national forests, state parks, wilderness areas and wildlife refuges. Montana's state parks offer recreational opportunities from boating and camping to wildlife watching. Nine national forests are filled with roads and trails for hiking, biking and horseback riding. Montana's wildlife refuges preserve thriving populations of waterfowl, big game and other creatures. And, Montana protects millions of acres of scenic splendor in some of the nation's most famous wilderness areas, including the

Bob Marshall and the Absaroka-Beartooth. But land and sky aren't all that's big in Montana. The state is filled with pure waters as well – ranging from some of the world's most famous blue ribbon trout streams to deep turquoise lakes.

In Montana, the wildlife outnumber the people. And you'll find a greater variety of wildlife in Big Sky Country than anywhere else in the lower 48 states. Antelope, elk, moose, mountain goats, bighorn sheep, eagles and trumpeter swans call Montana home, as well as some of the more 'celebrity' species like grizzly bears and wolves. Montana is active in the national 'Watchable Wildlife' program, which helps to educate people about native species.

The brochure also promotes scenic motoring:

Just about any Montana highway is a scenic drive. You don't have to visit a park or trek into a wilderness area to see some amazing sights. You just need a full tank of gas. Here are some suggestions:

- The Beartooth Highway connecting Red Lodge and Yellowstone Park. Here you'll cross the Beartooth Plateau, with altitudes nearing 13 000 feet.
- The Seeley-Swan Highway on MT 83 between Clearwater Junction and Bigfork. As you drive you'll be surrounded by dense national forests and inviting mountain lakes.
- The Pintler Scenic Route on MR 1 between Drummond and Anaconda. Traverse a mountain pass with views of the Anaconda–Pintler Wilderness.
- Kings Hill National Scenic Byway between White Sulphur Springs and Great Falls. Treat yourself to views of central Montana's Little Belt Mountains.
- Makoshika State Park bordering Glendive. A drive back in time through an 8123-acres preserve of badlands and prairie complete with fossil remains.
- C.M. Russell National Wildlife Refuge on US 191 north of the Missouri River. A two-hour backcountry drive through eastern Montana's wildlife-rich prairie and badlands.

The brochure presents the state's main tourist centres, attractions and main events in sections covering the six 'countries': Glacier, Gold

West, Russell, Yellowstone, Missouri River and Custer (in West to East order). The larger of these countries are approximately the size of Scotland. Each produces its own main brochure and other information. Two quotes from the Montana brochure exemplify the main appeals of the state – outdoor recreation and the history of the West:

Yellowstone country

Big Sky Ski and Summer Resort ... this lively resort is a year-round playground for outdoor recreationists. Golf, tennis, hiking, horse-back riding, mountain biking, white water rafting, skiing and snow-mobiling are all spoken here. Gondola rides offer spectacular views in the summer ...

Custer country

Little Bighorn National Monument ... The site memorializes one of the last armed efforts of Northern Plains Indians to preserve their traditional way of life against the encroachment of white civilization. On June 15–16, 1876, 263 soldiers and personnel of the 7th Cavalry were killed by an overwhelming number of Lakota, Cheyenne and Arapaho warriors. Among the dead was Lt Col. Custer. Battlefield includes visitor center, museum, Custer National Country, 7th Cavalry Memorial and Reno-Benteen Battlefield. Guided summer tours, interpretive programs and films.

Statistics

Around 95% of Montana's non-resident travellers come to the state by private vehicle. Around 95% are from other parts of the US and from neighbouring Canada; 5% are from further afield. A 1999 Report on 1998 performance notes:

- The state hosted 9.25 million Montana visitors.
  - Visitors to Montana spent $1.5 billion during their 1998 stay.
  - The $1.5 billion represents expenditures coming from the following groups:
    - 49% from vacationers
    - 22% from non-residents visiting friends and family
    - 11% from business travelers

9% from visitors simply passing through Montana
9% from people here for shopping, conventions, or other such as medical.

- Montana's travel industry payroll is $423.4 million annually.
- 28 500 Montana jobs are directly supported by non-resident travel.

Visitor Expenditures: Where does the $1.5 billion travel industry money go? (1998 figures)

- 24% Retail Sales, $368 million
- 26% Food, $396 million
- 17% Lodging, $262 million
- 22% Gas, $338 million which generates over $60 million in state gas taxes
- 10% Other Purchases and Transportation, $158 million.

Between 1991 and 1998:

- Montana visitor expenditures (including tourism and other types of non-resident travel) grew 39%, from $1.08 billion to $1.5 billion.
- Non-resident visitation to Montana grew 24% from 7.45 million travelers to 9.25 million travelers.

(Source: The Institute for Tourism and Recreation Research, University of Montana)

The Institute analyses separately key markets for particular product categories. In 1998 the fishing market spent $64 millions, the downhill skiing and snowboard market $21 millions and that for snowmobiling, $27 millions.

The same source gave economic data for an earlier year:

Size of the Industry
In 1996, expenditures by non-resident travelers accounted for approximately:
- 30 800 jobs (6% all jobs in the state);
- $400 million in employee compensation (4% of state total);

- $56 million in proprietor's income (income of self-employed persons) (3% of state total); and
- $135 million in other property income (industries' dividends, interest, rent and profits) (2½% of state total).

Taxes

In 1996, non-resident visitors:
- Paid approximately $60.2 million in gasoline and diesel taxes (35% of total state gasoline and diesel taxes);
- Generated an estimated $52.5 million in state and local taxes, which were paid by the businesses and employees supported directly by non-resident travelers' expenditures; and
- Paid additional accommodations, alcohol, cigarette, and other excise taxes.

In total, non-resident travel's contribution to state and local taxes is estimated to be more than $113 million, or more than 7% of all state and local taxes.

The survey report concluded that:
- Non-resident visitor expenditures represent new dollars to the state economy, and are an important element of Montana's economy.
- The activity associated with non-resident travel adds diversity to the economy.
- The figures for non-resident travel, in the context of all sectors of the economy, show that non-resident travel is an important part of the state's economy, on par with agriculture in terms of jobs and wood and paper products in terms of total income.
- The estimated tax figures suggest non-resident travelers contribute substantially to state and local taxes, generating a share of taxes disproportionately larger than its share of income or employment.

Organization

The OTA is the state's Department of Commerce. The OTO is Travel Montana, with five main departments and 26 staff. Travel Montana is guided by the Tourism Advisory Council which was created by statute in 1987 as a result of the inception of the Montana accommodation tax.

The Council is composed of no fewer than 12 members from Montana's private-sector travel industry, with representatives from each of the six tourism regions (countries) and representatives from the Indian tribal governments. Members of the council are appointed by the Governor. The duties of the council are:

- Advise the Governor on matters which relate to travel and tourism in Montana.
- Set policies and guide the efforts of Travel Montana within the Department of Commerce.
- Oversee distribution of funds and set regulations for non-profit regional tourism corporations and non-profit Convention and Visitor Bureaus.
- Prescribe allowable administration expenses for which accommodation tax proceeds may be used by non-profit regional tourism corporations and non-profit Convention and Visitor Bureaus.
- Direct the university system's travel research ...

The 1998/99 Plan stated that Montana's dramatic tourism growth since 1988 was directly tied to the legislature's creation of the accommodation tax. In 1999, around $10 million was to be raised from this tax. Montana funded its travel and tourism marketing plans solely from this source *with no dollars from the state's general fund.* The financial projections for 1999 showed that 90% of the proceeds from the tax would be available to Travel Montana and, subject to tight controls, to the regional/local organizations very largely for marketing, i.e. promotion and information, particularly the production of literature. But there is a new force which may affect the pattern of spending. The Chief Executive, Matthew Cohn, in his introduction to the 1998/99 plan, noted:

Three years ago, Travel Montana tested the waters with an experimental Internet site ... The results have been outstanding. Currently, 40% of our enquiries came to us electronically. Over 200 Montana organizations and businesses have created links to our site. Studies show that visitors that access our web site stay longer and spend more money while vacationing in Montana ... I see us evolving into an information broker.

By 1999, 83% of Travel Montana's enquiries were 'electronic'.

Travel Montana is overwhelmingly a marketing organization but there is a growing interest in development. In the text quoted above, the Chief Executive also referred to the organization's recognition that:

> we needed to take a lead role in dealing with tourism related infrastructure [facilities and amenities] issues. ... preserving our heritage and culture and diversifying the tourism 'product' for the enjoyment and benefit of both non-resident and resident visitors.

Small appropriations were available from the accommodation tax proceeds and from other sources in order, for example, to assist in the restoration and conservation of an important heritage site, Virginia City. Pump priming funds were also available for non-profit facilities such as information and interpretive centres. Modest spending in these areas might in fact help the private sector indirectly to generate revenue and profit.

Notwithstanding, heavyweight investment in infrastructure and facilities is predominantly a matter for other public, including federal, agencies and the powerful private sector. That Travel Montana should be involved is acknowledged. Its Tourism Development and Education Program has dedicated a staff person to coordinate and facilitate the numerous cooperative partnership projects and activities of the Montana Tourism & Recreation Initiative (MTRI). MTRI is an interagency coalition comprised of 13 state and federal agencies, whose 'membership' includes the state departments of Commerce; Agriculture; Transportation; Fish, Wildlife & Parks; Natural Resources & Conservation; Montana Historical Society; and the University Extension Service. Federal participants include: the National Park Service; Bureau of Land Management; Army Corps of Engineers; Fish & Wildlife Service; Bureau of Reclamation; and the USDA Forest Service.

The MTRI coordinator works to create effective interagency 'partnership teams' in an overall effort to establish and reach a true statewide tourism and recreation philosophy for Montana.

Controversial issues

The main focus of controversy, Yellowstone Park, was mentioned above. In common with many countries and regions, Montana experiences the phenomenon of spatial concentration and spreading, serious congestion in some areas and 'not enough tourism' in others. In Montana the West is under some pressure; the East does not benefit sufficiently economically. There is a population shift from East to West. This problem was among several aired at the 1999 Governor's Conference. Other issues included the indirect influence of tourism on permanent settlement bringing in wealthy 'outsiders' who privatised valued recreational land previously open to all; competition between residents and tourists for recreational space; and the negative effect of excessive visitation on the environment and wildlife not only in the National Parks. Other concerns included a possible change in 'traditional way of life'.

One of Montana's tourism leaders, William Bryan, discussed such issues in greater depth in a paper to the 1999 Governor's Conference, posing these questions:

What kind of tourism industry do we want to have? What are the appropriate characteristics of a Montana tourism brand?

But, what is appropriate?
- High end, high quality, locally controlled, more expensive, fewer numbers; or
- More numbers of people, low margins, consolidation rules, out-of-state interests dominate, lower quality; or
- A mixture of the best of these?

One speaker at the conference said that Montana was 'how Colorado used to be' and implied that it should retain its traditional values and a style of tourism consistent with this aim.

16

South East England

The region embraces the counties of Kent, East and West Sussex and Surrey. Like the majority of the English tourism regions, the South East is not a self-contained and coherent entity, although its boundaries on three sides are fairly clearly delineated by London, the Thames estuary and the English Channel. To the west, there is no such edge and West Sussex merges imperceptibly into Hampshire.

Within this area there are some common elements and themes which help to give the region a distinctive character and feel. These include:

- The use of brick, tile and flint; and white stucco in the resorts.
- The North and South Downs.
- An intimate, varied and attractive landscape.
- A rich heritage of old buildings, picturesque small villages and historic towns.
- The absence of large cities and conurbations.

■ Chalk cliffs and a mixture of sandy and shingle beaches.
■ A varied and vibrant arts and cultural scene.

A major research project conducted by the South East England Tourist Board (SEETB) and partners into the image and perception of the region concluded that whilst pockets of the region enjoy recognition, it generally has an unclear identity and there is general confusion about its credentials as a holiday/break destination.

The quality of the environment is one of the region's key assets and lies at the heart of its appeal. Much of the countryside adjoining London is Green Belt. There are five Areas of Outstanding Natural Beauty covering almost one-third of the area, including the High Weald and South Downs, whilst the countryside is generally varied and attractive. The region is rich in historic towns such as Canterbury, Chichester, Guildford and Rye, and contains numerous unspoiled picturesque villages. The coast is also a strong feature with its chalk cliffs, 16 miles of Heritage Coast, extensive harbours at Chichester and on the Medway, and good quality sandy beaches in Thanet.

On the downside, the region is associated with an image of congestion and over-development, particularly in the M25 corridor and North Kent. Bathing quality on the coast is also relatively poor, although major capital programmes in Folkestone, Brighton and Hastings are being carried out by Southern Water over the next 5 years which will help to alleviate some of these problems. The physical environment in some of the coastal towns and resorts also needs attention, although there have been some encouraging examples of recent investment in the town centres of Hastings and Eastbourne, and seafront improvements in Dover, Thanet and Brighton.

The car is by far the most important source of transport used by 79% of staying visitors and most day visitors to the region. The Dartford bridge was opened in 1994, improving access from Essex, and a number of trunk road schemes have been completed, including the widening of the M25, the completion of the M20 to Dover, improvements to the A3 and A27, and major improvements to the A229 Thanet Way.

There is a very extensive rail network in the region, primarily consisting of radial commuter lines to London but also with cross-country connections from Ashford to Guildford and the South Coast Route.

Whilst rail is used by relatively few visitors (9% of staying visitors), the rail network has tremendous potential for accessing the countryside, coast and towns of the region capitalizing on the huge underused capacity outside peak hours.

There have been major changes since the early 1990s, with the long awaited opening of the Channel Tunnel and considerable rationalization of ferry routes. Crossing the Channel has become easier, more comfortable, faster and cheaper. This has stimulated a growth in cross-Channel traffic through the region's seaports and the Tunnel from 19.8 million passengers in 1990 to 37 million in 1997. Whilst traffic through the Tunnel has not reached forecast levels, it carried some 15 million passengers in 1997 whilst the Port of Dover itself carried 21 million passengers.

Another significant port-related development has been the building of the cruise liner terminal in Dover Western Docks in 1996 and a second cruise terminal was added in 2000.

The airports are major generators of economic activity and create a huge demand for overnight stays and meetings in the surrounding area and further afield. Gatwick handled 25.8 million passengers in 1997, a growth of 27% on 1990, and has a planned capacity of 40 million. Heathrow, on the edge of the region, handled 57.8 million passengers in 1997, a growth of 36% on 1990. A new terminal (5) would increase capacity to 80 million.

There are over 500 visitor attractions. Most are small, but 53 attracted more than 100 000 visitors and seven received more than 0.5 million visitors. Compared to other regions, the South East has a particular strength in gardens, heritage and farm attractions. Canterbury Cathedral, Leeds Castle, Hever, Penshurst and the wealth of National Trust properties are a major draw for overseas visitors, as are places associated with great historic events such as the 1066 Battle of Hastings.

The region boasts a wide range of facilities for recreation and spectator sport, conference and exhibition facilities and English language schools.

Statistics

In 1997, 14 million tourists stayed in the region. Of the total:

- 7 million came for holidays;
- 4 million came to visit friends and relatives;
- 2 million came on business;
- 1 million came for other purposes, including English language tuition.

The number of tourism trips to the region grew from 9.5 million in 1990 to 14 million in 1997.

These tourists spent a total of 53 million nights and their expenditure amounted to £1.7 billion. In addition, there were 94 million day trips from home to the region, accounting for an additional £875 million of spending. According to an SEETB Report, total visitor spending was almost £2.6 billion, equivalent to £643 per resident, representing 7.5% of the region's GDP.

Of tourists, 20% came from overseas and 80% from the UK, but overseas tourists account for 42% of the spending (excluding that of the day trippers from other parts of the UK).

In total the region has 103 000 tourism-dependent jobs or 6.5% of the total.

Sources

The following commentary is based on a range of sources published by the SEETB, listed below, and a number of unpublished documents provided by the Board:

- Annual Reports for 1996/7, 1997/8 and 1998/9
- Meeting the Challenge – a tourism strategy for South East England 1999
- SEETB Marketing Plan 1998–2000.
- Building Business in the Millennium 2000/2001
- Tourism in the Countryside – a tourism development code
- Creating a World Class Tourism Destination – a vision for the South East Region, jointly published by the SEETB and the STB (Southern Tourist Board)

Organization

The South East England Tourist Board was formed in 1971 and was then incorporated as a company limited by guarantee in 1980. The Board was initially largely funded by the English Tourist Board but the contribution from this source in 1999/2000 is likely to be no more than 13%. Other sources are: commercial membership subscriptions (13%), local authority subscriptions and commercial activity (c.57%). Funding from all sources required over the forecast period is £1.662 million. The number of staff is 36. At the beginning of 1999 the Board had in excess of 1700 commercial members, its highest numerical support.

Whilst a membership scheme had been in existence from the early 1970s, a Commercial Members Group and a democratically elected Committee was not established until 1988. The latter has meant that the commercial sector is formally represented. Two private sector Chairmen have emanated from this nucleus of industry representatives and since the formation of the Group, membership has more than doubled.

All the county local authorities and 26, mostly city and town, local authorities are subscribing members. With few exceptions, these authorities have their own OTOs but subscribing to the SEETB reflects an agreement to pool efforts in recognition of the special character of tourism and the need to achieve economies of scale in some areas of activity.

A two-tiered electoral system ensures that the large number of members across the region contribute to policy and action. There exists a 60-strong Tourism Council, representing members, which plays an important part in choosing the Board of Management (12 Directors). The system provides for balanced public and private sector control. The Chairman of the Board is elected by all members of the Tourism Council while the Vice-Chairman is elected by its Commercial Members.

SEETB has stated that the Board is:

committed to providing a wide-ranging and superior service to its commercial members but at the same time it needs to change the perception that non-members are excluded from its activities. This is not true, not only because of its work with local authorities and the broad cross-section of business that they represent, but also the whole industry in the region benefits in many ways from the work of the Board including:

- its extensive support and involvement with local business part- nerships;
- its assistance with business start-up and other advice;
- its co-ordination of training delivery;
- its liaison with local associations.

In 1999/2000 the Board will continue to provide a wide range of services to members but there will also be a conscious effort to further engage with all parts of the diverse industry. For example, non-members will be actively encouraged to participate in the Board's campaigns, although subscribing members will enjoy dis- counted rates.

Programmes

The organization's two main functions are marketing and development. The first of these is primarily promotion to attract visitors to the region, although it also includes after-sales service mainly in the form of a regionwide network of Tourist Information Centres which the organi- zation help to co-ordinate and maintain to a high standard. Development includes the expansion and improvement of supply.

The organization has a more direct operational involvement in mar- keting, though this is still largely a matter of facilitating communica- tions between the consumers and suppliers of tourism products. Development is achieved largely through advocacy and expert guid- ance to developers (in the public and private sector), although the organization has a more direct hand in the development of the work- force and in the improvement of service quality through training. Other activities – e.g. research and corporate public relations – are essentially support for the twin pillars of marketing and development. These call for separate comment in more detail.

Marketing

The SEETB promotes a 'brand image' of the whole region developed, with the aid of the NTO, on the basis both of consumer research and consultation with the region's members.

Promotions are aimed at selected target markets both at home and abroad and are segments judged to be those from which visitors may be attracted most cost-effectively. The following is quoted from the current strategy to attract visitors from London:

What is the South East?
In a Branding Workshop completed in late 1998, a number of core values and themes were developed by SEETB and partners, which were felt to represent the core essence and identity of South East England. These were rigorously tested and explored in focus groups comprising two key segments – career couples and empty nesters. Broad agreement from the groups was achieved in response to the following themes:

- Lush, green and varied.
- Cosmopolitan.
- Connected (to Europe, gateways and near the capital).
- Rich in heritage and history.
- Wealthy/comfortable (in parts).
- Quality (in parts).

In order to assert the Region's identity and create distinctiveness, these themes will underpin future work at a regional level.

Asserting the region's identity
The research identified a need to create a clearer image for the Region and the work of marketing the Region at local and regional level will take note of this in the future. This will not be necessarily about creating a geographical entity called 'the South East' but it will revolve around reinforcing the core attributes of the Region in order to create a clearer picture of what the area stands for. In the long term the Region will not be able to expand its appeal if it continues to concentrate its efforts solely on destination marketing. The research supports this contention and is best demonstrated by the following chart which gives the primary holiday taking motivations.

DINKIES*
Looking for new experiences, good food, activities:

EMPTY NESTERS†
Looking for a change, good food, to relax, to be pampered:

Sporting activities
Interest weekends
Activity weekends
Lads or lasses weekends

Meeting friends
Eating and drinking
Special occasions
'Chill-out' weekends
Romantic weekends

Relaxed/easy exploring
Interest weekends
Themed weekends
Cultural, arts-orientated
activities
Activity weekends
Educational courses
Special occasions

*Dual Income No Kids
†Middle aged and older couples.

There are two main means of communication: a range of brochures and attendance at tourism exhibitions in source markets. The Board is making increasing use of the Internet. At exhibitions, the organization's specialist staff assist and co-ordinate the presence of local authority and commercial members who also want to attend. Bearing in mind that other (County and District) OTOs also produce brochures and attend exhibitions, how is duplication avoided? As a general rule the regional organization takes responsibility for and coordinates activity in more distant markets, the others concentrating on nearer markets and playing a more direct role in after-sales servicing. SEETB's priorities shifted in the 1990s towards overseas marketing. Towards the end of the decade the Board began a series of promotions in the USA. Working with 19 partners, American Airlines (AA) and American Vacations, this new regional campaign, which began in 1997, presents the South East as the 'Real England on London's Doorstep'. The partnership of local authority plus private sector partners is viewed as a salesforce and SEETB has trained partners with AA to act as regional representatives at over 50 travel trade and consumer events. The target market segment for this campaign is said to be 'baby boomers and seniors'. In the current phase of the programme the commercial sector is invited to take advertising space in a brochure to be distributed in the course of the campaign.

Development

The activity to promote and assist development may be conveniently divided into two: the first generalized and the second ad hoc.

The first is typified by the Board's ongoing campaign to promote improvements in the general quality of local destinations by means of 'benchmarking'. Through the Board, local authorities may buy into a national scheme to enable them to assess and improve upon their own performance. The Board's newsletter states:

> Benchmarking is undoubtedly one of the important new buzzwords of the 1990s, despite the fact that it has been well established in the manufacturing industry for over 20 years. Rank Xerox's widely accepted definition is 'the continuing process of measuring products, services and practices against the toughest competition of those recognised as leaders'. Benchmarking then, is an important first step towards improvement – measuring performance against competitors enables businesses to identify areas of their own product, service or process where they are under-performing and attention is required. It also helps identify strengths, which can be capitalised upon, and promotes the sharing of good practice.

> The same principles of benchmarking can be applied to visitor destinations such as towns, cities or seaside resorts. Fifteen pilot studies took place during 1998 in destinations throughout England to test and refine a standard methodology. This is based on obtaining the opinions of visitors through face to face surveys on a wide range of factors or indicators which together comprise ' the visitor experience', e.g. the cleanliness of streets and public toilets, adequacy of car parking, the quality of local restaurants and the friendliness of local people/traders. Indicator scores for similar types of destination are then compared to identify relative performance and best practice.

> The over-arching benefit of destination benchmarking is that it provides a customer-focused and competitor-related basis on which to set priorities for action and improve the destination product.

Another example of a generalized development activity is the Board's scheme for granting annually public awards for outstanding achievement in different sub-sectors of tourism. These name, for example, the Tourism Pub of the Year, the Caravan Holiday Park of the Year, the Hotel of the Year, the Visitor Attraction of the Year and so forth. Winners may go forward to compete for a national award. Both the regional and national schemes achieve substantial public relations exposure. The implied purpose is to motivate the industry as a whole to emulate exemplary performance. It is therefore essentially a development activity.

Another example of a general contribution is the Board's advice to rural developers on the land-use planning system.

Limited ad hoc advice on a wide range of development issues is available free to the industry from the Board's consultancy services while a fee is charged for projects requiring substantial time inputs. The 1998/99 Annual Report mentions, among others, the production of tourism strategies for Tonbridge and Malling (inland) and Thanet (seaside) as well as a Tourism Product Audit for Lewes and a Canterbury Visitor Information Centre Operational Audit. Several management consultancy commissions from private sector clients are also listed.

Cooperation

There are numerous bodies in the region which have an impact on visitor facilities and the visitor experience. These include organizations such as South East Arts, the Regional Sports Council, English Heritage, English Nature and the Countryside Agency. The Board's policy is to have an active dialogue with all these bodies and ensure that they understand the relevance of tourism to their remit. These key public agencies are outnumbered by a long list of public sector bodies, public–private sector partnerships and private sector associations with which the Board maintains continuous contact. Throughout the working year, conferences, meetings and seminars are convened or attended by the Board's specialist personnel to address development, marketing and conservation issues with the ultimate aim of achieving consensus on tourism in the region as a whole, in particular areas or in particular sub-sectors. Such activity is seen as essential to the sound development of the sector and to ensuring that the Board's programmes are continually adapted to changing needs. Central to SEETB's function are intelligence-gathering, analysis and synthesis. This function is dependent on dialogue, participation and teamwork, which require frequent human contact. Perhaps one of the most important arguments in favour of an organization with regional headquarters is that it is easily physically accessible to a large number of leaders and specialists who have a joint contribution to make to its tourism sector.

Central government's new approach

Reference was made in Chapter 14 to Regional Development Agencies, a new tier of government, inaugurated in 1999. The South East England Development Agency (SEEDA) covers a large area which includes the territories of the present SEETB and STB. The two Boards have worked together to produce a 'vision' for the whole new region as a first step to assist SEEDA to develop a policy for the sector. It is already on record that the Agency attaches high priority to tourism as one of the main future motors of the economy. Up to now SEETB and STB have aimed over many years to establish distinctive identities for their areas as separate brands. Whether there will be an attempt, long term, to merge the two into one new brand remains an open question. Both organizations have received commitments to separate funding for the three years from 1999. A merger in the medium term therefore is not envisaged.

Controversial issues

Issues common to both SEETB and STB regions are:

- Environmental issues such as growing traffic congestion, visitor pressure on sensitive sites and overdevelopment, which threaten the overall quality of the environment on which much of tourism is based.
- The creeping homogenization of towns and cities, with a growing dominance of multiples and the associated loss of local character, distinctiveness and sense of place.
- The plight of traditional resorts along the coast where the current product is out of line with market demand. Some have found it hard to adapt to changing circumstances leading to environmental and economic decline made worse by the limited scope for economic diversification.

Kent and the Région Transmanche

Different parts of Kent experience a different mix of markets.

Historic towns and cities
This principally includes Canterbury, Tunbridge Wells, Rochester, Dover, Maidstone, some smaller towns such as Sevenoaks, Sandwich and Tonbridge and larger villages like Tenterden. The main markets are UK and overseas short breaks, UK and overseas day trips, UK and overseas groups, business and conference trade, and visits to friends and relatives.

Seaside resorts
This includes the coast from Swale around to Shepway and includes the resorts of Whitstable, Broadstairs, Margate, Ramsgate, Deal and Folkestone. The main markets are UK longer main holidays, UK day trips, and visits to friends and relatives.

Countryside, historic houses and gardens
This includes the rural Heart of Kent, the North Kent Downs and quieter stretches of

coast such as Romney Marsh. The main markets are UK and overseas short breaks, UK and overseas longer additional holidays and UK and overseas day trips.

Motorway corridors and gateways

This includes the M2, M20 and M25 and the nearby towns such as Dartford, the Medway towns, Maidstone, Ashford and Sevenoaks, plus the gateways at Dover and Folkestone. The main markets are UK and overseas transit traffic and business and conference trade.

Other attractions

There are scattered throughout the county numerous attractions, many world famous. Although many – especially historic monuments and churches – are presented with a minimum of 'interpretation', others are highly organized to cater for and entertain visitors. Two entries in the leaflet 'Best Places to visit in Kent', featuring 54 major attractions, speak for themselves:

- Knole, Sevenoaks (National Trust): A great treasure house built in 1456 with important collections of portraits, silver, tapestries and world renowned 17th century Royal Stuart furniture. Set in picturesque deer park.
- Visit Dover Castle and witness Castle life as it prepared for a visit from King Henry VIII, in the new colourful recreation of Tudor life in the Keep. Experience a dramatic sight and sound presentation of life during a 1216 siege of the Castle ...

Statistics

In 1998 it is estimated that Kent attracted 4.56 million trips by UK residents and 940 000 trips by overseas residents. Together these visitors stayed 18.5 million nights in the county. The most recent data on tourism expenditure are:

UK visitor expenditure	£338 million
Overseas visitor expenditure	£216 million
Day visitor expenditure (estimate)	£575 million
Total visitor expenditure	£1129 million

UK trips increased by over 50% and overseas trips increased by 30%

between 1989 and 1998. Nights and real spend showed smaller increases.

The most recent data on tourism employment have been taken from the Kent County Council and Cambridge Economic Consultants survey in 1998:

- Total of 36 399 jobs supported by tourist expenditure.
- 25 516 jobs supported in establishments directly receiving tourist expenditure.
- 10 883 indirect (linkage and multiplier jobs).

Sources

The following commentary is based on:

- The section on tourism in the 1996 Kent Structure Plan;
- Kent Tourism Strategy 1999–2004;
- Transmanche Tourism Facts 1999;
- and other material provided by Kent County Council.

Organization

Kent County Council (KCC) is the UK's largest local authority, serving a population of 1.3 million people in a county covering 354 296 hectares. With a workforce of around 30 000, an annual budget of £1.14 billion and a diverse range of services, KCC is a major organization.

Given KCC's breadth of responsibilities, many aspects of its role involve working in partnership with other organizations, such as health authorities, local councils, educational establishments, businesses and business support agencies. These partnerships extend into Europe, and especially to Kent's membership of the Euroregion (a partnership between Kent, Nord-Pas de Calais in France and the three regions of Belgium).

Kent's unique position, with the UK's population of 56 million to one side and the rest of the Single European Market's 360 million to the other, affords it a blend of opportunities and challenges. Huge investments are being made in Kent's future, through its transport infrastructure (motorways, sea ports, the Channel Tunnel and its dedicated rail link), strategic developments such as the Bluewater retail and leisure park (Europe's biggest), and a wealth of business parks, educational, health and research centres.

KCC consists of four 'Directorates' (Corporate Services, Education and Libraries, Social Services and Strategic Planning), briefly described here.

- Corporate Services supplies services and support to all KCC stakeholders. Services include: corporate communication, legal, property management, facilities management, finance, personnel and development and IT.
- Education aims to raise standards and achievements in schools and other educational establishments, and ensure equality of access to educational opportunities.
- Social Services aims to help Kent's people live safely and independently in their local communities.
- Strategic Planning provides a county-wide service, with particular emphasis on challenges that require a holistic view, including: development of Kent's economy, highways and transportation, environment, land use and waste disposal.

KCC has a fundamental role in the shaping of tourism through the discharge of its responsibility, entrusted to it by central government, for structure (land-use) planning for Kent. The functions of structure plans are to:

- provide the strategic policy framework for planning and development control;
- ensure that the provision for development is realistic and consistent with national and regional policy; and
- secure consistency between local plans for neighbouring areas.

Structure plans must deal with nine *key strategic topics*, one of which is 'tourism, leisure and recreation'. Like all other councils responsible for structure plans, Kent County Council benefits from central guidance on the tourism sector (PPG 21, published 1992).

The two principal themes of the Kent Structure Plan, adopted in 1996, are to encourage the growth of economic activity and employment and concern for the environment. In order to achieve these objectives the county's tourism strategy is one of selective encouragement of development.

Kent Prospects Economic Strategy 1996–2006 provides a framework for development and sits alongside the Structure and Transport Plan to guide future development in the county. Kent Prospects is aimed at developing the economy of Kent over the next ten years. It focuses on the importance of improving the competitiveness of business and the workforce and sets a long-term vision for the county born of a partnership of both the public and private sectors. The strategy identifies 12 key sectors of industry, of which tourism is one, and three main priorities. The priorities are:

- To assist Kent firms to become more competitive.
- To develop the skills of Kent's workforce.
- To create the right conditions for new economic activities.

A new 5-year tourism strategy seeks to maximize the local income and employment generated by tourism; to encourage the provision of new tourist facilities and the upgrading of existing facilities to attract visitors in an increasingly competitive marketplace; and provide for development which can realize the potential of Kent's unique position between London and the Continent.

The strategy is built around four key principles:

- building on strengths, creating partnerships and developing external relationships;
- responding to change and ensuring high quality;
- maintaining a balance and contributing to the quality of life; and
- investing in the workforce.

Targets set in 1996 were to raise UK visitor expenditure by 45% from £392 million in 1997 to £568 million by 2003 and overseas expenditure by 40% from £210 million to £296 million over the same period. (There was no target for day trip expenditure.)

The Strategic Planning Directorate of Kent County Council incorporates the Economic Development Land Use and Transport Planning and Environmental Management Units. Tourism is recognized as a major contributor to the county's economy in the Kent Structure Plan. Kent

Tourism is part of the Economic Development Unit and it is effectively the OTO (Official Tourism Organization). There are 120 staff in the Directorate, of whom seven are in the OTO.

Tourism marketing activities concentrate on leading the county's overseas marketing campaign aimed at Northern Europe, on working with Kent's District Councils to co-ordinate and brand the domestic marketing campaign, and on developing sustainable tourism products such as walking and cycling. Kent Tourism also has programmes to raise awareness of tourism investment opportunities, to raise the quality of attractions and accommodation and to improve information on business performance and customer profiles.

Cooperation within Kent

Partnerships with the District Councils, cross-Channel carriers and the local industry are an important feature of the KCC's approach to tourism. Public sector funding for Kent Tourism's work is assisted by private sector support and European funds.

Specifically, Kent Tourism interacts within the KCC, with the Environmental Management Unit (on walking, cycling and heritage product development) and with the Highways Unit (on tourism signposting). The OTO also liaises with the South East England Tourist Board.

Learning and Business Link (LBL)

The new Learning and Business Link company operational from April 1999 is a merger between Kent Training and Enterprise Council, Business Link Kent, Kent Education Business Partnership and Kent Technology Transfer Centre. The focus of LBL is to grow business and people by delivering relevant, high quality products and services to build on the capacity of the local economy through sustained expansion. In relation to tourism, LBL will respond to the needs identified by regional and county bodies, equip businesses and individuals with the skills to respond to tourism, and assist the sector to identify project resources in relation to training and business development issues.

Kent Prospects and the Kent Economic Forum (KEF)

Kent Prospects is a ten-year economic development strategy launched in 1996 and approved by a large number of private and public sector organizations. The partner organizations have made a commitment to a shared vision and to a common approach to tackling the issues and priorities for action in Kent. Tourism is one of the key sectors identified in the strategy as being of importance to the future of Kent.

Kent Prospects is overseen by the Kent Economic Forum Board, which draws its membership from the public and private sector. The Board has no executive powers but is a partnership able to express an independent voice with regard to the implementation of Kent Prospects.

Kent Tourism Sector Group (KTSG)

The Kent Tourism Sector Group was set up in 1997 and represents both the private and public sector interests of the tourism industry in Kent including hotels, guest houses, pubs, transport operators, caravan parks, visitor attractions and public sector organizations such as Kent County Council, District Councils and the South East England Tourist Board. The KTSG has four working groups: Hotel and Leisure Investment, Quality Programme, Marketing (International and Domestic) and Research. These groups work to solicit views, thoughts and ideas on KCC and other agency projects and activities which affect the tourism industry in Kent.

The objectives of KTSG are to:

- drive forward the implementation of the tourism elements of Kent Prospects with an emphasis on measures that maximize the competitive potential of tourism businesses;
- provide a forum for all parties involved in Kent to meet and discuss key issues;
- provide a voice and a lobby for tourism in Kent;
- provide a focus for coordinating strategic initiatives and campaigns;
- promote best practice and encourage participation in initiatives by the widest possible number of tourism businesses and organizations.

KTSG has a vital role to play in the implementation, monitoring and review of this strategy.

District and Borough Councils

There are 12 District and Borough Councils in Kent: Ashford, Canterbury, Dartford, Dover, Gravesham, Maidstone, Sevenoaks,

Shepway, Swale, Tonbridge and Malling, Thanet and Tunbridge Wells. The District Councils operate 26 Tourist Information Centres in the county and have an important role to play in running museums, theatres and leisure centres and providing infrastructure such as public conveniences and car parks. Local planning policies provide control over new built development and environmental services provide a degree of quality control over standards in tourist accommodation and food outlets.

Medway Unitary Authority

Following local government reorganization in April 1998, a new unitary authority was created covering the former Districts of Rochester and Gillingham. The new Medway Council has separate strategies for economic development and tourism but continues to work with the County Council to ensure there is a coordinated approach to tourism marketing and other activities.

Local tourism groups

There are 16 local tourism or industry groups in Kent. The Association of Tourist Attractions in Kent (ATAK) is the only one operating across the county, established with the assistance of Kent County Council. This is a private sector membership organization run by volunteers and part-time staff support, which produces an attractions leaflet and attends exhibitions on behalf of the membership.

The Nord–Pas de Calais Region of France

Kent and a neighbouring county, East Sussex, are areas which receive European Union aid under the Interreg programme. Kent is linked closely with the Nord–Pas de Calais region on the other side of the Channel in this context. Kent also has one area – the Isle of Thanet – qualifying for European Objective 2 funds for the regeneration of areas seriously affected by industrial decline.

The Interreg programme is one of many financed from Structural Funds whose main purpose is to support development in less prosperous regions. Parts of Kent and of the Nord–Pas de Calais have suffered from severe decline in some industrial pockets and in declining seaside resorts. Interreg is used specifically to encourage cooperation and integration between neighbouring regions in different European countries.

Similar links exist, for example, between the border regions in Northern Germany and Denmark, Northern Spain and Southern France, and between Spain and Portugal. The total European budget for the second phase (Interreg II) 1994–1999 was ECU 2900 billions – around \$US3000 billions (data from European Commission, *Tourism and the European Union: A Practical Guide*, 1995a). Within this framework the Regional Tourism Committee in the Nord–Pas de Calais and Kent County Council have cooperated in the areas of research, marketing and development, including the encouragement of EU part-funded capital investment. Kent's budget under Interreg II was £12 millions. The programme is evolving against the background of vastly improved communications at the centre of which is the Channel Tunnel. A shared aim is to develop the two areas as destinations in their own right – or possibly as one destination for some markets – rather than becoming rapid transit areas.

Interreg funds have been used to finance substantial research. The year 2000 saw the publication of the bilingual Transmanche Tourism Facts, giving data on tourism resources, facilities, flows and expenditures in the two areas. A joint Research Unit, funded annually to the extent of £75 000 was established in Canterbury to undertake a three-year programme. Data are required *inter alia* to assist investment decisions, investment promotion being a key activity.

Under the rules the two areas may link up with neighbouring areas. Euroregion is a partnership with Flanders, Wallonia and Brussels. A specific example of cooperation in mutually reinforcing marketing and development activity is the Historic Fortifications Network. This is a collaboration between 17 towns in Kent, Nord–Pas de Calais and West Flanders (Belgium) linked by history, origin and evolution. The 'network' has been created by the towns themselves and co-ordinated by three partner organizations, Kent County Council, le Syndicat Mixte de la Côte d'Opale and the Province of West Flanders. A three-year promotional programme to market the network and to develop heritage tourism in the Transmanche Region is being funded by these organizations and the partner towns with the support of the EU Interreg II fund to 'promote cross border cultural partnerships'. A simultaneous capital programme to develop and improve interpretation and access to historic and fortified sites within the network is also being implemented.

There are other major individual projects under way within the

Transmanche cooperative framework. One of many is the long-term regeneration of the seaside resort and port gateway of Ramsgate. Here, among specific investments, are proposed a 'magnet' tourist attraction, a speciality retail centre, a hotel and housing. A total public investment of £100 million in the regeneration of Ramsgate is envisaged, including major infrastructure – a new access road, which opened in June 2000.

The influence of the OTO (Kent Tourism)

Kent Tourism is a small but highly skilled unit of seven persons within the Kent County Council, four concerned with marketing and three with research and development. The marketing budget – used largely for printed material, development of an Internet site, attendance at exhibitions and press relations – is modest at around £200 000 per year. But the significant fact is that it is integrated into a local government which deploys very considerable resources and powers to shape every aspect of tourism within the county and carries great weight with both public sector bodies (including the District Local Authorities) and private enterprise. Earlier chapters have highlighted the central problem of tourism development – the difficulty inherent in coordinating the many relevant policy areas and the physical bringing together of the different elements of an otherwise fragmented industry. Coordination and development must also be carried out in ways that are acceptable to local communities. Democratically elected local authorities are in a unique position to address such issues.

Kent County Council's influence may be illustrated by reference to a series of actions to improve the quality of services by promoting the application of the new government approved schemes to inspect, classify and grade accommodation throughout the county. In the words of an official statement:

> Kent Tourism has underlined its commitment to quality with a new programme monitoring standards at attractions across the county … most Kent districts have adopted the policy of only promoting inspected accommodation in their accommodation guides … Kent Tourism has worked closely with several destination areas over the last year in establishing accommodation improvement schemes for the Thanet resorts and Folkestone. The 3 year Thanet and Folkestone schemes are worth over £500 000 each, with grants of up to 30%

available for those prepared to upgrade and reach the standards of their choosing.

After the launch of the new harmonised scheme, consumers should be fully aware that they are being actively encouraged to select accommodation with quality rating and also what the new symbols – diamonds for guest accommodation and stars for hotels – indicate.

Controversial issues

The two main issues are of very different kinds. The first is the problem of spatial concentration and visitor pressure, as experienced in many parts of South East England. The second concerns duplication of effort between the different official tiers of the system and the private sector. The following quotes from Kent County Council's statement on the Strategy 1999–2004 explains them more fully:

Tourism in the future requires a careful balance between economic gain, the environment and overall quality of life. Whilst the emphasis will continue to vary from area to area the establishment of appropriate planning policies is essential to managing the environment. The quality of the environment particularly in rural and historic areas is a key part of the tourism product.

The greatest risk has emerged from the visitor pressures experienced at honeypot historic towns or rural sites of special scientific interest. Visitor pressures are experienced in Canterbury, a major heritage and cultural destination with 41 000 residents yet 1.6 million visitors to the Cathedral. The Canterbury City Centre Initiative was established in 1994 to work with residents, local businesses and statutory bodies to ameliorate the impact of visitors through better management of information, transport, signposting and car parking. (The name was changed to Canterbury City Partnership in 1999.) This project will require a long term commitment to help residents understand the benefit of tourism and help visitors to be aware of the difficulties of managing such a special town and to understand how they can minimise the impact of their visit.

The impact of additional motorway traffic en route to the Continent and fast rail proposals to London have brought new pressures to bear both to residents and visitors. The increase in continental road freight can have a negative impact on visitor activity and perceptions, particularly when political or social issues cause traffic delays and temporary motorway closure.

Sustainability is important to the public sector. This covers issues such as transport and environmental capacity, product purchasing and local supply chains, the use of resources and waste minimisation. Small businesses acknowledge these issues but do not necessarily understand them and are unlikely to jeopardise short-term commercial interests in preference to long-term sustainability of the product. This is a matter where awareness and education will be important.

On the second issue, under heading 'Reducing Marketing Overlap', the Kent County Council states:

The situation is becoming complex in the overseas market which is inevitable given the increasing sophistication in markets and promotions. Kent County Council is a key player working in conjunction with the local area partnerships, individual local authorities and the carriers. Market planning and communication between partners is therefore essential. There is not always clear division of responsibility, which runs the risk of duplication and fragmentation. Most organisations who are active overseas are targeting the same broad and relatively well established markets. Few are pioneering in new markets.

Whilst effective marketing has been carried out over the last decade, the majority of the activity has been brochure or print led and not necessarily campaign or market driven. Hence, disproportionate budgets are spent on brochures at the expense of campaigns. There is an over-dependency on bulk shipment of brochures to Tourist Information Centres in the UK and BTA overseas offices for distribution.

More could be done at the two ends of the marketing cycle:

- generating awareness in new markets in both the UK and overseas through a proactive public relations strategy and campaign;
- generating repeat business by direct marketing to a database of previous enquiries and customers;
- using the Internet to interface the Kent brand more directly to local destination web sites and facilitate direct booking.

In an interview with the author, Simon Curtis, spokesman for Tourism Kent, pointed out that most Districts wanted to publish their own guides even though this was not necessarily the most efficient medium. They were however 'politically important'. He confirmed that:

> for too many tourism organisations, marketing is still about producing brochures and attending exhibitions. However, there is now growing recognition that the Internet will become the main medium for marketing over the next 5 years, reducing dependency on print.

In this, in the author's experience, local destinations within Kent have much in common with others throughout the UK and indeed worldwide.

Part Four

Conclusions

18

Conclusions and reflections

This chapter is divided into two parts. The numbered points in Section I are matched by the numbered comments in Section II.

I: Recapitulation and discussion of salient points

1 The opening chapters of this book revealed the generally controversial character of tourism. The host community is rare that unreservedly welcomes all comers and is in favour of limitless expansion. The response of governments to growing pressures from tourism has also been marked by controversy.

2 The political debate in the 1960s and 1970s was animated by sharp disagreements between those who believed strongly in central (state- and government-directed) control of the industry's development and those who were convinced that the industry would only develop healthily when allowed to respond freely to market forces.

Under the interventionist option, the industry might be developed selectively or restrained by means of fiscal and regulatory measures, if policy so required. The industry might alternatively be stimulated by means of fiscal measures (incentives, subsidy and other privileges).

Under the liberal, free market option, whole destinations and individual enterprises would succeed and survive in fair and open competition insofar as they managed to supply, more effectively than their competitors, the products which consumers were prepared to pay for. Under this dispensation consumers would have a direct, decisive influence over the shape and character of the industry. Essential to the efficient working of such a system was consumer access to adequate information on the products available.

In the last quarter of the twentieth century and to the present day free market thinking has increasingly held sway in the global economy. Developments, including deregulation and privatization in the tourism industry, have been part of a more general economic revolution. However, the decline of one type of regulation has tended to be counterbalanced by new forms of regulation covering two main areas: the protection of natural and built environments and consumer protection. The former is exemplified by stricter land-use planning and by the increasing application of 'polluter pays' principles to the framing of legislation and regulation. The latter is exemplified by measures to prevent the emergence of private monopolies and cartels and to set minimum standards for the flow of information to consumers. Both types of regulation are relevant to the *leitmotiv* of modern tourism planning – the promotion of 'quality tourism'.

3 Chapter 8 suggested that states and governments cannot stand back from tourism and indeed that many have had strong motives for intervening or at least heavily influencing its development. But policy statements issued at the highest levels reveal less about policy and its justification than about the organizational mechanics of its implementation. The OECD review of 1989, quoted in Chapters 2 and 6, referred to the repeated questioning of structures throughout its member countries over several decades. Some observers, for example Elliott (1997), noted an excessive concern with organizational efficiency and little questioning of ultimate policy objectives. The many periodic Ministerial reviews in the UK, right up to the end of the 1990s, seldom resulted in measures of substance but unfailingly produced yet one more reorganization of the NTO to turn it allegedly into a 'leaner and fitter' body than its predecessor. The practice invites the suspicion that this was normally the only area over which the UK Minister for Tourism had any real authority.

Regarding overall governmental activity worldwide, the challenge to administrators has been threefold as follows:
(i)   interministerial and interdepartmental coordination of functions, including those not primarily concerned with tourism but having implications for the industry;
(ii) coordination and cooperation between the specialized agencies operationally responsible for tourism and other agencies with which they might have close affinities; and
(iii) the correct distribution of responsibilities and apportionment of resources between the national, regional, sub-regional and local parts of the tourism structure.

These items are now discussed in their numbered order.

There is scant evidence of any high level enthusiasm for or sustained success in the pursuit of interministerial coordination with the development of tourism as its specific objective. The reasons for this can only be matters for conjecture. The task itself is potentially very complex and demanding of substantial administrative resources. Perhaps in few countries is tourism *per se* so important that the regular joining up of all Ministries and Departments for the sake of this one sector is warranted. Tourism, leisure and recreation (international and domestic) could together command more attention for economic and social reasons. Of the countries studied in detail, France, with its long tradition of state intervention in all three fields, has done most in recent years to articulate formally and legally its coordinated structures – by means of the 1992 Loi Mouly in particular.

It is reasonable to expect that, where there is some degree of interministerial coordination, subsidiary agencies sponsored by ministries are also encouraged to cooperate closely. Cadieu (1999, p. 28) refers to the existence of 19 relevant parallel agencies or *Directions* in France from 1977 whose cooperation the Minister of

Tourism had the right to seek. But he does not comment on their relationships or the results achieved. The equivalent of this subordinate level of agency in the United States is to be found within individual states where formal machinery for cooperation exists, as illustrated by the example of the Montana Tourism and Recreation Initiative in Chapter 15. Some insights into the UK practice were presented in Chapter 9. But the workings of such machinery in general and in a range of countries are not well documented. They have evidently not been a major preoccupation for policymakers or academics.

The sharing of resources and power between the different geographical layers of the official tourism structure has been the subject of much wider debate and controversy. A long-term trend towards decentralization has been noted. The introduction of a layer between national and local is widely noted and questioned. There is publicly funded activity at three levels or more in most countries. (In this context, individual states in the US are analogous to nations in Europe.) One problem that is a potential source of conflict is the perceived overlapping of budgets and duplication of efforts. The detached observer may well ask why, for example, the hotels and attractions in a resort need to be promoted simultaneously by the marketing department of that town and by the marketing departments of the surrounding sub-region, region and country, that is, by the whole national pyramid of OTOs. Various approaches to the more efficient distribution of responsibilities and budgets have been attempted. In 1996 the USTTA was abolished. In 1999 in the UK New Labour withdrew all central funding from the English national domestic marketing campaigns and distributed available resources to regions. Within less than two years a Conservative Policy Group on Tourism was calling for the restoration of 'an England-wide marketing function' to the NTO (*Tourism*, Issue 106, Autumn 2000, p. 9). In France, the Loi Mouly, while allocating roles to French OTOs at every level from national to local, is claimed to provide a framework for debating and deciding more rationally than previously their respective roles. There is little published evidence as yet on this framework's effectiveness. As Chapter 9 indicates, these are difficult issues which in many countries are far from settled.

Whatever doubt attaches to the distribution of marketing responsibilities, there is virtually everywhere *de facto* recognition of the critical importance of local initiative. Local action can be strongly motivated by a number of factors: tourism can be the dominant industry at local, rarely at national, level; its impact is highly visible to the community; its visibility may be enhanced when, as is often the case, there is a strong element of specialization (in, for example, a winter sports resort or historic city). Proportionately, the resources devoted to the development and marketing of tourism are much higher at local than at other levels. In two of the three major countries studied, local hypothecated or dedicated taxes levied on the tourist contribute to this higher level of funding. The use of funds can be the subject of meaningful public debate locally. Where a wide range of functions is overseen by one powerful local government (for example, in Kent, England), there is a greater opportunity for achieving coherence between the many public agencies, associations and enterprises engaged in the sector. Interministerial and inter-agency coordination at national level is highly problematic. Attempting the equivalent at local level is prima facie more realistic. Pulling together effectively the heterogeneous collection of elements and activities that constitute a tourist destination is crucial for its success. Coherence is what local action can uniquely deliver in terms not only of development and marketing, but in overall tourism management.

4   Some policies and public sector action in several countries in the 1960s and 1970s were designed to produce spatial redistribution of tourism away from areas already noted as 'congested' or 'saturated'. This marked the beginning of a trend towards 'managed' tourism which was to receive in the long run new impetus from the 1992 'Earth Summit' of nations in Rio. Sustainability quickly became virtually the *sine qua non* of policy statements and interest group pronouncements. The concept also became the subject of a generous academic output. (See, for example, Stabler, *Tourism and Sustainability. Principles and Practice*, 1997.) An early and respected definition of sustainable development was development that 'met the needs of the present without compromising the ability of future generations to meet their own needs' (Brundtland Commission). There have been others. As Stabler remarks (p. 14):

Most commentators on the meaning of sustainable development, from whatever perspective they are considering it, agree that definitions of it are rather vague and open to different interpretations.

Pursuit of the concept implies a requirement to optimize rather than maximize tourism. Notwithstanding, governments and spokesmen for the industry have continued in major public pronouncements in the late 1990s to the present day to proclaim further growth as their primary aim in terms that can only be described as euphoric. Many have been quoted in this book. There is a widespread implicit assumption that growth and sustainability in this sector are by and large compatible given the right kind of intervention. Such an assumption is implied, for example, in the 1999 UK strategy which postulates both the maintenance of the UK's share of a growing world market over the ensuing 10 years through 'wise growth' and the promotion of 'quality'.

5 NTOs operate at the interface between the upper echelons of government and other levels. They function also at the intersection between the public and private sectors. Their record as overall coordinating bodies is not impressive. Arguably their greatest asset is their knowledge of the market and of the industry. They are important as sources of management information and market intelligence. But NTOs are small, poorly resourced organizations occupying a subordinate place within their government hierarchies. OTOs at regional, sub-regional and local levels also have junior status in their respective political and administrative contexts. While OTOs frequently provide platforms for discussion and have some research and advisory functions, most major on marketing in its narrower sense, that is, promotion. They coordinate a significant, though not dominant, part of the industry's promotion, which has a short-term to medium-term perspective.

II: Reflections

1 During a 25-year period, from 1970 to 1995, in which tourism became demonstrably more controversial, international arrivals increased threefold from around 166 million to 563 million according to WTO. The same source (WTO, 1998c, p. 3) forecasts a

further tripling of such arrivals worldwide to 1600 million (1.6 billion) within a further span of 25 years to 2020. WTO does not provide comparable information on domestic tourism.

WTTC (1998, p. 2) states that:

> Travel and tourism is a service business which has grown up in the latter part of the twentieth century as countries have opened their borders, businesses have globalized their markets, consumers have exploited their increased leisure time/disposable income and technology has produced faster cheaper transport.
>
> In the last 25 years international travel and tourism has grown more than 500%. Domestic tourism, which is by far the largest market, has also expanded dramatically during the same period. All forecasts point to continued dynamic growth ...

A report in *The Times* of 27 June 2000 (p. 11), refers to a government study which showed that in the UK three new airports the size of Heathrow would be needed to meet demand over the next 20 years. (Heathrow is already the world's largest international airport in terms of passenger movements.) *The Times* report refers to the forecast as a 'political time bomb'. The doubling in the use of fuel, pollution and noise and the loss of land likely to be caused by the increased number of flights, most over the South East, will, the report says:

> place the Government on a collision course with councils [local governments], sleepless residents and the Government's own environmental advisers ...

The community in South East England is likely to be only one among many which will step up the pressure to be better informed about and more involved in policies for travel and tourism which pass through or head for their territories. It will be in the interests of governments and the industry to listen carefully. Murphy (1985, p. 153) remarks that:

> Tourism, like no other industry, relies on the goodwill and cooperation of local people because they are part of its product. Where development and planning does not fit in with local aspi-

rations and capacities, resistance and hostility can raise the cost of business or destroy the industry's potential altogether.

It is reasonable to expect that long-term movements away from 'boosterism' to managed tourism, as noted in Chapter 2, will continue well into the twenty-first century. Host communities will be less impressed by promises of indefinite expansion in this sector than by credible schemes to manage its environmental, economic and social impacts. This will imply, *inter alia*, greater selectivity – the attraction of certain categories and patterns of tourism in preference to others. Governments will also be well advised to consult host communities more closely than in the past on priorities for development. The industry is well locked into consultative structures but host communities are not evidently well represented except at the local level in countries with strong democratic traditions and adequate administrative resources. Local communities in poorer countries have tourism thrust upon them by external interests (Burns, 1997). Brown (1998, p. 112), referring to developing countries, considers that:

> at least some current research seems to be based on the researchers' own (usually Western based) perceptions of what is best for people, without attempting to consult them.

2 If the state's involvement is inevitable and indispensable, it follows that the state and governments should be heavily engaged in the relatively new and important task of managing the ever-growing impacts of tourism. It is time to abandon the cliché that it is mainly a matter for the private sector. Both heavy public sector and private sector engagement is required.

As emphasized by a senior spokesman for WTO, quoted at the end of Chapter 8, the key is to identify the dividing line between the two. The evidence presented in this book suggests that at the destination the public sector must take the lead role in the development and management of the natural, built and human environments in which tourists are interested, including many key assets which are primarily cultural assets and secondarily tourist attractions, most obviously major historic monuments. The principal contribution of the private sector is the basic product, as defined in Chapter 4, notably in the form of transport, hotel, restaurant, recreational, sporting and entertainment facilities together with guiding and other specific services.

The above does no more than indicate very broadly where the main emphasis of public and private sector action might be placed, but some attempt must be made to sketch in an answer to this difficult issue.

The state has an important part to play in consumer protection, especially by ensuring that the prospective buyer has adequate information on basic products available and their prices. The prospective buyer often has to make a commitment before being able to inspect or experience the product. Government regulation not of the product but applicable to standards of information would seem to be essential ultimately to the efficient operation of the free market. There are 18 800 officially classified *hôtel homologués* in France and 2890 hotels in the latest English classification and grading (quality assurance) scheme (*sources*: Direction du Tourism, Paris and English Tourism Council, November 2000). The French authorities would surely argue that they have a competitive edge.

3 If tourism is to continue to grow massively there must surely be a case for improving its planning and coordination at national level where evidence suggests they are at their weakest. The present primary concern of the authorities is with liaison and a form of governmental good housekeeping. The tone has been set by the Tourism Policy Council in the USA, quoted in Chapter 9, which aims to:

> bring together high-level agency officials with direct program operating responsibilities to consult and discuss needed improvements, to examine specific tourism related programmes and to assist in resolving inter-agency conflicts should such arise.

Credible strategic plans, rather than safety nets, may be required as tourism grows and presents more opportunities and problems for resolution. Currently the great breadth and complexity of the sector are obstacles to bold action.

A simplified statement outlining the government's intentions in five main areas affecting tourism with an indication of their expected specific effects on the industry might be an improvement on past 'strategies'. These areas are: public investment in transport infrastructure and operations; transport regulations; land-use planning; taxation; and consumer protection. Whether it is the government's policy to encourage unfettered free market expansion or to develop 'quality' tourism highly selectively, it is in these areas where it is likely to have most influence. A well thought out, coordinated strategy embracing all five in a single document would be an advance on those 'strategies' that have concentrated on the budget and structure of the NTA or NTO.

Public discussion of the distribution of responsibilities among the different geographical layers has focused on marketing. There are some marketing tasks which are clearly the responsibility of the NTO. For example, it makes sense for the NTO to promote and service market segments disposed to make circuits of the whole country and to make convenient contact with one central information source. The consumer who is firmly committed to visit one specific, named location may on the other hand need only to dialogue with the OTO at that location and no other.

Much depends on the geographical dimension of destination components being sought by the consumer or being developed and promoted by OTOs. There may be a variety of typical itineraries from countrywide through those covering several regions to centre-based stays in single locations.

The information and booking processes of different market segments are highly relevant to the apportionment of marketing responsibilities among OTOs. The point at which the prospective tourist makes, or is persuaded to make, contact with the OTO system during the planning of the trip is relevant. The consumer who settles at a very early stage on the country to be visited but is undecided on the specific location or locations to be included in the visit may require to be put in touch with a number of competing local OTOs directly or through the conduit of the NTO. Another quite different type of consumer may have a clear requirement, at an early stage in trip planning, in terms of the category of trip envisaged – a shopping weekend in a capital city, a golfing weekend, a winter sports holiday, a windsurfing holiday – but may wish to compare a number of countries' offerings. There is a *prima facie* case for allowing the NTO to facilitate this type of 'sectoral shopping', in competition, of course, with other NTOs.

Spatial patterns of production, tourists' perceptions of destinations and their decision making processes have implications for the apportionment of marketing responsibilities. Current approaches to their study are not manifestly scientific. OTOs would appear to proceed largely by trial and error, guided partly by the industry's perception of 'what works', as reflected in its financial participation in OTO marketing at various levels. The areas described could be researched more systematically. One result could be the rationalization of expensive printed material which can clog up OTO marketing networks.

4   In seeking sustainable development, 'wise growth' and managed tourism, host communities may be in danger of falling foul of the cherished tenets of 'market-driven management' and of committing the marketing sin of 'excessive product orientation'. There is no point in trying to develop a tourism industry, acceptable to the community in terms of its character and location, if there is not an adequate demand for its products. Does the community's vision of the tourism it wants correspond to what markets want to buy? In reality host communities, like corporate enterprises, usually have a number of production options. Policymaking and planning may involve choosing from among these options a smaller number that best suit the needs of the community and at the same time have adequate market appeal. Only some may be at once acceptable to the community, cost-beneficial for the public sector and sufficiently attractive to markets to be profitable for the private sector.

Two key types of expertise that need to be put together to identify the best options are those of the land-use planner and the marketer, though other disciplines are obviously relevant. Sound land-use planning (producing, for example, structure plans and local plans in the UK) indicates the future capacity, character, quality and location of the hotels, attractions and facilities required. In effect, in outline it determines the spatial framework into which the industry is expected to fit and the physical standards to which it must conform. In democratic systems local communities are empowered to scrutinize and propose modifications to land-use plans before they are finalized. Such plans, however, are most sensibly drawn where they take full account of market realities. There is a potentially important role for marketers to play in the search for a better understanding of the market potential and the competitive position of the destination and of any proposed developments. Market knowledge should be a routine input into land-use planning. Local governments might consider making greater use of marketers in cross-disciplinary teams for land-use policy formulation, following the lead of advanced, market-driven corporate organizations described by Kotler and noted in Chapter 4. Both the industry and the community would stand to benefit. The perils of 'excessive product orientation' – majoring on what the producer prefers to sell rather than what the consumer wants to buy – have been illustrated in the UK by the Millennium Dome *débâcle* and other Lottery-funded developments, regarded by communities as 'good causes' but based on over-optimistic projections of market potential.

5   Where NTOs and their equivalents are closely identified with the industry, the latter is usually well represented on controlling Boards and Committees. Such NTOs are biased towards short-term and medium-term marketing. There are other functions which merit consideration: the R and D function concerned with long-term development and innovation and general research into market potential. In Chapter 5 reference was made to the need for improved categorization of tourist products which might assist in improved assessments of market potential, share-of-market calculations and competitive positioning, in line with practice in other industrial sectors.

Regular data on the production and consumption of tourism by meaningful categories of producers and consumers could be the basis of improved dialogue between land-use planners and marketers, as suggested above, as well as useful to investors in the industry. Other candidates for further research, so far greatly neglected, are the spatial patterns of tourism production as well as consumers' information-gathering and booking processes. Indeed, these might become in the long run subjects for periodic monitoring and reporting as part of a country's regular statistical output. While the costs of NTOs' short-term marketing might be increasingly borne by the beneficiary elements in the private sector, greater emphasis could be placed on public funding for research and data collection given their relevance to policymaking in the public sector and their potential value to host communities. If tourism is to grow massively over the next 20 years, now is the time to invest more in a fuller understanding of its complex requirements and impacts.

Appendices

Appendix 1

Parliamentary (House of Commons) Debates 27 February, 23 June and 24 June 1969: selected quotations from Hansard

Intervention versus liberal economics

Member for Moray and Nairn: The President of the Board of Trade began his speech by pointing out the great service which the tourist industry gives to the United Kingdom economy. However, we have just witnessed what to me was an outstanding spectacle, the Right Hon. Gentleman introducing the Bill as if the Government were kindly benefactors to the tourist industry. Nothing could be further from the facts of the recent past. ...
I remind the House of what the Government have done. During their first one-and-a-half-years in office they imposed a restrictive building licence procedure which did not apply to industrial buildings but which did apply to hotels. This caused delays and uncertainty. Then

they withdrew investment allowances – except on buildings – the investment allowances on hotel equipment of all kinds. At the same time, they made the hotels and the tourist industry ineligible for the investment grants which they introduced for manufacturing and other industries in place of the allowances. Shortly afterwards there was a severe and unexpected blow. Selective Employment Tax, an ill-conceived and iniquitous impost, was brought in. ... The Government have behaved like a thug who, having battered someone to the ground with blows, kicks him in the teeth. The kick was the Selective Employment Tax. ... After perpetrating this violence the Government reappear in the role of the Good Samaritan with a stretcher and medicine – the present Bill. But the medicine which is proposed is not the best which could be prescribed. (Second Reading)

Member for Blackpool South: The Government should put the tourist industry on a par for tax purposes with manufacturing industry. (Second Reading)

Member for Eastbourne: I regard the Bill as a typical Socialist approach to legislation. If the Government had not mucked up the tourist trade in the first place ... the Bill would have been unnecessary ... If the tourist industry were recognized as really important, if the burden of SET were removed, and there were a general easing in the granting of planning consent for new ventures, with only one Government Department instead of eight to deal with, the industry would go ahead under its own steam, with its own enthusiasm and enterprise. (Second Reading)

Member for Wolverhampton South West: It would be a pity if the Bill were to leave this House without at least one Member on this side laying his curse upon it ... It has all the classic features of a Socialist Measure. It establishes bureaucratic boards in order to perceive commercial opportunities and promote commercial operations. ... Then there is the use, of course, of public money for various schemes which, if justifiable at all, are justifiable commercially, and to enable the State to buy its way into and take a share in private enterprise undertakings ... public money is used to pay grants towards new capital expenditure, in all cases expenditure which is justified only, if at all, by the prospect of a profit comparable with that which the same resources applied in any other way would attain. ... I was glad that my Right Hon. Friend [main spokesman for the Opposition] ... sought to justify the Bill only on the ground that there were distortions already existing which might be counteracted to some extent by the Bill... . But it seems to me that if we are faced with distortions of that kind the proper remedy is to remove the distortions and not superimpose a new set of distortions on top of them. (Third Reading)

Member for North Cornwall (Liberal): Other countries have very substantial subsidies for the tourist industry. Those of us who have stayed in foreign resorts know this only too well. ... The Conservatives may well come back to power, but they will not remove all the distortions. The distortions that make some parts of the Bill necessary are not just the distortions of the tax system, which the Conservatives may put right, but if they were to come back as a Free Trade Government committed to a floating exchange rate they would have no use for these subsidies. ... But no Government we are likely to get in the foreseeable future will come back committed to these views. It will probably be necessary for us to carry on distorting the economy *ad infinitum* to catch up with the subsidies of other Governments overseas.

Scottish and Welsh affairs

The Minister of State, Scottish Office: As a Scotsman I do not accept that Scotland and Wales are regions. They are nations ... (Third Reading)

Member for Orkney and Shetland: In Scotland, there have been widespread complaints about the projection of Scotland overseas by English authorities. At the moment there is widespread strong demand in Scotland that Scotland itself should be allowed to explain its own advantages, its own beauties to the world at large. ... there are some occasions and some aspects of tourism on which the Scottish want their country to be projected by themselves in their own way. The Minister will be making a very grave mistake if he thinks that this can be met by saying they have a seat or two on a British authority and can make representations to that authority. (Third Reading)

Coordination

Member for Westmorland: The economic planning councils already have a function in tourism. The Northern Planning Council produced a great book with a chapter on tourism. It makes studies and surveys of golf and water sports facilities, all part of the tourism functions of an economic planning council. In the North of England now the Rural Development Board is being set up under the Agricultural Act, 1967 and this body, too, has powers to give assistance to tourist facilities. In the Lake District, another amenity proposed for tourists is a theatre at Windermere. The Arts Council will help there. (Second Reading)

Member for South Shields: ... the Countryside Commission is concerned with the whole of the countryside and the sea coast. It is concerned not only with conducting surveys of facilities available for tourists but with those facilities themselves and their provision in a way which will do least damage to the natural beauty of the countryside, and also with ensuring that adequate provision will be made ... The last thing we want is confusion about the role of these two bodies. (Third Reading)

Regional boundaries

Member for Blyth: I do not consider that the regions which are necessary for local authority or industrial development purposes are necessarily the same as those which should be set up for the tourist trade and the holiday industry. (Second Reading)

Regulation and hotel classification

Member for Leeds, North East: We on this side of the House find that the voluntary system has worked extremely well, that there are a number of guides and that the guides are improving. We find it hard to justify registration, let alone classification, grading or even, perish the thought, inspection. What justification can there be, in the light of the growing and improving guides, for all the paraphernalia of staff, cost, inspection and penalty? (Second Reading)

Member for Eastbourne: Both the British Hotels and Restaurants

Association and the Catering Association have said that they regard the Bill as unnecessary and wholly unacceptable in its present form. (Second Reading)

Member for Wolverhampton, South West: ... Finally, we have provision made for the registration, classification and grading by a State authority of hotels, something which, if it is justifiable at all – that is to say, if it enhances the commercial efficiency of the industry – will be undertaken voluntarily on the initiative of the industry itself as indeed it is already to our knowledge here and in many other countries .... (Third Reading)

Constituency advocacy

The Member for Bury St Edmunds: First, the Government ought to help the tourist industry by providing the infrastructure – the roads, the communications, and so on. They have done the opposite. They have helped to reduce these things.

Second, they should be encouraging private investment in hotels and in tourism. But by their tax policy they have reduced and limited that investment.

Third, they should get out of the way of the private sector, which would be perfectly capable of providing what the Bill seeks without all the provision that the Government are making. But they are not getting out of the way of the private sector. On the contrary, they are getting in its way.

I am bound to conclude on a slightly different note. I have to change gear, because every hon. Member of this House has two obligations. He has an obligation clearly to state his view on national policy, which I have now done. But the Government have their majority and they will pass the Bill. Therefore, at that stage, every hon. Member of this House must accept two other obligations: first, if this public money is to be spent – and I regret that it is to be spent – to see that it is spent well; second, if any money is to be spent at all, it is part of my job to see that some of it comes to Bury St Edmunds. I want this money, which I do not think should be spent at all, to be spent well. If it is to be handed out, the English Tourist Board would be very wise to recognize the enormous advantages of spending some of it in East Anglia. (Third Reading)

Appendix 2

BTA backs hoteliers' claim for industry status (Caterer and Hotelkeeper, 6 August 1970)

The British Tourist Authority this week strongly backed the hotel industry's demand to be classified as an industry and not as a service trade.

It is recommending to the Government that the present grants and loans scheme should be extended for a year as an emergency measure, but that it should be followed by fiscal benefits similar to those enjoyed by the manufacturing industries.

BTA's recommendations were outlined on Monday by Sir Alexander Glen, BTA chairman, and Mr Michael Pickard, managing director of Trust Houses Forte and chairman of the authority's infrastructure committee.

Saying that the Government, 'as a matter of urgency', should extend the grants and loans scheme by a further 12 months, Mr Pickard pointed out that the scheme only became operative early this year, which means that only eight months remain for projects to obtain approval.

'The Authority is very fearful that a number of important projects will fail to qualify unless the terminal date is extended', he said.

BTA suggests that this should be followed by a system of capital allowances in regard to depreciation and obsolescence of hotel structures. When the grants scheme finally finishes, hotels should also benefit from investment grants similar to those paid to manufacturing industries, or from investment allowances should these be introduced in place of grants.

BTA and the three national boards are particularly concerned at the 'extreme difficulty' experienced by independently owned hotels in obtaining funds for development.

It is pointed out that these hotels play a vital part in tourism in Britain and that banks are not generally able to make loans available over a suitable period for capital purposes, a problem further aggravated by credit restrictions over recent years. The medium or longer term market has also been effectively closed to the independently owned hotel.

BTA's recommendations call for the establishment of a hotel development fund which would help independent hoteliers. They suggest something similar, but separate from, the scheme operated successfully by the Council for Small Industries in Rural Areas.

Mr Pickard said that no other industry had such a bad record of investment over the past 30 years. Of the 200 000 hotel bedrooms available in the UK only 15 000 were built in the past 30 years. Of those 14 000 had been built since 1959 and most of them were in London.

BTA is convinced that these measures are required if sound profitability is to be achieved by the hotel industry and if it is to obtain adequate finance for expansion. They are 'confident that Britain can double by 1975 the revenue which we earn from overseas visitors' if the recommendations are carried out.

The editor says ...

The recommendations being put to the Government by the British Tourist Authority are not new. As regularly as clockwork, the British Hotels and Restaurants Association, Caterers Association, *Caterer* and many individual hoteliers have called for similar action.

But this is the first time that the official Government bodies have made such a powerful plea on behalf of the hotel industry. Let's hope they are heeded.

BTA is calling for the re-classification of tourism as an industry instead of a service trade and for it to receive the appropriate recognition and benefits. The present temporary grants and loans scheme is no substitute for putting the industry on a proper capital basis with a workable taxation system.

Sir Alexander Glen and his team are giving the industry support where it needs it most. The potential rewards of tourism are rich and the Government would be foolish to disregard their views.

Appendix 3

A paper to the British Tourist Authority Conference on Tourism and the Environment (Royal Festival Hall, London, 11 November 1971), by Sir Mark Henig, Chairman, English Tourist Board

Please allow me to put you at ease from the beginning and assure you that I have no intention, either personally or in the name of the English Tourist Board, of intervening in fields which are specifically the responsibility of others, nor of discussing the techniques of conservation and preservation on which so many people in this audience are experts. I am moved to saying this, I must admit, out of a certain nostalgia for my days in local government. I am well aware that people in local government are jealous – and I believe rightly so – of local powers in regard to planning and I am still firmly of the opinion that local authorities must have these powers.

Tourist Boards are of course able to offer advice on tourism trends if needed, but on the other hand should be careful not to interfere in planning policy. For example, I regard it as important that the English Tourist Board keep out of any special pleading on behalf of individual applicants for planning permission.

The Tourist Board's top priority is to concern itself with the satisfaction of tourists and holidaymakers and with the sound economic performance of an industry. Tourism is one of the country's biggest employers. Its relative contribution to employment may increase, and, heaven knows, that is important. Tourism is potentially a powerful contributor to regional economic revitalisation.

Now, in looking to our own priorities, we find ourselves allies rather than opponents of those who are interested in planning and conservation. We are interested in the success of our planning system and in assisting the experts engaged in it when we can. We want to see that England's tourist resources are conserved – for example, that fine scenery is unspoilt, that historic buildings and streets are preserved and that the growth of tourism in itself does not upset the environment.

This would only be sensible. From the point of view of the tourist industry, an attractive environment is a saleable commodity and only a short-sighted industry would dare to put it at risk. One of the jobs of a tourist board is to help the industry take the longer view.

As far as the work of the planners is concerned, we can contribute then in two ways: by accepting realistically that the needs of tourism are only part of the so-called 'inputs' to the planning process and by feeding in our knowledge about tourism at the right stage. Also we can contribute by ensuring that environmental considerations are taken into account in our long term tourism marketing strategies.

How can the work of the English Tourist Board and the English regions produce this contribution and what is actually being done?

Right from the beginning of its existence, the English Tourist Board opted for regional organization which 'provides a framework for maximum possible involvement and closest possible co-operation'. This means the official tourist set-up is close to local planners and indeed closer to local opinion than a central organization could be.

As an illustration of these intentions, model regional constitutions which we drew up indicated that the purposes, among others, of the regional boards would be 'To stimulate the development of facilities and amenities for tourists in association with local authorities possessing planning powers ...'.

Further, regional boards (for example, Northumbria, South East, West Country) have taken an early opportunity to establish Tourist Development Panels whose members include representatives of planning authorities. Within a fairly flexible national framework we are able to recommend regional variations in tourism development policy because, clearly, tourism is at very different stages of development from one region to another. In one region the board might recommend minimal expansion in the capacity of tourism facilities and concentrate on spreading the season or increasing profitability; in another, priority might be given to expanding capacity and stimulating the growth of new markets.

It so happens, then, that the regional structure, created primarily to develop and market tourism efficiently, can also provide machinery whereby the impact of tourism on the environment can be discussed where discussion most counts – that is at the regional and local level. But let me emphasize: final decisions on planning rest with the planning authority and the Department of the Environment.

The regional framework is now established and early in 1972 eleven regional tourist boards will be operational. They will mostly, of course, be in their infancy but by 1973 they should be greatly strengthened. It has come through very clearly to us as we have helped to set up and develop regional tourist boards that the time had indeed come, not only to strengthen existing organizations and create new ones for some regions, but to suggest a new emphasis in their work. May I be allowed a generalization here and say that the pioneers of official tourist organizations in this country perceived them in almost exclusively promotional terms and a fine job they did. Tomorrow's professionals will see the job of a tourist board – for instance a regional tourist board – in the round: they will consider themselves engaged in a thinking, planning, managing activity at least as much concerned with encouraging the sound development and operation of tourist attractions and services as with promoting them.

At a national level, environmental considerations form an integral part of the English Tourist Board's future planning.

Let me quote from a document we published last May and which outlines, among other things, the strategy which we are adopting. In this we recognized the constraints on tourism growth.

While London can accommodate more overseas visitors we are assuming that a ceiling will be approached if not reached in the 1970s and that we must immediately look for growth in the flow of traffic to the provinces.

Any further marked expansion of peak traffic (in the resorts) would tend to put up capacity and exert pressure on such basic amenities as roads, parking facilities and beaches.

These factors influence the direction of future tourism strategy:

The main long term requirements would seem to be to spread tourism in space and time and to increase and spread the economic benefits of tourism.

Our first steps towards implementing these requirements have been:

- In our publicity campaigns aimed at encouraging our own people to take their holidays in England. We are emphasizing in our advertising those places and facilities which have sufficient capacity to take the numbers of tourists likely to be attracted. We are promoting more remote places with limited capacity to 'minority' markets which are unlikely to generate too many tourists in relation to the facilities available.
- We are opening a series of points-of-entry bureaux for overseas visitors – the first is already in operation in Dover – which gives the opportunity of influencing the direction of tourist movements and of promoting regions outside London.
- In operating the scheme of financial support for financial projects in Development Areas we are taking the opportunity to use our financial powers to back developments which help relieve pressure in crowded tourist areas (for example, in the northern part of the Lake District).

The guidelines published by the English Tourist Board suggest that projects for which our financial assistance is sought should be 'designed to extend the season and help relieve overcrowding at peak times'.

In the last analysis, however efficient or knowledgeable the official tourist bodies may be, tourism cannot be developed in isolation and its growth must depend on what the community wants, and in deciding what it wants, the community will undoubtedly be very conscious of the impact of tourism on its everyday life. The English Tourist Board considers this relationship between tourism and the local community very important and worthy of study. Let me give you an example.

We have commissioned a survey of residents' attitudes towards tourism in York where we are carrying out, in conjunction with the City Council, a large study of the City's tourism business. We wanted to know how York residents felt about tourism.

The most concise single expression of residents' opinion emerges from results to the question 'taking everything into account, both the good things and the bad things, should York try to attract more visitors, try to cut down the number of visitors, take any other action or leave things as they are?'

There was a decisive opinion that York should attract more visitors, with an average of three-quarters of residents expressing this favourable attitude towards an expansion of tourism.

Yorkists were asked whether, from the residents' point of view, they thought there were any advantages from tourists coming to their city. Most of them spontaneously mentioned some advantage and most mentioned more than one. The advantage cited by far the most frequently, both in the off-peak period and the peak period, was the extra money that tourists bring to York.

The social advantages, as seen by the citizens of York, were many and varied. There were those who said it was nice to meet people from other parts of Britain, and from other countries, others who said visitors made York more lively or interesting; and others that the special tourist events attracted them too. Many other amenities such as buses, parks and theatres, were mentioned as being improved by the influence of the tourist, and one in ten referred to the consequent preservation of old buildings.

On average each person named about five advantages with the

emphasis on the financial aspects, social benefits, and preservation and improvement of the built environment.

To ensure that we had a balanced opinion of tourism residents were asked if there were any disadvantages. There is a contrast between the nature of the advantages described above, and the nature of the disadvantages, which centre round three things: traffic blocks, pavements too crowded, parking problems.

It was more the newest residents, those who had lived in York no more than ten years, and particularly – but not surprisingly – those who were themselves car users, who mentioned such disadvantages.

The research at York is an example of formal research into community reactions to tourism. We will probably do similar research on a regional basis. This will supplement the knowledge we have gained in many meetings up and down the country, which I have chaired, and which have been an essential preliminary to the setting up of regional tourist boards. Consultations will continue and will greatly enhance our knowledge of the regional and local views as the structure consolidates.

One of the principal functions of the official tourist body – at local, regional, or national level – is to help the community to discuss tourism and to say what it expects of tourism development. We have a machinery that permits the sum total of local views and expectations to influence the regional view, and the sum total of regional views to determine the national view.

With the prospect of a steady growth of tourism by our own people within their own country plus an enormous growth of overseas visitors amounting to perhaps fifteen millions per year by 1980, it will be increasingly important for us to understand how the community in England as a whole views tourism, what it expects of tourism in economic and social terms and how it wants tourism to develop. It will be up to us to get this information feeding up from the grass roots, where tourists and the local communities really come together, via the regional structure, to formulate a national view, and it will be up to us to communicate this view to all those who are interested.

Appendix 4

Memorandum on National Parks and Tourism, issued by the Countryside Commission and the English Tourist Board, 1978

National Parks and Tourism

1. In paragraph 53 of Circular 4176 the Secretary of State for the Environment fully endorsed the Sandford Committee's recommendation that respect for the environmental qualities of the national parks should be a primary aim in the development and management of tourist accommodation, and referred to the establishing of 'heads of agreement' between the Countryside Commission and the national tourist boards, This document is an endeavour to meet that point.

2. The national parks were designated under

the National Parks and Access to the Countryside Act 1949 for the twin purposes of preserving and enhancing their natural beauty and of promoting their enjoyment by the public.

3. The Countryside Commission replaced the National Parks Commission under the Countryside Act 1968 as the independent statutory agency responsible for designating national parks in England and Wales. They advise Ministers and others on national park policies, planning, administration and finance. They also have statutory duties to keep under review all matters relating to the conservation and enhancement of the natural beauty of the countryside generally, to the provision and improvement of facilities for its enjoyment and to the need to secure public access for open-air recreation.

4. The English Tourist Board was established under the Development of Tourism Act 1969 with a statutory duty to promote tourism to and within England, in particular to encourage people to visit England and people living in England to take their holidays there; and to encourage the provision and improvement of tourist facilities and amenities in England. The English Tourist Board has the statutory duty to advise government, local authorities and other statutory undertakers on tourism matters.

5. The Countryside Commission and the English Tourist Board note:

a. the obligations of Section 11 of the Countryside Act 1968 which says: 'In the exercise of their functions relating to land under any enactment every Minister, Government Department and public body shall have regard to the desirability of conserving the natural beauty and amenity of the countryside';

b. the acceptance by the Government that there will be situations where the two statutory purposes of the national parks are irreconcilable, and that when this happens, priority must be given to the conservation of natural beauty.

6. The Countryside Commission and the English Tourist Board accept that:

a. the social and economic well-being of the residents of the national parks is an essential consideration in achieving the statutory objectives of national parks, and employment in the tourist and related service industries is an important part of the economy of most national parks;

b. recreation and tourist use of national parks must be maintained in such manner and at such levels as not to impair natural beauty and amenity;

c. constraint should be placed on the growth of bed space and associated tourist facilities in those national parks with heavy visitor use. It is also important to ensure that there are areas where peace and quiet should predominate. There is scope for promoting off peak holidays and improving visitor facilities and services to strengthen the economy of tourism;

d. when constraints are exercised, alternative facilities and services will need to be provided to meet the demand for facilities elsewhere, possibly outside the national park;

e. close co-operation and integration of services as between national park and tourist authorities is essential to give better guidance to visitors and to avoid duplication of effort and a conflict of aims;

f. national park and regional tourist boards should agree, and incorporate within the national park plan, policies on the signposting of tourist facilities and the means of providing information about the availability of tourist accommodation;

g. improved public transport systems are a help to visitors, and a benefit to the local community.

7. The Countryside Commission and the English Tourist Board consider that:

a. the national park plan is likely to be a most effective mechanism for the harmonization of policies within national parks, and commend to the national park boards and committees, and the regional tourist boards, the worth of close, patient and continuing dialogue;

b. the structure plans covering the national parks should relate policy for tourism and day recreation in the national parks to adjoining areas and the national park authorities and the regional tourist boards, acting together with local authorities, should co-operate in achieving that objective.

Countryside Commission
John Dower House
Crescent Place
Cheltenham, Glos GL50 3RA

English Tourist Board
Grosvenor Gardens
London SW1W 0DU

April 1978

Appendix 5

Memorandum of Understanding between the British Council and the British Tourist Authority, 1998

Summary

The British Council ('The Council') and the British Tourist Authority ('the BTA) will initiate a programme of collaboration designed both to support the Government's drive for a more up-to-date and coordinated promotion of Britain overseas and to assist each organization to achieve its objectives more effectively. The collaboration will focus on local sharing of overhead costs, research and market intelligence in areas of mutual interest, and promotional activity on behalf of Britain determined on an individual country basis.

It will be led for the Council and the BTA by Regional and Overseas Directors who will ensure that the benefits of collaboration are closely monitored and reviewed.

Context

The Government has established a working group, Panel 2000, of which the Council and the BTA are members, to make recommendations for the more concerted promotion of Britain overseas, including closer collaboration between national agencies. Both the Council and the BTA welcome this initiative and propose to set exemplary standards of consultation and collaboration between their organizations.

Activities

The Council, which promotes a better understanding of Britain overseas through educational, scientific and cultural co-operations and the teaching of English, and the BTA, which promotes and markets Britain abroad as a tourism destination, believe that by practical working together they can better serve their own individual objectives and the national interest.

The Council is represented in 230 cities in 110 countries. It has over 200 information centres and 118 teaching centres, all of which attract potential visitors to Britain. It provides a range of market intelligence and services in English language teaching, education and training and other sectors, to UK suppliers through its international network.

The BTA has 43 offices in 36 countries. These offices provide:
- Information to potential visitors about Britain and to the local travel trade about selling Britain, including extensive print
- Intelligence for British suppliers about local markets, their needs and potential, based on consumer research
- Public Relations and media activity to promote Britain

In addition, selected offices carry out a range of tactical marketing activities, often with trade partners, targeted at specific market segments; some offices also carry out major consumer advertising campaigns, often with partners.

Principles

The Council and the BTA are separate organizations with separate objectives and purposes. Both organizations need to deliver maximum value from their grant-in-aid budgets. They look for opportunities to share costs with appropriate partners and to co-finance market research, publications and other activities where their respective programmes suggest that this would be useful.

Both the Council and the BTA attach priority to building strong partner relations in Britain, and to ensuring that their partners know about, use and value their services. In many sectors, such as education and English language teaching, these partner groups are shared by both organizations.

There are opportunities for practical collaboration in cities where both agencies are present; in addition, the Council wishes to explore ways in which the BTA might use the Council's network in appropriate markets where the BTA itself does not have a separate presence.

Both the Council and BTA believe that the proposals for practical co-operation must be worked out at the level of individual countries, be based on high quality market research and be under regional direction within the spirit of this Memorandum.

Both the Council and the BTA, whilst working in co-operation in the areas outlined below, will retain their own distinct identities.

Areas for cooperation

The Council and the BTA propose to cooperate in the following areas subject to their individual assessments of market needs, their respective objectives and priorities, the availability of resources, and subject to agreement by Regional and Overseas Directors:

General:
- Regular cross-briefing of each other's promotional strategies, plans and initiatives.
- Collaboration/cooperation on individual initiatives where this is appropriate for local market needs.

- Sharing, and where appropriate commissioning, qualitative and quantitative consumer research.
- Joint activities to encourage overseas students to study in Britain at accredited English language schools, and other schools, colleges and universities.
- Showcasing of Britain in selected markets as agreed, for example in arts, cultural activities and education.
- Development and cross-promotion of websites.

Physical:

The provision of:

- Cross-signalling of each other's offices with contact information, based on a consistent style of presentation.
- BTA information corners in Council offices.

A staffed information desk in the Council's offices in countries where there are common objectives and where the Council is present and the BTA is not.

Jointly-managed Britain information centres.

Co-location of offices.

Priority will be given, in the first instance, to cooperation in Central and Eastern Europe, Latin America and Asia.

Implementation

The overall programme of collaboration will be led from Britain by:

- Edmund Marsden, Assistant Director-General of the Council and Jonathan Griffin, Marketing Services Director of the BTA.

Detailed implementation will be supervised, at the country level, by the British Council's Regional Directors and the BTA's Overseas Directors. Currently these are:

British Council

John Hawkins	Africa and South Asia
Michael O'Sullivan	East Asia and Pacific
Peter Sandiford	Americas
Ray Thomas	Middle East and North Africa
Jim Whittell	West and Southern Europe
Anne Wozencraft	East and Central Europe

British Tourist Authority
- Jeff Hamblin   The Americas
- Roger Johnson   Europe
- Rob Franklin   Asia Pacific, Middle East and Africa

Review and follow-up

British Council Regional Directors and BTA Overseas Directors will report annually on collaborative activities and the benefits delivered. Attention will be given to four key areas:
- Strategic issues
- Premises
- Joint working
- Information Services

This Memorandum will be reviewcd after three years.

Signed for the British Council
Dr David Drewry
Director-General

Signed for the British Tourist Authority
David Quarmby
Chairman

Date: 27 July 1998

Appendix 6

The members of the Tourism Forum, convened by the Department of Culture, Media and Sport (UK) and the sectors represented, October 1997

Tourist Boards

David Quarmby	English Tourist Board (ETB) and British Tourist Authority (BTA)
Anthony Sell	BTA
Tim Bartlett	ETB
Patrick McKenna	BTA Board
Michael Elliot	Heart of England Tourist Board
Dorothy Naylor	North West Tourist Board

Business Groups

Peter Agar	Confederation of British Industry
Brendan Burns	Federation of Small Businesses

Trade, Industry and Professional Bodies
    Michael Hirst   Joint Hospitality Industry Congress
    Jeremy Logie   British Hospitality Association
    Ken Robinson   Tourism Society
    Stephen Moss   Restaurateurs Association of Great Britain and Springboard UK
    James Spencer   British Holiday and Home Parks Association

Local Authorities
    Peter Hampson   British Resorts Association
    Phillip Swan   Local Government Association
    Cllr John Price   Local Government Association
    Ken Male   Bournemouth Tourism

Larger Hospitality Businesses
    Charles Allen   Granada Group
    Peter Chappelow   Holiday Cottages Group and ETB
    Peter Moore   Centre Parcs and ETB
    John Jarvis   Jarvis Hotels and BTA
    David Thomas   Whitbread
    Sir Denys Henderson   Rank Warner

Visitor Attractions
    Michael Jolly   Tussauds Group
    John Lee   Association of Leading Visitor Attractions and ETB

International Tourism   Geoffrey Lipman World Travel and Tourism Council
    Stephen Freudmann   Association of British Travel Agents
    Richard Tobias   British Incoming Tour Operators Association

Heritage and Culture
    Pam Alexander   English Heritage
    David Beeton   Historic Royal Palaces Agency
    Martin Drury   National Trust
    Graham Devlin   Arts Council
    Tim Mason   Museums and Galleries Commission

Environment and Countryside
    Richard Wakeford   Countryside Commission
    Margaret Clarke   Rural Development Commission
    Bill Breakell   North Yorks Moors National Park

Training and Education
David Harborne	Hospitality Training Foundation
Conrad Lashley	Council for Hospitality Management Education
David Wood	Hotel Catering and International Management Association

Trade Union   Donna Covey   GMB

Travel and Transport
Robert Ayling	British Airways and BTA
Brian Barrett	Virgin Rail Group
Sir John Egan	BAA, London Tourist Board and ex-BTA
Alan Britten	BTA and ex-Mobil
Peter Ford	London Transport

Consumers
Patricia Yates	*Holiday Which?*, Consumers Association

People with Disabilities   Tourism for All Consortium
and Special Needs
Bob Taylor

Small Tourism Operators
Nicola Hayward	Seaview Hotel
Gulshan Jaffer	Hotel La Place
Akbar Verjee	Oki Hotel Kensington

The role of the new Forum was to: provide a conduit for consultation between DCMS Ministers and the tourism, hospitality and leisure industry; assist coordination of the efforts of all the various parties with an interest in developing the success of tourism; advise DCMS and the Tourist Boards on the development and implementation of a strategy for the further development of tourism; assist with implementation of the various action plans arising out of the overall strategy, through working groups of experts on specific issues; and monitor, review and update the strategy as necessary.

(Source: DCMS Press Release, 10 October 1997)

Appendix 7

Department of Culture, Media and Sport. Tourism Division Staffing and Subjects Covered

Head of Division
Personal Assistant
Tourism Advisor

Government and Industry Branch (7 staff):
Tourism summit and support for cross-Whitehall Steering Group, liaison with ETC in respect of Tourism Forum, education, training, skills development issues (including NTOs and TECs), New Deal and employment issues, competitiveness (including all DTI related issues such as Business Links, small firms, trade associations, benchmarking), sector challenge, consumer issues, widening access and social inclusion, all fiscal and regulatory issues, whether EU or OGD related, hospitality and catering, food and drink issues, planning, sustainable tourism, rural and urban issues, beaches and bathing water, transport (excluding APD), RTBs (includ-

ing casework, visits correspondence) – Heart of England, North West of England, Cumbria, Southern England.

Domestic Tourism Branch (7 staff):

Sponsorship and monitoring of ETC, London policy and casework including GLA, ETC strategy and planning, accommodation rating schemes, regional structures and regional development agencies, Local Authority issues, seasides, piers, honours, divisional finance and administration, appointments – East of England, London, Northumbria.

International Tourism Branch (5 staff):

Sponsorship of BTA (including strategy, business planning, financial monitoring and appointments), overseas promotion and Britain's image, international issues, UK representation in European Union, policy on EU regulation, business tourism, IT applications and booking systems, tourism research and statistics, devolution, language schools, tourist guides, creative industries, heritage, arts and culture, visitor attractions, sport and leisure, public expenditure, divisional business planning, public enquiries, RTBs – South East of England, West Country, Yorkshire.

Stats Branch:

Statistical information, advice and briefing for DCMS, including tourism policy.

(*Source:* DCMS, June 2000)

Bibliography

The bibliography lists over 200 books and documents relevant to the study of governments and tourism. A small number of the papers listed are unpublished. Teachers and researchers may obtain copies via e-mail on application to: judgedjj@aol.com.

Adam, T.R. (1995) *Modern Colonialism: Institutions and Policies*, Doubleday and Co., New York

Advertising Works 10 (1999) Cases from the IPA Advertising Effectiveness Awards, Institute of Practitioners in Advertising (N. Kendall, ed.), NTC Publications, Henley-on-Thames

AFCI (1989) *Hôtellerie et tourisme: 50 ans de normes hôtelières françaises*, Assemblée des chambres françaises de commerce et d'industrie, Paris

Airey, D. and Butler, R. (1999) *Tourism at the Regional Level*, Report of the 49th AIEST Congress, Editions AIEST, Vol. 41, St-Gall, Switzerland

Anon (n.d.) *Amish Farming in Knox County*, Kenyon College, Gambier, Ohio
http://www.kenyon.edu/projects/famfarm/whatis/amish.htm

Ashworth, G.J. and Voogd, H. (1990) *Selling the City: Marketing Approaches in Public Sector Urban Planning*, Belhaven Press, London and New York

Association of District Councils (1988) *It's the District Councils who Deliver*, ADC, London

Australian Bureau of Statistics (n.d.) *Framework for the Collection and Publication of Tourism Statistics*, Belconnen ACT

Baker, M.J. (1983) *Marketing: An Introductory Text*, Macmillan Press, London

Barthes, R. (1972) *Mythologies*, Jonathan Cape, London

Beaver, A. (1993) *Mind Your Own Travel Business*, Beaver, London

Bellamy, D. and de Savary, P. (eds) (1990) 'Land's End', unpublished report for the Land's End & John O'Groats Co. Ltd

Bender, T. (1996) 'Transforming tourism', *Context 44*, Summer Issue

Bieger, T. (1998) 'Reengineering Destination Marketing Organisations – the Case of Switzerland', Discussion Paper, 33rd TRC Meeting at Brijuni, University of St-Gall, Switzerland

Boniface, B.G. and Cooper, C. (1995) *The Geography of Travel and Tourism*, Butterworth-Heinemann, Oxford

Bramwell, B. (1998) 'User satisfaction and product development in urban tourism', *Tourism Management*, Vol. 19 (1)

Bramwell, B. and Broom, G. (1989) 'TDAPs', *Insights*, BTA/ETB, London

Bramwell, B. and Rawding, L. (1994) 'Tourism marketing organizations in industrial cities', *Tourism Management*, Vol. 15 (6)

Bramwell, B. and Sharman, A. (1999) 'Collaboration in local tourism policymaking', *Annals of Tourism Research*, Vol. 26, No. 2

Brewton, C. and Witham, G. (1998) 'United States tourism policy. Alive but not well', *Cornell Hotel and Restaurant Administration Quarterly*, Vol. 39 (1), pp. 50–9

British Tourist Authority (1971) Annual Report 1970/71, BTA, London

British Tourist Authority (1972) Annual Report 1971/72, BTA, London

British Tourist Authority (1973) Annual Report 1972/73, BTA, London

British Tourist Authority (1974) Annual Report 1973/74, BTA, London

British Tourist Authority (1977) Annual Report 1976/77, BTA, London

British Tourist Authority (1984) Annual Report 1983/84, BTA, London

British Tourist Authority (1974) *Britain – The Broad Perspective*, BTA, London

British Tourist Authority (1975) *The British Travel Association, 1929–1969*, BTA, London

British Tourist Authority (1982) *Legislation Affecting Tourism in Britain*, BTA, London

British Tourist Authority (1984) *Strategy for Growth, 1984–88*, BTA, London

British Tourist Authority (1989) *Strategy for Growth, 1989–1993*, BTA, London

British Tourist Authority (1999) *Digest of Tourist Statistics*, No. 22, BTA, London

British Travel Association (1968) Annual Report, 1967/68, British Travel Association, London

British Travel Association (1968) Annual Report, 1968/69, British Travel Association, London

Brown, F. (1998) *Tourism Reassessed: Blight or Blessing?*, Butterworth-Heinemann, Oxford

Burkart, A.J. and Medlik, S. (1982) *Tourism Past, Present and Future*, 2nd edn, Heinemann, London

Burns, P. (1997) 'Master Planners and Master Planning and Development in the Third World', PhD Thesis, University of Surrey

Cabinet Office Enterprise Unit (1985) *Pleasure, Leisure and Jobs*, HMSO, London

Cadieu, P. (1999) *Droit et politiques du tourisme local*, La Lettre du Cadre Territorial, Voiron

Cassen, L. (1994) *Travel in the Ancient World*, Johns Hopkins Paperbacks, London

Caterer and Hotelkeeper, weekly, issues for the years 1970 to 1972 inclusive, Quadrant House, Sutton, Surrey

Chachage, C.S.L. (1998) 'Land, Forests and People in Finnish Aid in Tanzania: Some Preliminary Observations', FAD Working Paper 2/98, Institute of Development Studies, University of Helsinki in collaboration with Department of Sociology, University of Dar es Salaam

Chambre régionale de commerce et d'industrie, Provence–Alpes–Côte d'Azur–Corse (1997) *Le tourisme, Mémento*, Marseille, France, 1997

Chartered Institute of Public Finance and Accountancy (annually) *Leisure and Recreation Statistics*, London

Chesterton, G.K. (1936) *Autobiography of G.K. Chesterton*, Sheed and Ward, New York

CHL Consulting (1998) 'Regional Air Travel Review, South Pacific' (unpublished), Dublin

Chon, K.-S. and Olsen, M.D. (1990) 'Applying the strategic management process in the management of tourism organizations', *Tourism Management,* September.

Chon, K-S. and Singh, A. (1995) 'Marketing resorts to 2000: review of trends in the USA', *Tourism Management*, Vol. 16, No. 6

Choy, D.J.L. (1991) 'Tourism planning. The case for "market failure"', *Tourism Management*, December

Clarke, A. (1981) 'Coastal development in France', *Annals of Tourism Research*, VIII (3), pp. 448–60.

Commission of the European Communities (1998) 'A European Strategy to Support the Development of Sustainable Tourism in the Developing Countries'. Communication from the Commission to the Council and the European Parliament, CEC, Brussels

Cook, F.P. (1981) *Ombudsman,* BKT Publications, London

Cooper, C., Fletcher, J., Gilbert, D. and Wanhill, S. (1993) *Tourism: Principles and Practice*, Pitman Publishing, London

Countryside Commission (1997) *UK Day Visits Survey 1996*, Countryside Commission, Cheltenham

Daily Telegraph, Leaders of 23 and 24 May 2000, and article of 25 May 2000, p. 30

Davidson, T.L. (1998) 'What are travel and tourism: are they really an industry?', in W.F. Theobald (ed.), *Global Tourism*, 2nd edn, Butterworth-Heinemann, Oxford

Department of Culture, Media and Sport (1998a) *Measuring the Local Impact of Tourism. An Introduction to the Main Issues*, DCMS, London

Department of Culture, Media and Sport (1998b) *Practical Guide to Local Area Tourism Models*, DCMS, London

Department of Culture, Media and Sport (1998c) *The EU Tourism Statistics Directive*, DCMS, London

Department of Culture, Media and Sport (1998d) *Tourism Forum Bulletin*, March, DCMS, London

Department of Culture, Media and Sport (1999a) *Tomorrow's Tourism – A Growth Industry for the New Millennium*, DCMS, London

Department of Culture, Media and Sport (1999b) *A New Cultural Framework*, DCMS, London

Department of Culture, Media and Sport (2000) Report on Tourism Summit, April 2000, DCMS, London

Department of Employment (1986) *Action for Jobs*, DoE, London

Department of the Environment (1979) *Local Government and the Development of Tourism*, Circular 13/79, HMSO, London

Department of the Environment (1992) *Planning Policy Guidance 21: Tourism,* Department of Environment and HMSO, London

Department of the Environment, Transport and the Regions, Department of National Heritage (1994) *Planning Policy Guidance 15: Planning and the Historic Environment*, HMSO, London

Department for International Development, Environment Policy Department (1999) *Changing the Nature of Tourism*, Department for International Development, London

Department of Trade and Industry (1998) *A Guide to Working Time Regulations*, DTI, London

Downes, J.J. (1997) 'European Union: progress on a common tourism sector policy', *Travel and Tourism Analyst*, No. 1, Travel and Tourism Intelligence, London

Dryden, J. (trans.) (n.d.).Plutarch's *Lycurgus*, The Internet Classics Archive: http://classics.mit.edu/Plutarch/lycurgus.html

The Economist (1999) 'Undoing Britain?', *The Economist,* 6–12 November

Economist Intelligence Unit (various dates) International Tourism Reports on Fiji: No. 2, 1994; No. 1, 1996; No. 1, 1998, EIU, London

Edgell, D.L. (1990) *International Tourism Policy*, Van Nostrand Reinhold, New York

Edwards, A. (1992) *International Tourism Forecasts to 2005*, Economist Intelligence Unit, London

Edwards, A. (1993) *Price Competitiveness of Holiday Destinations*, Economist Intelligence Unit, London

Elliott, J.(1997) *Tourism Politics and Public Sector Management*, Routledge, London and New York

English Tourist Board (1971) 'Towards a National Tourism Marketing and Development Strategy', BTA/ETB Archives

English Tourist Board (1972) Annual Report, 1971/72, ETB, London

English Tourist Board (1973) Annual Report, 1972/73, ETB, London

English Tourist Board (1974) Annual Report, 1973/74, ETB, London

English Tourist Board (1983) England's North Country Campaign: National Opinion Poll Survey for the English Tourist Board, BTA/ETB Archives

English Tourist Board (1987) *A Vision for England: Tourism Development*, ETB, London

English Tourist Board and Employment Department Group (1991) *Tourism and the Environment. Maintaining the Balance* (synthesis: *Report of the Historic Towns Working Group*; *Report of the Heritage Sites Working Group*; *Report of the Countryside Working Group*), ETB and Employment Department, London

English Tourist Board (1988a) *Visitors in the Countryside*, Proceedings of a Rural Tourism Conference, ETB, London

English Tourist Board (1988b) *Visitors in the Countryside. Rural Tourism: A Development Strategy*, ETB, London

English Tourist Board (1997) 'Understanding the Domestic Tourism Market', unpublished report, BTA/ETB Archives

English Tourist Board (1999) *Opening Pandora's Box*, Report of a Conference to Discuss a Statutory Registration Scheme for Tourist Accommodation, ETB, London

English Tourist Board, Countryside Commission and Rural Development Commission (1990) *Shades of Green: Working Towards Green Tourism in the Countryside*, Conference Proceedings, ETB, London

English Historic Towns Forum (1994) *Getting it Right – a Guide to Visitor Management in Historic Towns*, EHTF, The Huntingdon Centre, Bath

European Commission (various dates) Publications of the Tourism Unit, DG XXIII, European Commission, Brussels

European Commission (1995a) *Tourism and the European Union: A Practical Guide* (eds Bates and Wacker), Office for Official Publications of the European Communities, Luxembourg

European Commission (1995b) *The Role of the Union in the Field of Tourism*, Commission Green Paper, European Commission, Brussels

European Tourism Action Group (1999) *Europe's Tourism. How Important Is It?*, Hensel Press Ltd, Great Britain

European Travel Commission (1999) *Survey of 22 Member NTOs*, ETC, Brussels

Ferras, R., Picheral, H. and Vielzeuf, B. (1979) *Languedoc Roussillon*, Flammarion et Editions Famot, France

Gee, C.Y., Choy, D.J.L. and Makens, J.C. (1984) *The Travel Industry*, AVI Publishing Co., Westport, CT

Gillmor, D.A. (1998) 'Republic of Ireland: expanding tourism sector', in A.M. Williams and G. Shaw (eds), *Tourism and Economic Development,* John Wiley and Sons, Chichester

Glen, Sir Alexander (1975) *Footholds against a Whirlwind*, Hutchinson, London

Global Town's Ni'ihau (1999) web site: http://www.global-town.com/about_hawaii/niihau.htm

Gold, J.R. and Ward, S.V. (1994) *Place Promotion. The Use of Publicity and Marketing to Sell Towns and Regions*, John Wiley and Sons, Chichester

Gork, L. (1998) *Mea Sharim*, BikeAbout web site: http://www.bike-about.org/resource/israel10.htm

Gorman, Teresa (2000) *A Parliament for England*, June Press, England

Greater London Council (1974) *Tourism in London: A Plan for Management*, GLC, London

Heeley, J. (1989) 'Role of National Tourist Organizations in the United Kingdom', in S.F. Witt and L. Moutinho (eds), *Tourism Marketing and Management Handbook*, Prentice Hall International (UK) Ltd, Hemel Hempstead

Heeley, J. (2000) 'The English Experience of Public–Private Sector Partnerships in Tourism, and the Primacy of the Local Level', full text unpublished

Hewison, R. (1987) *The Heritage Industry*, Methuen Paperback, London

House of Commons (various dates) *Parliamentary Debates* (Hansard), HMSO, London

House of Commons (1969) Report of Standing Committee E, 13 March 1969, HMSO, London

House of Commons: National Heritage Committee (1997) Third Report, Tourism: The Government's response to the Committee's first report of Session 1996–97, The Stationery Office, London

House of Commons: Culture, Media and Sport Committee (1997) Fourth Special Report, Session 1997–99, HMSO, London

House of Commons: Culture, Media and Sport Committee (1999) Sixth Special Report, 1998–99, HMSO, London

Huckshorn, K. (1997) 'As visitors discover Sapa, minority peoples find ways to boost once-meager incomes', *Asia Report*, 26 December, Mercury Centre, Silicon Valley, California

Jefferson, A. and Lickorish, L. (1991) *Marketing Tourism. A Practical Guide*, 2nd edn, Longman, Harlow

Jeffries, D.J.(1968) 'BTA Paris Office Marketing Proposal', unpublished

Jeffries, D. (1971) 'Defining the tourist product and its significance in tourism marketing', *Tourist Review*, Vol. XVII, No. 1

Jeffries, D. (1978) *The British Away from Home*, Tourism Society, London

Jeffries, D.J. (1985) 'The Development of Tourism', Inaugural Lecture, University of Strathclyde, Glasgow, Scotland

Jeffries, D.(1989) 'Selling Britain– a case for privatisation?', *Travel and Tourism Analyst*, No. 1, Economist Intelligence Unit, London

Jeffries, D.J. (1993) 'Terms of Reference for the Preparation of a Tourism Master Plan for Tanzania', unpublished

Jeffries, D.J. (1999) 'Personal Memoir on the History of Regional Tourist Board Financing in England', unpublished

Jeffries, D.J. (2000) Draft EU Financing Proposal: 'Use of the Logical

Framework in Programme Planning for the Development of Cultural Tourism in Syria', unpublished

Jowett, B. (trans.) (n.d.) Plato's *The Laws*, The Internet Classics Archive: http://classics.mit.edu/Plato/laws.html

Judd, D.R. (1995) 'Promoting tourism in US cities', *Tourism Management*, Vol. 16, No. 3

Keller, P. and Smeral, F. (1997) Background Paper, WTO/CEU–ETC Joint Seminar on Tourism Responsibilities of European Governments, World Tourism Organization, Madrid

Kent County Council and Comité Régional de Tourisme Nord – Pas de Calais, *Transmanche Tourism Facts 2000*, Maidstone, Kent

Klemm, M. (1996) 'Languedoc Roussillon: adapting the strategy', *Tourism Management*, Vol. 17, No. 2

Kotler, P. (1988)1997 *Marketing Management*, 8th edn, Prentice Hall International, Englewood Cliffs, NJ

Kotler, P. (1991) *Marketing Management: Analysis, Planning and Control,* 7th edn, Prentice Hall International, London

Kotler, P. and Armstrong, G. (1999) *Principles of Marketing*, 8th edn, Prentice Hall International, Englewood Cliffs, NJ

Kotler, P., Haider, D.H. and Rein, I. (1993) *Marketing Places*, The Free Press, New York

Lane, B. (ed.) (2000) *Tourism Collaboration and Partnership: Politics, Practice and Sustainability*, Channel View Publications, Clevedon, England

Leiper, N.(1990) *Tourism Systems*, Department of Management Systems, Occasional Paper 2, Massey University, New Zealand

Lonely Planet (2000) *Destination Italy*, Internet edition: http://www.lonelyplanet.com/dest/eur/ita.htm

MacCannell, Dean (1999) *The Tourist. A New Theory of the Leisure Class*, rev. edn, University of California Press, Berkeley and Los Angeles

McClaren, D. (1998) *Rethinking Tourism and Ecotravel*, Kumarian Press, West Hartford, CT

McIntosh, R.W., Goeldner, C.R. and Ritchie, J.R.B. (1995) *Tourism Principles, Practices and Philosophies*, 7th edn, John Wiley and Sons, Chichester

March, R. (1994) 'Tourism marketing myopia', *Tourism Management*, Vol. 15 (6)

Meades, J. (1999) 'We're on the road to nowhere', *The Times,* 'Weekend', Saturday 11 September, p. 1

Medlik, S. (1996) *Dictionary of Travel, Tourism and Hospitality*, 2nd edn, Butterworth-Heinemann, Oxford

Medlik, S. and Middleton, V.T.C. (1973) 'The tourist product and its marketing implications', *International Tourism Quarterly*, No. 3

Meethan, K. (1998) 'New tourism for old? Policy developments in Cornwall and Devon', *Tourism Management*, Vol. 19, No. 6

Michaud, J-L. (1995) *Les Institutions du tourisme*, Presses Universitaires de France, Paris

Middleton, V.T.C. (1994) 'Managing the marketing mix. Overall tourism product', in S.F. Witt and L. Moutinho (eds), *Tourism Marketing and Management Handbook*, Prentice Hall, New York

Middleton, V.T.C. (1996) *Marketing in Travel and Tourism*, Butterworth-Heinemann, Oxford

Middleton, V.T.C. and Hawkins, R. (1998) *Sustainable Tourism. A Marketing Perspective.* Butterworth-Heinemann, Oxford

Mill, R. and Morrison, A. (1992) *The Tourism System*, 2nd edn, Prentice Hall International Editions, Englewood Cliffs, NJ

Millennium Commission (1999) Annual Report and Accounts, 1998–99, The Millennium Commission, London

Molner, J. (1989) 'In an era of mass travel, tourism becomes the new colonial power', *Seattle Times*, 10 September

More, Sir Thomas ([1516] 1901) *Utopia*, The Internet Wiretap edition from *Ideal Commonwealths*, P.F. Collier & Son, New York; http://www.piracy.com/works/utopia.txt

Morrison, A.M., Bruen, S.M. and Andersen, D.J. (1998) 'Convention and Visitor Bureaus in the USA', *Journal of Travel and Tourism Marketing*, Vol. 7, No. 1

Municipal Yearbook (1982) Newman Books, London

Municipal Yearbook (1995) Newman Books, London

Murphy, P.E. (1985) *Tourism. A Community Approach*, Routledge, New York and London

Mutch, A. (1996) 'The English Tourist Network Automation Project: a case study in interorganizational system failure', *Tourism Management*, Vol. 17, No. 8

Neil, J. (1990) *Bellrive Foundation – Save the Alps*, press information from the Bellrive Foundation, 2 June

Nicholson-Lord, D. (1997) *The Politics of Travel: Is Tourism Just Colonialism in Another Guise?*, The Nation Digital Edition: http://www.thenation.com/

Organisation for Economic Co-operation and Development Tourism

Committee (1989) *Tourism Policy and International Tourism*, OECD, Paris

Organisation for Economic Co-operation and Development Tourism Committee (1993) *Tourism Policy and International Tourism in OECD Member Countries, 1990–1991*, OECD, Paris

Parker, Sir Peter (1979) *British Tourism – the Next 50 Years*, BTA, London

Pearce, D. (1988) 'Tourism and regional development in the European Community', *Tourism Management*, March

Pearce, D. (1989) *Tourist Development*, Longman, Harlow

Pearce, D. (1992) *Tourist Organizations*, Longman, Harlow

Pecqueux, J-L. (1998) *Tourisme et collectivités territoriales*, SOFIAC, Paris

Pimlott, J.A.R. (1947) *The Englishman's Holiday*, Faber, London

Richter, A.K. (1985) 'Fragmented politics of US tourism', *Tourism Management*, Vol. 6, No. 3, September

Saffigna, L. (1999) 'Focus on Macquarie Island', Adventure Associates digital newsletter: http://www.adventureassociates.com/newsletter/Macquarie.htm

Scottish Tourist Board (1999a) Annual Report, 1998–99, STB, Edinburgh

Scottish Tourist Board (1999b) Scottish Tourism Strategic Plan: Interim Review, STB, Edinburgh

Seaton, A.V. and Bennett, M.M. (1999) *Marketing Tourism Products*, Thomson Business Press, London

Shackley, A. (ed.) (1998) *Visitor Management. Case Studies from World Heritage Sites*, Butterworth-Heinemann, Oxford

Smith, K.S. (1997) 'Penguin colony not disturbed', cited on S/Y 'Sara W. Vorwerk' website:
http://dive-info.com/antarctica/antarctica.htm

Sonpal, C. (2000) 'Tourism Satellite Accounts', *Tourism*, Issue 103, Autumn, Tourist Society, London

Stabler, M.J. (ed.) *Tourism and Sustainability. Principles to Practice,* CAB International, Wallingford

Swarbrooke, J. (1997) 'The role of the European Union in UK tourism', *Insights,* BTA/ETB, London

Swarbrooke, J. and Horner, S. (1999) *Consumer Behaviour in Tourism*, Butterworth-Heinemann, Oxford

Taylor Nelson and Associates Ltd (1974) 'Extra Holiday Break Survey, 1974', BTA/ETB archives, London

Thompson, D. (1999) 'Domesday 2000: Brighton', *Daily Telegraph* 'Weekend', 11 September

Tourism (1998) Issue 98, Autumn, Tourism Society, London

Tourism (1999) Issue 101, Summer, Tourism Society, London

Tourism (1999) Issue 102, Autumn, Tourism Society, London

Tourism (1999) Issue 103, Winter, Tourism Society, London

Tourism (2000) Issue 106, Autumn, Tourism Society, London

Tourism Council of the South Pacific (n.d.) 1993 Annual Report, Suva, Fiji

Tourism Society (1998) DCMS's Comprehensive Spending Review: The Society's Formal Response to the Proposals, Tourism Society, London

Travel Industry Association of America (1997) 'Market share indicators', *International* (Newsletter), Vol. 3, No. 1

Travel Industry Association of America (1998a) *The Economic Review of Travel in America*, TIA, Washington

Travel Industry Association of America (1998b) 'From Strategy to Success': A Final Report on the White House Conference on Travel and Tourism, TIA, Washington, DC

Travel Industry Association of America (1999) *Newsline*, April, TIA, Washington, DC

Travis, A. (1979) *The State and Leisure Provision*, The Sports Council and Social Science Research Council, London

Tuppen, J. (1998) 'France: Tourism comes of age', in A.M. Williams and G. Shaw (eds), *Tourism and Economic Development*, John Wiley and Sons, Chichester

United Nations (1994) *Recommendations on Tourism Statistics,* UN, New York

University of North London (1998) 'The economic and social impact of the National Lottery', *Research Digest*, Vol. 2, London

United States National Tourism Organization Act (1996) *Legislative History*, HR 2579 (S.1735), Public Law Act 104–288, approved 11 October, Washington, DC

US National Tourism Organization, Inc. (1998) Addendum to the report of the USNTO Board and USNTO Inc. to the Committee on Commerce, Science and Transportation, US Senate and the Committee on Commerce, US House of Representatives, February, Washington, DC

Valenzuela, M. (1998) 'Spain: from the phenomenon of mass tourism to the search for a more diversified model', in A.M. Williams and G.

Shaw (eds), *Tourism and Economic Development*, John Wiley and Sons, Chichester

Walton, J.K. (1983) *The English Seaside Resort: A Social History 1750–1914*, Leicester University Press and St Martin's Press, New York

Wanhill, S. (1987) 'UK politics and tourism', *Tourism Management*, Vol. 8, No. 1

Wheatcroft, S. (1994) *Aviation and Tourism Policies*, Routledge, London and New York

Williams, A.M. and Shaw, G. (eds) (1998) *Tourism and Economic Development,* John Wiley and Sons, Chichester

World Resources Institute (1998) 'Mombasa Marine National Park', published on the Internet at: http://www.econet.apc.org/wri/indic-trs/kenya.htm

World Tourism Organization (1993) *Tourism Development and the Responsibility of the State*, WTO, Madrid

World Tourism Organization (1994a) Seminar on GATS Implications for Tourism, WTO, Madrid

World Tourism Organization (1994b) *Privatization Papers*, Themes I, II and III, WTO, Madrid

World Tourism Organization (1996a) *Budgets of National Tourism Administrations*, WTO, Madrid

World Tourism Organization (1996b) *Implications of the UN/WTO Tourism Definitions for the US Tourism Statistical System*, WTO, Madrid

World Tourism Organization (1996c) *Towards New Forms of Public–Private Sector Partnership. The Changing Role, Structure and Activities of National Tourism Administrations*, WTO, Madrid

World Tourism Organization (1997) *Tourism Responsibilities of European Governments*, WTO/CEU–ETC Joint Seminar, WTO, Madrid

World Tourism Organization (1998a) *Asian Tourism Experiences*, WTO, Madrid

World Tourism Organization (1998b) *Guide for Local Authorities on Developing Sustainable Tourism*, WTO, Madrid

World Tourism Organization (1998c) *Tourism 2020 Vision*, revised and updated, WTO, Madrid

World Tourism Organization (1999a) *The Economic Impact of Tourism*, WTO, Madrid

World Tourism Organization (1999b) *The Future of National Tourism Offices*, WTO, Madrid

World Tourism Organization (1999c) *Compendium of Tourism Statistics, 1993–97*, WTO, Madrid

World Tourism Organization Business Council (1998) *Tourism and Taxation – Striking a Fair Deal*, WTO, Madrid

World Travel and Tourism Council (n.d.) *Agenda 21 for the Travel and Tourism Industry*, produced jointly with WTO and the Earth Council, London, Madrid and San José, Costa Rica

World Travel and Tourism Council (1994a) *Issues in Tax Policy*, World Travel and Tourism Tax Policy Center, Michigan, USA

World Travel and Tourism Council (1994b) *United Kingdom Travel and Tourism. A New Economic Perspective*, WTTC, London

World Travel and Tourism Council (1998) *The Economic Impact of Travel and Tourism in the APEC Region*, WTTC, London

Wright, P. (2000) 'Regenerating seaside resorts: learning from Spanish practice', *Tourism*, Issue 101, Winter, Tourism Society, London

Yale, P. (1985) *The Business of Tour Operations*, Longman Scientific and Technical, Harlow

Young, Sir George (1973) *Tourism: Blessing or Blight?,* Pelican, London

Index